Simon Somerville Laurie

Report on education in the parochial schools of the counties of Aberdeen, Banff and Moray

Simon Somerville Laurie

Report on education in the parochial schools of the counties of Aberdeen, Banff and Moray

ISBN/EAN: 9783337277093

Printed in Europe, USA, Canada, Australia, Japan

Cover: Foto ©Paul-Georg Meister /pixelio.de

More available books at **www.hansebooks.com**

REPORT ON EDUCATION

IN THE

PAROCHIAL SCHOOLS OF THE COUNTIES OF ABERDEEN,
BANFF AND MORAY

ADDRESSED TO THE

TRUSTEES OF THE DICK BEQUEST

BY

SIMON S. LAURIE, A.M.

VISITOR FOR THE DICK BEQUEST TRUSTEES; MILNE BEQUEST INSPECTOR; SECRETARY
TO THE EDUCATION COMMITTEE OF THE CHURCH OF SCOTLAND.

EDINBURGH: PRINTED BY THOMAS CONSTABLE,
PRINTER TO THE QUEEN, AND TO THE UNIVERSITY.
MDCCCLXV.

NOTE BY THE TRUSTEES.

In giving forth the usual decennial Report of the administration of Mr. Dick's Bequest, for the information of the clergy and schoolmasters of the counties which benefit from its funds, the Trustees are painfully reminded of the loss which has been sustained since the period when the last Report was published. They allude to the death of Professor Menzies, who, from the commencement of the operations of the Bequest in 1832 to the year 1856, when he died, held the combined offices of Clerk to the Trust and Visitor of the Schools.

The very important part taken by Mr. Menzies in fixing the principles and maturing the plans for the distribution of the Bequest, is well known to those acquainted with its early history. Those especially can, perhaps, best appreciate his value, who witnessed the deep and never-failing interest which their late Clerk took in all that tended to the elevation of the literary and religious standard of education in the three counties, proving thus, by his zeal and untiring energy, the conscientious feeling he ever had of the onerous and important duties of his office. As it must then be felt, by all connected with the Bequest, that to Mr. Menzies's exertions much of the success which has attended its administration is attributable, the Trustees feel that they cannot allow this opportunity to pass without thus publicly recording their sense of the great value of his services, and the deep and lasting regret with which they must ever look back on the loss of one so esteemed and respected.

At the close of other ten years in the history of the Bequest, it affords satisfaction to the Trustees to believe that the influence it has exerted on education within the favoured district, during the period from 1854 to 1864, has proved in all respects as beneficial as in former years. The original intention of the Trustees, when arranging for the preparation of their usual Report on the present occasion, was to limit it as far as possible to a narrative of the facts of their administration during the decennial period, with a statement of its results, as shown by the present condition of the schools, and a brief notice of the changes which have taken place since the date of the last Report on the regulations affecting the distribution of the Fund. Their views in this respect, however, were afterwards altered in consequence of a strongly expressed wish on the part of Mr. Laurie, the Visitor of Schools, that either the "Principles and Theory of Teaching" should be introduced as an additional subject in the examination of new teachers, or that a statement, directing attention to their importance as a subject of careful study, should be prepared and circulated among the schoolmasters generally. The first of these alternatives the Trustees were unwilling to adopt, seeing that the two days set apart for the annual examination are already fully occupied, and that, as the time could not be extended without serious inconvenience, it would be difficult to arrange for the introduction of any additional subject, unless at the cost of partially neglecting or wholly setting aside some other of the prescribed branches of study. They felt themselves constrained, however, so far to give effect to the recommendations of the Visitor, as to invite him to prepare, for circulation among the schoolmasters, such a treatise or other paper on the " Theory of Teaching," as his large experience and thoughtful consideration of this important subject might lead him to deem calculated to accomplish the object in view. It was therefore arranged that Mr. Laurie should embody his views and suggestions in a Special Report, to be printed along with the Report of 1864 ; and it will accordingly be found that these form the First Part of the Report, while the Second Part brings down the history of the Bequest and its administration for the decennial period, and it is for this

Second Part alone that the Trustees hold themselves responsible.

In Part First the schoolmasters have the benefit of Mr. Laurie's extensive knowledge and experience on all matters connected with the teaching art ; and the Trustees feel assured that the great talent displayed in its preparation cannot fail to recommend it to their most anxious study, and that its fruits will ere long be exhibited in a more widely diffused knowledge of the principles of the art of teaching and of school management, and a still further improvement in the condition of the schools connected with the Bequest.

JAMES HOPE, D.K.S.,
Chairman of the Trustees.

CONTENTS.

PREFATORY NOTE, . . 1

PART FIRST.

THE FUNCTION OF THE PAROCHIAL SCHOOLMASTER, AND THE SUBJECTS AND METHODS OF HIS TEACHING.

The Purpose of the School, ... 5

    The ultimate purpose of the parochial school—The importance of keeping this purpose in mind—The consequences of keeping this purpose or practical ideal in view: Moral; Intellectual; Personal to the teacher.

The First Qualification of the Parochial Teacher, . 14

    The knowledge necessary to enable the teacher to conceive the practical ideal—Protest against the opinion that there are no principles in education.

The General Method of Education, . . . 17

    To attain the ideal we must have method—Nature of mind and its growth in relation to methods of instruction and training—Philosophic aptitude rather than philosophic knowledge necessary in the teacher—Auxiliaries of the teacher, viz.: Natural operation of mind; Moral accesses to the intellect; Class-sympathy.—The sympathetic teacher may dispense with philosophy—Character in the teacher himself.

Restrictions of the Parochial Teacher, . . . 27
   Shortness of attendance—Irregularity of attendance—Number of classes—Character of pupils' homes—Utilities of pupil's future life.

The Lessons to be drawn from the Restrictions of the Parochial Teacher, ... 37
   Contraction of teacher's work—Principles of selection—Subjects in order of importance, primary and secondary.

METHODS OF TEACHING.

THE CONCURRENCE OF GENERAL METHOD AND PARTICULAR METHODS, . . . 51

OBJECTS AND METHOD OF TEACHING READING, . 53

Initiation in the Art of Reading, ... 53
   The Phonic, the "Look and Say," and the Alphabetic methods—Spelling.

The Juvenile Stage in Teaching Reading, . . 65
   Mental progress and Progress in Reading should be concurrent—Intelligent reading—To teach to read properly is to educate—The imagination and the moral and religious sensibilities of children—Intelligible reading.

OBJECTS AND METHOD OF TEACHING WRITING, . . 77
   The practical purpose, namely, facility and distinctness, to be kept constantly in view—Letters to be turned to use as they are learned—The power to be applied to copying on slates—Writing from dictation.

OBJECTS AND METHOD OF TEACHING ARITHMETIC, . 83
   Intellectual discipline of Arithmetic—School Arithmetic should be practical and economic—Method of teaching: the concrete method—Moral uses of School Arithmetic.

	PAGE

The Secondary Subjects of the Parochial School, . 93

   Education an extensive as well as an intensive process—Order of importance of secondary subjects.

MUSIC IN THE PRIMARY SCHOOL, ... 97

   General effect of Music on the school—Sympathy as an educative agent—Sympathy and simultaneity contrasted. (The simultaneous system.)—Singing a moral and religious agency—Effect on the children—Method of teaching singing.

GEOGRAPHY, AND THE METHOD OF TEACHING IT, . 103

   Chief error in teaching Geography—Practical purpose of teaching Geography—Theoretical purpose—The two harmonize—Indirect uses of Geography—Method of teaching Geography.

ON DRAWING, . . 111

THE HIGHER INTELLECTUAL INSTRUCTION OF THE PAROCHIAL SCHOOL, ... 113

   Advanced Reading—Analysis of Sentences—Advanced Writing or Composition—Method of teaching Grammar and Composition, . . . 113

   History, ... 123

   Latin and Greek. (*Middle Schools.*)—Language *versus* Science, ... 124

      On the Method of teaching Latin and Greek, . 140

   Mathematics, ... 145

ORGANIZATION, . . . 146

   Classification—Time-Tables.

SCHOOL DISCIPLINE, . . . 151

   Indirect Moral Teaching—Rewards and Punishments.

		PAGE
MORAL INSTRUCTION,	. . . . .	174

　　Initiatory stage—Direct Moral and Suggestive Moral Teaching—Juvenile stage (Laws of Health, etc.)

MINOR MORALS OF THE SCHOOL, . . 186

　　Courtesy between Boys and Girls—Influence of Female Schools—Politeness—Order—Cleanliness, etc.—Personal habits of teacher.

THE TEACHING OF RELIGION, . 195

PART SECOND.
HISTORICAL AND STATISTICAL.

CHAPTER I.

ORIGIN AND AMOUNT OF THE BEQUEST, . . . 207

　　Mr. James Dick—Professor Allan Menzies—Trustees and Office-Bearers—Terms of Bequest from Mr. Dick's Will.

CHAPTER II.

CHARACTER OF THE BEQUEST AND OF ITS ADMINISTRATION, 215

　　The Bequest not a Charity—Historical sketch of Parochial School system—Outline of the principles of administration.

CHAPTER III.

PRINCIPLES OF DICK BEQUEST ADMINISTRATION, 224

1. The Teacher, ... 224
2. The Heritors and Minister, and Presbyterial Superintendence, ... 228
3. Plan of Distributing the Fund, . 230
4. Assistant-Substitutes, 233

CONTENTS. xiii

CHAPTER IV.

ADMINISTRATIVE AND OTHER CHANGES SINCE 1854, . 237

Assistant-Substitutes—Temporary Substitutes—Music—Side-Parochial Schools.

CHAPTER V.

THE RELATION OF THE BEQUEST TO THE PRIVY COUNCIL, 241

CHAPTER VI.

VISITATION OF THE SCHOOLS, . 245

CHAPTER VII.

NOTES OF VISITATION, . . . 251

1. Reading. Examination on the Reading Lessons. Course of Lessons, . . 251
2. Writing (Dictation Exercises), 268
3. Arithmetic, 273
4. Music, . 276
5. Geography, 277
6. History, . . 280
7. Grammar and Composition, . 281
8. Organization. Specimen Time-Table, . 287
9. Discipline and Minor Morals, 292
10. Direct Moral Instruction, . . . 296
11. Direct Religious Instruction, . . . 298
12. The Higher Instruction of the Parochial Schools:— English Composition—Latin—Greek—Mathematics, 304

CHAPTER VIII.

THE CLASS OF PAROCHIAL TEACHERS IN ABERDEEN, BANFF, AND MORAY, 310

CHAPTER IX.

PRESENT STATE OF THE SCHOOLS—SPECIMENS AND CLASSIFICATION—CHIEF DEFECTS IN RESPECT OF RESULTS—PROGRESS MADE DURING THE LAST TEN YEARS, . . 316

CHAPTER X.

THE BEARING OF FEES AND DATE OF ENTRY ON ATTENDANCE AND ORGANIZATION—GRATIS SCHOLARS, 330

CHAPTER XI.

SCHOOL ACCOMMODATION — FURNITURE — APPARATUS—SCHOOL LIBRARIES—TEXT-BOOKS USED, . . 335

CHAPTER XII.

GENERAL STATISTICS OF EDUCATION IN THE COUNTIES OF ABERDEEN, BANFF, AND MORAY, . . . 339
   Parochial Schools, ... 339
   Non-Parochial Schools, ... 342

CHAPTER XIII.

PAROCHIAL SCHOOLS IN CONNEXION WITH THE BEQUEST, 344

CHAPTER XIV.

COMPARATIVE STATEMENT, HAVING REFERENCE TO PREVIOUS REPORTS—STATISTICAL TABLE, . 347

APPENDIX.

		PAGE
I.	RULES OF EXAMINATION AND SPECIMEN OF EXAMINATION PAPERS,	353
II.	RESULTS OF EXAMINATION OF SCHOOLMASTERS AND SUBSTITUTES,	371
III.	SPECIMEN OF PRESBYTERIAL REPORT TO TRUSTEES,	377
IV.	ABSTRACT OF REGULATIONS OF THE DICK BEQUEST TRUSTEES,	380
V.	STATEMENT TO PRIVY COUNCIL REGARDING THE ENDOWMENT CLAUSE OF THE REVISED CODE,	385
VI.	LIST OF PAROCHIAL SCHOOLS, AND OF THE SCHOOLMASTERS AND ASSISTANT-SUBSTITUTES IN THE COUNTIES OF ABERDEEN, BANFF, AND MORAY, FROM 1854 TO 1864,	391

PREFATORY NOTE.

ABOUT two years ago I was asked by the Trustees of the Dick Bequest to put in writing such a statement of the methods of school-work as might be of service to teachers admitted to participation in the Bequest. Anticipating the instructions which I afterwards received, to lay before the Trustees the usual decennial Report on the working of the Trust, and the state of the schools inspected by me, I proposed to embody in that Report all that it was necessary to say on the art of teaching.

When, however, I began to write the Report, I found that scraps of method and disjointed suggestions, occurring in the midst of details of school work, would not secure the object I had in view. Methods and expedients, I felt, were of no real and permanent value, except in so far as they were referred back to principles. Moreover, every successive year's experience had more deeply impressed me with the belief, that the object of any writing addressed to teachers ought to be, not so much to provide them with weapons which they could turn to immediate use, as to inspire them with a large conception of their task; to convince them that their business is to educate their pupils while instructing them in a few technical arts; to show them that every part of their work is instinct with a moral purpose; and, with a view to these ends, to bring into prominence the harmony that subsists between the special methods of teaching and the general method of education. In addition to this, it seemed not out of place to take the opportunity which this my first public Report afforded me, of stating explicitly the grounds of my annual Reports on individual schools, and the point of view from which I criticise them. Accordingly, I have separated all that has general reference to the function of the teacher from the survey of the operation of the Trust, and of my experience of the schools in the three north-eastern counties. The actual working condition of the schools in these counties is recorded in the second part of the Report.

I need scarcely say that the general question of Education is not the subject of the following pages: my business is with education as it ought to be conducted within the walls of a Parochial School. Should my remarks sometimes appear to teachers to be simple and obvious, and indeed anticipated in the practice of a large body of the teachers of the three north-eastern counties, my apology is that I am confident that, by young teachers at least, they will be found not superfluous.

REPORT TO THE TRUSTEES OF THE
DICK BEQUEST.

PART FIRST.

THE FUNCTION OF THE PAROCHIAL
SCHOOLMASTER.

PART FIRST.

THE FUNCTION OF THE PAROCHIAL SCHOOLMASTER, AND THE
SUBJECTS AND METHODS OF HIS TEACHING.

The Purpose of the School.

The ultimate purpose of the parochial school—The importance of keeping this
purpose in mind—The consequences of keeping this purpose or practical
ideal in view: Moral; Intellectual; Personal to the teacher.

I FIND that the defects of conscientious teachers are for the most part to be traced to the want of a purpose, both as regards the general object of the school and the particular result of special studies.

"What is it that I propose to myself in School-keeping?" is the first question which a young teacher should put to himself. His first duty is to form a purpose or practical ideal. A clearly defined purpose is not only the indispensable condition, but it is also the measure, of progress. The question is, as it seems to me, best answered thus: The object which the schoolmaster ought to propose to himself is the Formation of Character. This is the ultimate purpose of the Parochial School, as it is of all education.

It is true that the objects of education, and even of such education as the parochial school affects to give, are, in their details, various, and seem at first sight to be inadequately summed up by the words "Formation of Character." The child, for example, has to be taught how best to preserve through life a sound mind in a sound body. In teaching him this, we must furnish him with the knowledge necessary for earning a livelihood ; we must provide him with a certain amount of intellectual food ; and, above all, we must instruct him in those moral duties, which it behoves him to know and practise. The moral teaching, again, can have due efficacy and adequate sanction only if we connect it with the will of the Unseen Power which sustains and administers the Universe : it thus becomes religious teaching, and this long before it assumes that more definite form of Christian faith which the school also inculcates. The necessities of the case thus demand that the pupil's mind shall be *informed* as well as *formed*.

But what is the purpose of all this instruction ? It is to make men lead better lives ; better, intellectually, by giving greater activity, vigour, and precision to the powers by which they know and do ; better, morally and religiously, by causing them to live in obedience to the laws of God as revealed in the nature of man and the visible order around him, and in harmony with the will of God as communicated in his Word. The bettering of men's wills, and the bettering of men's intellects,— these are the great objects which we have in view.

Accordingly, if asked to sum up in a few words

the end of Education, and to do so in words which will indicate its ultimate aim at the same time that they furnish the practical teacher with a criterion by which to measure every detail of his work, I can find no better or more exhaustive answer than that which has been given :—" The Formation of Character."

But since the invigorating of the understanding, and the training of the will, are operations which cannot be conducted without materials, we are bound, in determining the nature of these materials, to allow ourselves to be controlled by the needs and facts of man's daily life.

The materials of parochial school education thus forced on us are at first sight so humble that it may with some show of truth be contended that they do not admit of a treatment in relation to a larger purpose outside themselves. If this be so, they are unsuited for the work they have to do, and the schoolmaster, since no other material is available, inevitably sinks into a mere mechanic. This antagonism happily does not exist. The necessities of the pupil's future life and the necessities of sound training can easily be shown to harmonize. For, although in such formal matters as arithmetic and grammar the ideal may mean only a certain perfection of acquired knowledge in the pupil, accompanied by a certain amount of mental power developed in the process of acquisition ; yet, when even these subjects are ethically taught,—that is to say, so handled as to be brought into close concrete connexion with their ulti mate uses in common life, they pass into a higher category, and contribute their full share to the attain- ment of the ultimate purpose of the school. In the elementary school, if nowhere else, purely formal studies have, when rightly understood, a moral significance.

If the purpose of the parochial school has been correctly stated, something has already been done towards defining the position and work of the schoolmaster. If it be true that he is set apart by society, in order that he may direct his daily energies towards the formation of character in the children of the people, he cannot fail to feel that he is engaged in an elevating, an inspiring, nay, more, a *creative* task. He is in truth, if he will but believe it, a kind of moral artist. He has a plastic work to do,—the work of moulding the rude untutored nature of peasant and city boyhood into a shapely form. Nor will any one regard this as an exaggeration of the teacher's office, who has had opportunities of contrasting the uncombed, untamed young barbarian of civilisation, distinguished for his loose and insolent carriage, his lawless manner, licentious speech, and vagrant eye, with the same child, sitting on the school-bench, well-habited and clean, his manner subdued into fitness with the moral order around him, his tongue under a sense of law, his countenance suffused with awakening thought, his very body seeming to be invested with reason. That such transformations are effected by the best schoolmasters, all know who have come into direct personal contact with educational agencies.[1] And surely the man who can point to such results as the product of his labour, rightly claims to have in some sense a creative function. Is not his work, in point of fact, creative in a high and peculiar sense ? This at least is certain, that, except in so far as it is felt by him, consciously or unconsciously, to have this character, it may be safely said to be a drudgery the most dreary and soul-tiring in the whole round of human labour—an occupation for slaves.

I speak exclusively of the elementary teacher; for the departmental instructor in this or that science or language stands on a lower moral eminence than that which is occupied by the parochial schoolmaster. The former makes only a partial contribution to the final result of character, and he does so at an age when the pupil's unconscious moral tendencies are already declared, and the bent of his intelligence is already given. The latter, on the other hand, has to rear successive generations of children, during the years in which they are most open to impressions. These children he has, in the widest sense, to train as well as

[1] " From culture unexclusively bestowed,
. . . . .
Expect these mighty issues ; from the pains
And faithful care of unambitious schools,
Instructing simple childhood's ready ear—
Thence look for these magnificent results."
Wordsworth's *Excursion*, B. ix.

to instruct. His duty is to operate on their faculties and capacities, to stimulate these into life, and to give them their first direction. The intellect of the child is thus dependent on its earliest instructor more than on any other,—on his wise understanding of the manner of its natural operations, the limits of its legitimate exercise, and the objects most readily seized and assimilated at the different stages of its growth. Still more is the moral destiny of the child in his hands ; for the extent to which the sentiments and imagination are to enter into the future character, and give it balance and harmony, depends more on the way in which they are respected and judiciously fostered in the child's earliest years, than on any future influences whatsoever.

If this be the work of the national schoolmaster—if his function be to elaborate out of rude, but not unpliable material, some approximation to a good intellectual and moral habit, how indispensable is it that he should be guided as well as sustained by the conscious possession of this the ideal aim of his profession ! It is only when he has a clear comprehension of the real nature and the large bearings of his work, that the little things of the schoolroom—and it is precisely these that require his attention— assume their rightful importance. All the details of his arrangements are then felt to promote or retard the realization of the educative purpose of the school, and, in so far as they contribute to the final result, to have a moral value. Small things are no longer petty. Things which would otherwise be considered trivial—such as cleanliness, order, light, ventilation—acquire a new significance. Those daily incidents, so apt to be regarded as merely harassing and vexatious, and as traversing the steady onward progress of his work, are now beheld by him in a new light, and what were formerly only obstructions, become transmuted into auxiliaries of his general method or into felicitous opportunities for applying it. The teacher, on the other hand, who is ignorant of the true nature of his function, and is unfurnished with a practical ideal, can at best take only a partial and technical view of his duties. His various classes and subjects of instruction do not present themselves to his mind as parts of one whole. The organization is probably loose and disjointed, the subjects taught and the classes operated on seeming to have no intimate connexion with each other; for where no ultimate unity of general result is conceived, none can exist in the particular details. The multifarious operations of the schoolroom hang in clumsy juxtaposition, instead of being woven together by the power of a common purpose. Such a teacher looks at his work piecemeal, and does it in fragments. A portion of this, that, or the other subject, has to be taught to a certain number of pupils, and the day's work is over. Each lesson seems to terminate in itself, without reference either to the past or the future; to-day seems to have no necessary issue in to-morrow. Every passing event, every collateral circumstance attending his intercourse with his pupils, is to such a man obstructive and irrelevant, if it do not forward the sole object of the day—"getting through the lessons." That done, the day's duty is also done: and we may be sure that where the teaching is not animated and controlled by any higher purpose than this, by something which can neither be questioned out of the pupils nor communicated to them in didactic shape, even the mere lesson-saying will be perfunctory and barren.

But not only are the possession of an ideal, and of the desire to attain it, indispensable qualifications of a primary teacher; they also point out the easiest and shortest road to his end. They may almost be said to supersede every other qualification; for where there exist the imagination and the precision of apprehension necessary to give definite shape to the final aim of his work, and along with these the will to realize in his school what he entertains in his thought, the teacher may almost be said to be fully equipped for his task. So equipped, he cannot wander very far from the right track; and, should he deviate, his errors will quickly turn to use. Even the principles of organization and of discipline, and all scholastic methods, are of little value compared with a distinct conception of the ultimate aim of the school, sustained by an earnest purpose. These things, if they are not quickened by the independent thought of the teacher, deal with the scholastic art from the outside; while the teacher we have in view has already a firm grasp of a central idea, which not only gives validity and force to the methods which he may adopt, but is itself the fertile source of new expedients.

Again, the possession of a practical ideal enables the teacher to give fair proportions to the various parts of his work. The subjects to be taught, their relative importance, the limits within which they are to be kept, and the direction which is to be given to them, can be determined only by the help of the foregone purpose. Even good teachers frequently exhibit a certain helplessness in giving to each subject of instruction its due prominence or subordination. They are too often the slaves of traditions; and when new subjects are admitted into the schoolroom, they seem to be allowed to elbow their own way, jostling out of their fair share of attention, by no means the least important studies, but probably only the least clamant.

Further, the possession of the school-ideal sustains and animates the teacher. Without unduly magnifying his office, he feels a just pride in the reflection that he is one of the moral agencies of society. The knowledge that it is his special duty to aid in forming the character of others, is a never-failing source of strength. It is well that it should be so; for in no profession or occupation is there more need of the consolation which a high purpose gives. The teacher is denied the fresh source of courage and hope which a completed work so often yields to other labourers. He is constantly toiling towards an intellectual and moral unity of result which he never reaches. He is always producing, but there is never a completed product. His fondest hopes are being constantly frustrated ; weakness, folly, wickedness cropping out where and when least expected, breaking down his most cherished beliefs in his success, and undermining his best-laid schemes. Even his successes it is seldom given him to know, because the pupils pass out of his hands before the fruit of his training is visible. Harassed by petty exactions and unrefreshed by the reward of generous recognition, he is often depressed, if not despairing. In such circumstances it is manifest that he can find renovation of zeal in the magnitude and moral aim of his professional task, and in the trust that he is humbly co-operating with a higher Power in whose hands are the issues.

The First Qualification of the Parochial Teacher.

The knowledge necessary to enable the teacher to conceive the practical ideal — Protest against the opinion that there are no principles in education.

The Formation of Character, which is the great end and aim of the parochial school, presents itself to the schoolmaster in two aspects : the formation of a good habit of the intelligence, and of a good habit of the will. All the materials of instruction which he uses, he must regard as nothing more than the implements with which he works towards these ends. It is fortunate that, however mechanically he may use his tools, they possess, even in the hands of the incompetent, an inherent power of producing some appreciable disciplinary result in the minds of learners. But they can have their full and proper effect only in the hands of one who has a clear conception of their precise relation to the results at which he aims, and of the peculiar kind of handling necessary for each different instrument.

Now it is evident that the schoolmaster cannot in any adequate sense conceive either the habit of intelligence or of will which is the end of his teaching, or the relation of his instruments to the production of these habits, unless he himself has some knowledge of the nature of the intelligence and the will. Indeed, only to the extent that he has that knowledge, can he form any *rational* conception of his vocation at all. In other words, it is only through a knowledge of psychology and ethics that he can render to himself an account of what he is doing, and can see to what point his labours are tending. These are the two pillars on which the whole fabric of education rests. I do not mean to say that it is necessary that the teacher should be a philosopher, but it is quite indispensable that he should philosophize. All good teachers do this, whether they are aware of it or not. They propose to themselves certain specific intellectual and moral ends in teaching each subject of their somewhat extensive curriculum, and to this extent they necessarily construct for themselves a kind of crude and undeveloped doctrine of mind. They cannot move a single step without doing so, although the reasons which determine their objects, and guide them in attaining them, may assume to their own minds no formal or scientific shape.

If this be so, and it seems almost superfluous to endeavour to establish its truth by argument, it is surely of some importance, that that knowledge which underlies the work of every schoolmaster should be included in his self-preparation for it. It is manifestly better for his school and for himself that he should know, with some approach to accuracy, that which he *must* apply, whether he will or not. Doubtless, some are still to be found, among those who vaunt their purely "practical" views on education, who are of opinion that the primary teacher's work has no intimate connexion with the philosophy of the human mind, and that consequently it has no principles and deductive methods worthy of the name. It is not my business here to combat this opinion. It is enough for me if I gain the thoughtful teacher's assent to the proposition, that the extent to which he can realize in his own thought those formed habits of the intelligence and the will which constitute the objects of his professional existence, depends on his knowledge of human nature. If he does not admit this, he degrades himself from the position of an educated worker striving by means of intellectual processes to reach certain well-defined moral and intellectual results, to that of a mere retailer of the alphabet, and of an inferior (because male) nurse, and converts what is a profession, in every sense in which that distinctive term is applicable, into a trade so unutterably petty and vexatious, that only men of mean natures would willingly adopt it.

The General Method of Education.

To attain the ideal we must have method—Nature of mind and its growth in relation to methods of instruction and training—Philosophic aptitude rather than philosophic knowledge necessary in the teacher—Auxiliaries of the teacher, viz. : Natural operation of mind ; Moral accesses to the intellect ; Class-sympathy.—The sympathetic teacher may dispense with philosophy— Character in the teacher himself.

The teacher may have a knowledge of the nature of human intelligence and will, sufficiently clear and precise to yield to him a distinct conception of that good habit of both, which constitutes the purpose of education, but may be so ignorant of the manner, the conditions, and the periods of mental growth, as to be unable to construct for himself a road to the goal which he desires to reach. It is true that if the clear perception of the goal be united with an earnest endeavour to reach it, a man whose character is itself formed, or, which is better, consciously forming itself, in accordance with the highest standards of life, will not deviate very far from the right track. A steady eye, already to some extent practised in the field of moral and intellectual exploration, requires little more than the visible prominence of a goal, to enable it to map out a chart of the country which has to be traversed before that goal be reached. But the devising of *some* practicable path through the intricacies of the yet untraversed ground, is the first demand on the powers of the teacher, and one involving too many delicate and important questions to be left to the improvised and haphazard solutions which the pressure of necessity may from time to time force from him as he proceeds. It is therefore incumbent on him to consider the principles which must determine the path to be chosen, and which lie at the foundation of Method ; in other words, the principles which point out the way by which he may reach his end.

The mind exhibits its life in various forms—forms easily distinguished from each other in the rough, and seeming frequently to have nothing in common, save that they are the manifestations of the same indivisible conscious power. These forms of sensibility or activity emerge into life at different periods of the child's growth, and claim, therefore, from the educator at those different periods the right of exclusive attention or careful neglect. Practically speaking, these sensibilities and activities of the child have no existence except in so far as they have objects ; and accordingly, the materials of instruction which the teacher employs are, in the first instance at least, to be contemplated solely as the aliment necessary for the due sustenance and growth of these powers. The development of them tends to produce that mental character which it is his business to form. But the wise development of them, such a development as will cause them to consolidate into a healthy and harmonious whole, can be promoted only by presenting the materials of aliment at the right time and in the right way. The chronological appearance of the phenomena of mind must not be anticipated, and their *modus operandi* must not be misunderstood. *That* food alone must be presented which the mind has acquired sufficient vigour to assimilate, and it must be presented in such a shape, and according to such processes, as harmonize with the manner in which the mind itself works. Such a presentation is a presentation according to method. Methods of teaching, therefore, are, if rightly understood, the times and ways of using the materials of instruction and discipline, and of presenting them to the mind of the learner ; and *right* methods are such times and ways of using and presenting our materials as accord with the times and ways of mental growth. Methods of teaching, on the one hand, are those processes by which we convey instruction and discipline, with a view to the formation of a right habit of the intelligence and the will ; mental growth, on the other hand, is that series of processes by which the mind attains to its maturity, and to that tendency to repeat itself which we call habit. Now, these two processes must run parallel : there must be a mutual understanding and consentaneity between them if the work of education is to be rightly done.

It is true that a teacher, himself possessed of a disciplined intelligence and of a will fortified by religion, reason, and experience, may be working wisely towards the production in others of that which is in himself, and be *unconsciously* adapting his processes to a sound method ; but even one so rarely endowed as to be able to dispense with a knowledge of mind, loses the consolation and invigoration which a man draws from the knowledge that he is working in conformity with certain mental laws of growth, towards an end which he can distinctly conceive and enunciate.

It may be urged, that to make such high demands on the parochial teacher, is to imagine him in possession of a psychology, completed in the large sense of furnishing him not only with an analysis of our emotional and intellectual nature, but also of its mode of growth, and that, inasmuch as no such recognised philosophic scheme exists, we require impossibilities. The reply to this may be found in what has been already said : it is not necessary that the schoolmaster be a philosopher, either in the sense of elaborating a scheme of psychology for himself, or fully comprehending those which others offer for his acceptance. But if he is to be a good and a living teacher, it is indispensable that he should philosophize, and that he should do so in the direction above indicated. A constant spirit of inquiry, with a view to understand the objects of his care, and to adapt fresh means to those ends which experience and reflection enable him from day to day more distinctly to perceive and more largely to comprehend, is essential to the right conception of his duty and to his own sense of manliness and dignity in the discharge of it. Given this, and we have all that it is essential for him to have ;

for where the master-mind of the school is itself thus open, living, and progressive, an intellectual and moral movement is communicated to the pupils, which could never flow from a man whose pretensions to theoretic knowledge were greater, and who laboured on in conscientious but dull obedience to a stereotyped system of mind, and to rules of conduct deduced from it. The habitual *study* of the capacities and growth of mind is necessary to the teacher, not the mere *possession* of a series of dead classifications, which he vainly imagines to be knowledge. Accordingly the mental requirement, seemingly so high, is not really greater than we are entitled to expect; for it does not involve profound knowledge or various attainment, but only an average amount of intellectual capacity, to which, under a sense of duty, a certain direction has been given. A certain amount of knowledge, but that easy of attainment, is indispensable, but it is the habit of mind, and the attitude which it takes up with respect to its work, which are the chief requisites. Of this the schoolmaster may be assured, that unless he take the "philosophic" view of his profession and its duties, he will never fully understand the significance of his daily task, or raise himself, either in his own eyes or in those of others, above the position of a soul-vexed mechanic, whose occupation the world will persist in regarding as petty, because the objects of it are small.

In the natural instinct of acquisition, so conspicuous

in children, and in the irrepressible love of activity, the teacher will find co-operating agencies ready to aid him in his labours, and to supply his own shortcomings in a knowledge of the processes and growth of mind. In truth, nature is hourly striving to do the work which he, in his impatient ignorance, is too often thwarting. For it is a fact in the operation of mind, that however awkward, inverted, or confused may be the way in which an object—whether it be grammar, geography, or the alphabet—is presented to the mind of child or adult, there is a strong and almost irresistible, though not always successful, analytic effort on the part of the intellect to fall into the proper acquiring attitude towards it,—to grope its way through the confusion, setting aside the irrelevant, until it seizes firm hold of the right end of the thread by following which it may find its way to knowledge. In this fact, the teacher may find much encouragement, the best teacher as well as the indifferent, for none are independent of its aid. It is this self-curative energy of mind which makes ultimately educative in their effect, facts and reasonings which, at the time of presentation, fail to touch either the understanding or the feelings of the pupil, and are utterly barren of any immediate result whatsoever, except the exercise of the memory.

Nor is the spontaneous energy of the mind the only auxiliary which the teacher finds ready to supply his defects and correct his errors. He has command over the moral avenues to the understanding. It is this fact which explains the success of those teachers who seem to begin everything at the wrong place, and prosecute it in the wrong way. They happen to possess a strong will and an earnest desire to instruct and discipline the minds of their pupils. The constant manifestation of their intellectual and moral energy is contagious : it communicates a wholesome shock to the pupil, and his powers are stretched to the utmost, in order to keep pace with a master whose earnestness and strength so conspicuously call forth respect and confidence.

Further, the schoolmaster has the potent ally, sympathy of numbers, on his side. All help each in the intellectual effort or moral discipline which occupies the passing moment. The perplexity or the kindling of the eye, as the mind of each member of the class works its way to apprehension and utterance, has a subtle power of co-operating with the master. Class-sympathy furnishes that mental stimulus which a common pursuit, supported by generous emulation, always communicates to those who are engaged in it.

Such, in outline, ought to be the schoolmaster's mode of operation, and such are some of the natural auxiliaries which never fail the conscientious teacher, —aiding his efforts, repairing his blunders, and supplying his deficiencies.

I can imagine only one case in which some knowledge of mental processes and a philosophic attitude of mind can be safely dispensed with,—the case of the master who is endowed with sympathetic sensibility. Where this is strong, formal philosophic methods are at once superseded, and the qualifications for understanding their organic connexion with mind are, if not superfluous, at least unnecessary. The *sympathetic* adaptation of means to ends is the most subtle and successful of all school-methods. There are some teachers to whom the impressions made on the minds of their pupils, or the intellectual efforts they may be making, communicate themselves instantaneously. The mental processes of others are realized by them, apparently without the intervention of any rational process. They seem to possess an intuitive power of forgetting their own individuality, in order to become sharers in that of their pupils. Such men are, even out of school, free from obtrusive self-assertion, and from dogmatism and arrogance of character : their simplicity and geniality of disposition are the genuine expression of a soul which has no ulterior " interest" to serve, and which is therefore free to enter, with single-heartedness and with wholeness of mind, into the sentiment or duty which may at the moment be exacting their service. Such a man was Pestalozzi, and such are many men silently eminent in school-life at this day, whose powerful instincts justly discard, without contemning, formal methods, because of the secret of success with which a happy mental constitution has already endowed them. That lively sympathy which leads them to live less in themselves than in the lives of others, furnishes them with a private key with which to unlock the intellects and hearts of their pupils.

There is something feminine in the character of mind which I have been describing, and it is in women that we find it most commonly. The sympathetic self-abnegation of the woman, consequently, makes her the best teacher of the young up to a certain age. She has *unconsciously* what a man for the most part acquires *consciously*, and what he must therefore, even when he has the best intentions, give out consciously. This implies an effort on his part which the subtle senses of children are so quick to detect, that he cannot, if he would, establish a perfectly harmonious relationship with them.

To teachers who apprehend the high purpose of the school, and strive to understand their own operations and to bring their teaching more and more into accordance with philosophic methods, school-keeping may be a labour, but it is not a toil; while to the teacher of genial and sympathetic power, whose processes are a continual and unconscious inspiration, it is scarcely even a labour, but rather the continuing, under special conditions, of his usual habit of life.

But neither philosophic methods nor sympathetic intuition can contravene or supersede the influence of the teacher's own character. The power which a vigorous character has of producing its likeness in another is a fact which requires only to be adverted to. In this, doubtless, lay the secret of the moral and intellectual successes of distinguished schoolmasters, who, with clear conceptions of their final aim, went straight at it without recognising, or perhaps caring to recognise, the fact, that the minds which they were educating lived and grew as independent organisms and according to certain laws. Such men, it is true, fail to succeed with the mass of their pupils, for they throw on their unripe minds, the burden not merely of learning, but also of analysing and reducing into method, what is taught. The strong intellects of the school come out perhaps the stronger for the difficulties overcome; but the ordinary intellect is perhaps never fairly reached by discipline to any appreciable extent, though doubtless morally benefited by the dominant will of the master and his irresistible exactions.

Character without methods never fails of at least partial success; but the most clearly conceived ideal and the most skilful methods, without the element of personal character, will, however successful in particular directions, invariably fail to attain the great object of the school. An uncontrolled will and an inaccurate and undisciplined intellect can never contribute a stone to the edifice of intellectual and moral character in others. An honest understanding, on the other hand, even though limited in capacity and attainment, if combined with a habit of will in accordance with the highest sentiments, unwittingly exhibits a reality and earnestness which do not fail to repeat themselves in the pupils. Nay, even where sound methods are in operation, it is character which does more than half of the work, or insidiously undoes it all, producing effects precisely in proportion to the unconsciousness of its operation, and affording a visible exemplar up to which, or down to which, the pupils grow. Limited powers and half-knowledge may, under a love of praise, or some other not unworthy but unstable motive, strive with a certain measure of success to convey instruction, and through it discipline; but the lesson which character teaches is apart from all intention, and above the will. What he morally *is*, that the schoolmaster morally *does*. Nor will any mere desire—should such occasionally visit him—to convey a higher moral influence than *himself*, give him the power to convey it.

Restrictions of the Parochial Teacher.

Shortness of attendance—Irregularity of attendance—Number of classes—Character of pupils' homes—Utilities of pupil's future life.

A schoolmaster may have a definite purpose, he may perceive the relation of all the various parts of the work to this purpose, he may grasp method in its fullest sense, or possess that sympathetic power which supersedes method; yet with all these qualifications he as yet stands only on theoretic ground. His most sanguine professional anticipations will be unfulfilled, and he will find that each successive year brings him only blighted hopes and fresh chagrin, if he do not from the first fairly face and measure the inevitable obstructions that strew his path, rendering necessary a modification of his route, his school appliances, and his expectations. While maintaining his ideal, it is his fate to work towards it under the severest limitations, and in the face of constant discomfitures. There is, in truth, no profession or occupation surrounded by so many discouraging and harassing difficulties as that of the primary teacher —difficulties, moreover, which have to be daily encountered, but which, by their very nature, can never be overcome.

(1.) The greatest of these is the short period of attendance at school. The average age at which children leave school is about ten years in England, and in Scotland about twelve. Short as this term of attendance is, if we take in view the work to be done, the primary teacher might bravely and hopefully undertake the task imposed on him if the attendance were continuous. So far is this from being the case, that days, weeks, months, and even years of absence intervene, breaking up the school so completely as practically to renew its constituent parts every two or three years. This is an evil for which no efficacious remedy has yet been proposed, except a compulsory law. Until we have some such law—a law, that is to say, which makes it penal for any capitalist to employ the labour of children under a certain age who cannot produce a certificate of a certain term of attendance at an elementary school—the evil can only be palliated.

I am not aware that any very serious efforts have been made in Scotland to remedy the evil as far as it admits of being remedied. With a few exceptions, neither the teachers nor the school-managers exert their full influence to induce the parents to abstain from withdrawing pupils. It is certainly impossible to imagine a more legitimate domestic subject for the exercise of a little local despotism. The teacher, being pecuniarily interested in steady attendance, may feel some delicacy in openly endeavouring to coerce the children of the parish into the schoolhouse; but the motives of the school-managers cannot be misinterpreted. In aid of the exhortations and pressure of the managers, various devices may be resorted to in different parts of the country for reducing the amount of absenteeism. In some districts, for example, the absentees are kept at home for two or three months in the year, not because the children are hired by large farmers for field-labour, but merely because their parents require a few hours' assistance on their crofts or in herding. It would surely be possible to come to an understanding in such cases with the parents, and by closing the school for the younger and unemployed children at noon, after two or three hours' instruction, and re-opening it towards evening for those who have been occupied in the fields during the day, if only for one hour, to combine attention to the material necessities of the parents with consideration for the mental needs of the children.[1]

[1] Elementary country schools in Scotland generally open about ten and close about half-past three or four, with an interval varying from half an hour to an hour,—usually the latter. It is, of course, presumed that the hour's evening tuition is obtained by *shortening the field-labour to that extent*.

A daily attendance so short could, it is true, effect nothing more than the maintenance of the knowledge previously acquired, but every earnest teacher would hail even this small instalment of a full attendance as a satisfactory solution of his chief difficulty. For, it is not the mere fact that the pupils have made no progress during a three or six months' absence that afflicts the master, but that they have visibly retrograded, not only in actual knowledge, but in intellectual facility. They have barely succeeded during the winter months in re-acquiring the latter, with a view to the recovery of the former, when their time of withdrawal for field-labour again approaches. So universal is this custom, that the children, after they have attained a certain age, professedly come to school only for what is locally called the winter "*spate*," which means an attendance of from ten to fifteen weeks. It is therefore worth considering whether evening schools for lads above thirteen could not to be held in *summer*, the teacher being set free from his other duties at an early period of the day, in order to carry forward at a later hour the training of his elder pupils, who are hopelessly lost to him without this supplementary instruction. If the parish will not adapt itself to the school, the school must adapt itself to the parish.[1]

---

[1] The above suggestion for mitigating the evil of irregularity, has reference solely to those children who are above a certain age, and are withdrawn for purposes of remunerative labour, in the service either of their parents or of large farmers and other employers of child-labour. To give effect to it requires the co-operation of the leading inhabitants of

The teacher has also to deal with an evil even more vexatious and more destructive of discipline than labour-caused absenteeism, if not so difficult of cure. I mean the habit of irregularity of attendance for trivial reasons, or for no reason at all. The teacher who can rely on the attendance of those of his pupils who are under ten years of age for 150 days of the school year, has reason to congratulate himself. I doubt if this amount of attendance is given by one-third of the children on the school register, taking Scotland as a whole, though in the three counties which benefit by the Dick Bequest the irregularity is by no means so great. A little thought might suggest expedients for correcting this evil; these necessarily varying with the circumstances, social or industrial, of each parish.

(2.) The number of classes which a primary schoolmaster has to superintend, and even personally to instruct, is seldom sufficiently considered by those who criticise his results, and seems frequently to be lost sight of even by himself. If we bear in mind that the average number of classes in an elementary school is six; that every one of these, if properly taught, is obtaining instruction in three subjects, and two, if not three of them, in six or seven subjects, during a school-day not exceeding five hours; in other words, that five-and-twenty distinct lessons have to be given daily, and time allowed for assembling, dismissing, and for the

the parish with the teacher; but inasmuch as it fairly admits an existing difficulty, and endeavours to make the best of it, an attempt to give effect to the proposal, would, I think, be met by fewer obstructions than encompass almost all other expedients for obviating a great evil.

formation of classes, the necessity of limiting the range of work, if work is to be effectually done, is sufficiently manifest to allow of my passing at once to the next obstruction besetting the teacher's path.

(3.) This obstruction is the character of the homes of the mass of his pupils. The uncontrolled will, the coarse language, the want of kindliness and of gentleness of demeanour, the dirty, wasteful and therefore demoralizing habits, the almost total disregard of intellectual family life, which may be seen in too many of these, counteract the teacher's labours, and seem more than any other difficulty to justify his despair. But it is needless to dwell on a moral obstacle which the teacher must be contented to endure, working in the face of it as hopefully as he can. It is pointed out chiefly because it has afterwards to be used for the enforcement of some of his duties.

(4.) The next limitation under which the elementary teacher works requires to be stated; not because of its presenting insuperable difficulties, but rather because he is himself very apt to omit it altogether from his calculations, setting it aside, not deliberately with a view to the better attainment of his own ideal, but in unthinking slavery to tradition and routine. This limitation is the necessity of selecting the materials of education which is imposed by the requirements of the pupil's future life. Outside the two prime subjects of moral and religious instruction, we are not left free in the elementary school to choose the materials best fitted to promote the formation of a good habit of the intelligence and the will: and for this reason, that both the moral and intellectual nature require to be *informed*, with a view to the actual needs of life. Nor is this to be regretted by the theorist intent on character only, for through information rightly given the mind gains much of its best discipline. The instruction which is too often omitted is needed for the support and direction of the conscience. We may perchance find among those who have left school a trained habit of the intelligence enabling them to perceive, distinguish, and reason with accuracy (or rather I should say with a conscious effort after accuracy); but if the materials on which the intelligence has been trained have no connexion with the demands of daily duty, the work it has to do will be done painfully and with very doubtful results. We may perchance find a trained habit of the will enabling the pupil to assert himself and his own resolution against and above the temptations which hourly beset him from within and from without; but if the materials with which the will has been informed have no direct bearing on the questions which have to be daily answered for others as well as for himself, the pupil will be quite abroad in his conclusions if a new thing has to be done; or, which is more probable, he will at once succumb without resistance to the bad habits which he may have inherited, and which belong to his class.

The above remarks have reference specially to the pupils of our Parochial Schools. The traditionary motives and inherited customs of the families of those boys who belong to the middle and upper classes of society, modify, if they do not indeed quite alter, the bearing of the whole education question on their training. This distinction is, perhaps, too much lost sight of in discussing questions affecting middle and public schools. Elaborately to impress on boys who come from homes in which baths, daily used, may be found in every bedroom, the physiological necessity of cleanliness, is to carry billets to the wood. Again, with boys from eleven to seventeen, whose characters are determined, by their homes and the class to which they belong, into the groove of honour, moral principle, and respect for religion, the idea of a *free discipline* ought manifestly to dominate over all others. Unrestricted mutual education in the open air under certain general rules and supervision, but without any vigilance that savours of espionage, the repression of luxurious habits, submission to law, and the development of a vigorous morality, probably do more to give wholesome exercise to the intellect as well as the will than any possible combination of literary or scientific pursuits. These must continue to be the main characteristics of the public school for the wealthier classes, in the case of all boys above twelve years of age. The chief blunder committed in the education of children of this class is to be found in their training during their earliest years. At the age of twelve, a boy of the wealthier classes must be either unusually dull, or have been much neglected, who, with uninterrupted opportunities of learning, cannot read well, write a well-spelled and grammatical letter, travel accurately in imagination and without the help of the map, over every part of the world, work any reasonable sum in Simple Proportion, give an intelligible, though perhaps rough account, of the more common natural phenomena, and have his memory stored with some of the finest characters in history and some of the best narrative poems in the language. All this, except the geography and arithmetic, can be easily acquired in the course of rightly learning the art of reading, if the reading-books be well selected. And if the practice of English reading be continued in the classical school for an hour or two weekly, this rough elementary knowledge of nature and its laws will gradually become more accurate and precise, and as much science will be conveyed as a boy can really absorb. After the age of twelve, and when a boy has fairly embarked on the current of a public school, the great object of the school-room should be to counteract the disadvantages and temptations incident to his social position by giving him hard intellectual work—something which will cost him a good deal of labour, however carefully it may be taught, and, along with the labour, confer the blessing of intellectual discipline. What will best accomplish these two objects is the main question, if not the only one, to be answered.

But if we turn to the Parochial School, we find ourselves on very different ground. The objects of the teacher's care are dispersed at the age of ten or twelve years, not drawn into an upper school which will carry onward the instruction and training of childhood, but driven into the labour of life. They are already little men and women, alive to the material responsibilities of existence, and called upon at once to exhibit a certain practical capacity and a certain quantity of usable knowledge. Before many years more have passed, they are compelled to take sole direction of their own conduct, unrestrained and unsupported, as the middle and upper classes are, by strong family ties and hereditary obligations.

We have already dwelt on the abrupt conclusion to the teacher's labours caused by the early removal of children from school, an evil which he must face by at once contemplating and arranging for the premature termination of his course of instruction and discipline. The limitation last adverted to imposes on him the further obligation of endeavouring to satisfy the ideal purpose of the school by means of *such a course of instruction* as will fairly meet the inevitable circumstances and requirements of the future life of his pupil. This naturally leads us to consider next—

The Lessons to be drawn from the Restrictions of the Parochial Teacher.

Contraction of teacher's work—Principles of selection—Subjects in order of importance, primary and secondary.

It was impossible to point out the limitations under which the primary teacher has to do his work, without, by implication at least, suggesting the obligations which these limitations impose on him; and not on him alone, but on all who have to do with the management of elementary schools. In looking more closely at this subject, we shall find that the limitations imposed by the brief period of school life, the irregularity of attendance during that period, the numerous classes demanding the master's constant attention, and the requirements of after life, all combine to teach the same lesson—the *contraction of the teacher's aim*. To maintain this, even in the face of the clamant demand for the admission into the school curriculum of all sorts of sciences and arts which has distinguished the last thirty years, would be more unpopular than difficult. Drawing, Music, the Physiology of Man, Physiology of Plants, Political Economy, Astronomy; every department of Natural Philosophy, Geology, and Mineralogy; Military Drill, Agricultural Chemistry, Natural History, Constitutional Law, Technology, Phrenology, have been all, or each in its turn, strenuously advocated in addition to the current and almost universal subjects of Reading, Writing, Arithmetic, Geography Political and Physical, History, Grammar, Writing from Dictation, and Religious Knowledge. The most conclusive answer to such theoretical projectors would be to assemble them in the same committee-room, and allow them to extinguish each other. Any thinking man is competent to *suggest* the subjects to be taught in our primary schools; but there is only one point of view from which all these subjects must be estimated, and that is the school-floor itself. And from this point of view a fair consideration of the limitations to which we have adverted, will force on every one the conviction that the education of the primary school cannot be general education at all, in the large and theoretic sense, but must be rather special and technical education. Given the facts of age, of irregularity of attendance, and of numerous classes, there is no alternative open, save to select, for the purposes of training and discipline, those subjects a knowledge of which is most essential to the practical and immediate needs of the child's future life.

The teacher is not, on this account, for one moment to lose sight of the great aim of his work,—the Formation of Character; nor does he require to curtail those direct religious and moral instructions which bear immediately on this his final aim. These instructions must be held sacred. Happily, they are as indispensable to the child here as to his preparation for a hereafter. They are the *direct* efforts made to form and inform the will of the child, towards which all other school-teachings contribute only *indirectly*. The limitations under which the schoolmaster works, accordingly, do not necessarily affect either his scholastic ideal or his moral teaching; they touch only the *intellectual* materials or implements with which he works. He is not permitted to be either discursive, encyclopædic, or from the theoretic point of view, eclectic; he is under the stern law of necessity, which points out, with unwavering finger, the path in which he is to walk. I do not mean to say that the idiosyncrasy of a teacher's intellect may not justify occasional deviation from the course pointed out to him. A special love and knowledge of botany or of natural history, or of any department of physics, or of poetry or music or drawing, ought to be allowed free play in the work of the school. In such exceptional circumstances, the subject which the teacher peculiarly affects will be so well taught as to do more to give a healthful stimulus to the intellects of the children, and a real and lasting interest in objects outside themselves and their daily wants, than any other. Such a result will fully compensate for the loss of what would probably be merely routine instruction in some other department of study. But allowing for an occasional divergence of this kind, the circumstances of which furnish its own best justification, it is from the limited and irregular attendance and future needs of the pupil alone that we must learn the leading subjects of primary-school instruction. And these subjects are the time-honoured branches—Reading, Writing, and Arithmetic.

But let it not be supposed that in confining intellectual school-work, in the first instance, to purely *technical* instruction in these, the three instruments whereby knowledge may be afterwards attained by the pupil himself, we omit from our consideration two things :—

First, the universally admitted fact that, unless the mind of the pupil be interested in attainment for its own sake, as well as qualified to acquire it, the work of the teacher will find its termination on the day on which the pupil leaves the school, and on that day a fatally retrograde process will begin. So far are we from forgetting this, that we shall show that the schoolmaster's craft consists in *so* teaching the technical subjects as to avoid this too common result, and also to attain certain higher ends. Reading, writing, and arithmetic, it is true, must form the groundwork of all purely intellectual primary instruction; nay, more, every other subject must be subordinated to the paramount claims of these. But precisely at this point *education as such* insists on being heard in relation to these subjects, and the art of teaching steps in with its suggestions, its aids, and its methods. At first sight, necessity seems to subvert the very idea of education in any large sense by compelling almost exclusive attention to certain technical acquirements; but the art of teaching intervening, demonstrates that even these technicalities will fail to be taught with practical effect unless they be taught in such a way, and in so large and comprehensive a spirit, as will virtually subordinate them in their turn to the idea of education. Thus theory and practice are reconciled. The way and the sense in which these formal subjects are to be taught with a view to the educative result, falls properly to be considered under the head of "Methods."

Secondly, we do not omit from our consideration the necessities of the future life of the children of the labouring population, already adverted to, and the nature of their home-training, both of which point to instruction in the duty and the means of preserving the bodily health of themselves and those dependent on them, and in the principles of conduct which should actuate them as members of a complicated social organization. These things fall properly under the moral instruction, which we presume to be sacred from interference. My experience, such as it is, has given me very strong convictions as to the vital necessity of insisting on this side of primary-school work. To train a child under a constant admonition to obey the laws of God and man, and to act as a Christian ought to act, and then to leave him to grope his own way to the fulfilment of his duty, is a mockery. A command is a merely formal utterance, and contains nothing. It is an outline to be filled up with the details of reasons, motives, and purposes.

The inherited habits of the middle and upper classes, and their superior education and intelligence, may possibly enable them to dispense with the details of a manual of morality: they certainly have a tendency to blind them as to the need of specific and detailed instruction on these subjects to the less-favoured members of society. The *how* and the *why* of moral laws, in their relation to the practical routine of daily life, require to be explicitly enunciated and deliberately and emphatically enforced in the school. To teach physiology and political economy would be absurd, simply because there is no time for them, and because the teacher, if he abstracted the time from other subjects, would waste himself in the futile effort to build up in an unripe mind a pseudo-scientific knowledge, and in laying foundations which the conditions of time, age, and circumstances under which he worked would prevent ever rising above the level of the ground. But to take up gravely and seriously the three great questions of air, food, and cleanliness, in relation to the three organs, the lungs, the stomach, and the skin; to show what these organs are, and why they exist, and how they work; to show that, so far as this natural fabric of ours is concerned, *we are these organs*, and that to disobey the divine laws under which alone they can healthily operate, is, in the gravity of its consequences, a moral offence—to do all this is to enter on a kind of instruction which those familiar with the domestic life of the mass of the people of this country know to have a more important bearing on every higher question of man's life, as a spiritual and immortal being, than any other, save the direct inculcation of spiritual truths themselves. The laws of health, then, which simply mean the rules of health taught with reference to the principles on which they repose, ought never to be absent from the primary school, and ought to be handled by the teacher with all the earnestness and solemnity of moral teaching. Again, although the duties which a man owes to his family, and to the society of which he is a member, defy all attempt at explicit teaching, unless we enter on the ground of elementary political economy, it is not necessary to go beyond truths obvious and trite. The moralities of getting and spending and selling involve a whole series of questions demanding detailed and impressive treatment and reiteration. Frugality, economy, saving, life insurance, the duty of educating children if only from purely prudential motives, the social and economic effects of lying and unfair dealing, all fall into the moral curriculum of the elementary school as leading subjects. The relation of employer and labourer, a clear understanding of what capital is, and of the fact that wages are paid out of capital (and the consequent importance of holding sacred the rights of property, of rejoicing in the accumulations of others, and of avoiding strikes), the causes of the rise and fall of wages, the effects of machinery, and the advantages, in some cases the duty, of emigration, are all momentous questions for the future operative, and attractive to him, if properly handled by the schoolmaster.[1] The present practice is to inculcate *the doing of the right;* the kind of instruction which I (following others who have given their thoughts to the objects and working of primary schools) consider to be indispensable, will show *what* the "right" is and *how* it can be done. Such instruction covers almost the

[1] Children leave school so young that the last-named subjects must generally be left to the teachers of the Evening or Continuation schools, now happily increasing in number.

whole field of practical morality. Its relation to religion, and the further and supreme task which special religious instruction has to accomplish, will be considered in its proper place. We are not called upon to introduce the above practical moralities pompously, as separate sciences or studies. In acquiring the technical arts of Reading, Writing, and Arithmetic, sufficient opportunities are afforded of instilling all the truths necessary to the future well-being of the pupil. If the reading-books are well constructed, they will suggest at least the text, if they do not supply the detailed evolution, of the moralities of our physical constitution and of our social relations.

As soon as the teacher has given such prominence in his school work to Religious Instruction, to the three technical subjects of Reading (in its larger sense), Writing, and Arithmetic, and to such teaching as can be given through these in practical morality in its detailed application to the duties which physiological laws and social life impose, he is then, but only then, at liberty to turn his attention to other subjects. The subjects here specified are indispensable and primary, and if others be introduced, they must be kept in strict subordination to the magistral studies. And here one word may be said on the vexed question of Grammar.

To teach English Grammar systematically before the child has reached the age of eleven is, it seems to me, a waste of time. I do not mean to say that it cannot be done, but that the pressure of other subjects makes it a waste of time to do it. Nor, perhaps, at any age is the teaching of English grammar in the primary school worth the time expended on it, except where it is made distinctly, and at every stage of the pupil's progress, to subserve two purposes, namely, *first*, facilitating the understanding of complex propositions, especially the language of poetry, by bringing into view and enabling the child to bring into view, the relation of the several parts of sentences; and, *secondly*, enabling the child to write sentences of his own composition accurately. Thus practically viewed in close relation to its real purpose, Grammar becomes a part of the reading-lesson, and by far the most useful intellectual discipline, *when taught with knowledge and precision*, to which a child can be subjected. Whatever may be said of boys above eleven years of age, it is certain that before they reach this age, they should know nothing of grammar save in the above purely practical sense. So limited, it is properly a part of the instruction in Reading and Writing, and essential to a thorough teaching of these arts, presuming that thorough teaching invariably aims at reaching and cultivating the understanding of the pupil.

The *secondary* subjects that can put forward the best claim for adoption into the school curriculum are Music and Geography. The moral and disciplinary effects of Music are so remarkable, that its judicious introduction is in reality a means of saving time;

and it is this fact which completes the numerous arguments which may be urged in its favour. Geography, again, occupies time ; but as it is a subject acquired chiefly through the eye, and therefore both attractive and easy, two or three lessons a week draw little on the time or disposable working power of the pupils. Its more solid claims for admission into the school are that, when taught with distinct and constant reference to climate, peoples, and industries, it is the least artificial of all the exercises of mind that can be presented to the young. For not only is it important as a discipline, it is the most fruitful of all possible subjects in facts ; and although an education which turns on absorption of facts is misnamed education—is not even instruction—yet the facts involved in a straightforward description of the earth we live on, its climates, peoples, and productions, are so *natural* an extension of the child's existing stock of knowledge, that they enter into his intellect as if part of his personal experience, insensibly broaden his understanding, and give greater depth and solidity to his future judgments. Moreover, the important relations of geography, when well taught, to the economic lessons already spoken of, by enabling the pupil to realize the nature and extent of industries and the mutual dependence of all mankind, strengthen the argument in favour of putting this subject next to music among the secondary subjects of the elementary school.

Here it is necessary to stop ; for beyond these subjects the primary school cannot go during the ordinary school hours, save in a few exceptional cases. It is true that a clever teacher may also give some instruction in the objects of nature by which his pupils are surrounded, and explain the more ordinary machines and physical phenomena which daily come across the pupil's path; but these he will find treated of in the school reading-books with sufficient fulness, and he cannot thoroughly teach the lessons there given, even as mere reading exercises, without eliciting their full meaning, and working them into the pupil's understanding in such a way as to imprint them firmly on his memory. The same remark applies to the elements of natural history, to geology, and accounts of industrial processes: they are to be treated as entirely subordinate to the technical subjects; that is to say, not treated at all, unless they enter into the reading-books by means of which the art of reading is taught.

The elements of Drawing one would fain see enter into the time-table of every primary school where the master is possessed of that organizing skill which converts subjects of this kind into time-savers rather than time-occupiers. But on no other condition can it find a place, for the simple reason, that if other more important subjects have their due, there is no place for it. It is necessary, however, to except those initiatory attempts at copying outlines of common objects on slates from the black-board, which are wisely interposed in the midst of other work in the case of very young children. These exercises properly belong to the infant school. They occupy and refresh the jaded mind, while giving facility to the unpractised fingers, and accuracy to the vague and undisciplined infant eye. To this extent Drawing is in reality a timesaver, and therefore constitutes no exception to the general condition of its introduction already specified.

History last and least claims attention in the elementary school.

So much for the lessons to be drawn by the schoolmaster from the chief of the inevitable limitations under which he works. But I cannot leave the subject without again adverting to the most serious limitation of all—the habits of life in the homes from which the children daily come, and the lesson which the teacher should draw from them. It will be observed that, next. to religious instruction and the acquisition of a certain facility in the three main technical subjects of the school, I have been guided in giving precedence to other topics by their moral relations, because the moral purpose in forming character must always maintain a strict ascendency over the intellectual. The latter serves man in this life, and can be at best only the basis on which his intellectual progress elsewhere can rest; the former is the man himself, his personality and will, without which he is nothing in this world, and apart from which he can be nothing hereafter. Nor does the will ever fail to justify its claim to supreme attention in the work of education, even in its relation to the understanding. For the most superficial observer must have noticed that a vigorous will sends a stream of clearness, perspicacity, and force into the operations of even an ordinary intellect, and is thus a constant source of real discipline. The necessity of this supreme regard to the moral aims of the school is, however, mainly forced upon us by the consideration of the domestic influences under which so large a proportion of the children live. The frequent wrangling, the ungracious demeanour towards each other, the careless ignoring, or what is even more common, the rude repression, of the gentler sensibilities of the young, are sufficient in themselves to divert the genial current of a young child's life into a hard and stony channel. To these demoralizing influences we have to add the too common disregard of cleanliness, decency, and order, the perpetual domestic struggle for mastery, determined ultimately by brute force alone, instead of the considerate command and eager submission which are the fruit of a paternal authority resting on moral superiority, and of a filial obedience prompted by respect and sustained by affection. If this be a fair summary of the counteracting agencies limiting, if not overturning, the teacher's work in the mass of the pupils' homes, the lesson which it enforces is the necessity of giving even exaggerated importance in the school to the cultivation of the feelings and imagination of the young, and of those ready civilities and mutual courtesies which do so much to confer happiness and dignity on the life of man. Here, again, the reading-books of the school will be found a useful auxiliary to the teacher, if, while furnishing the means of necessary discipline and instruction, they make provision for the starved imagination and repressed sensibilities of the children of the poorer classes.

Enough has been now said, by way of suggestion at least, on the lessons to be drawn from the limitations under which the primary teacher does his daily task; the result of all which is that he must confine his work within very narrow limits, and at the same time overrule it to certain moral and intellectual educative ends.

Nor is the result to which we have been led such as to discourage the ardent schoolmaster; for although he is excluded from such a choice of educational implements as might most efficiently promote the theoretic idea of the school—the Formation of Character—he is yet supplied with instruments good enough for the attainment of his purpose, if they be rightly used. The right use of these is such a use as will coerce them into submission to the ultimate educative purpose of his work. The consideration of this brings us to Methods of Teaching. For, having pointed out the subjects into which it is imperative that the teacher should throw his main strength, it becomes necessary to show in what way he is to regulate and apply that strength in the narrow field open to him, with a view to train his pupils to those good habits of the intelligence and the will which constitute the sum of his professional task.

METHODS OF TEACHING.

THE CONCURRENCE OF GENERAL METHOD AND PARTICULAR METHODS.

A method is a way towards the attainment of an end. The general method on which all education proceeds we have already spoken of. Our duty now is with the particular methods whereby certain special ends may be best attained. For the schoolmaster, inasmuch as he is precluded, by the circumstances under which he works, from selecting the materials of his craft with sole reference either to the ultimate educative end which he has in view, or to the best conception of general method, is driven to consider the question, whether it be possible to teach the subjects to which he is limited in such a way as to make them contribute directly to his ultimate purpose,—the formation of a good intellectual and moral habit,—and to bring the expedients he adopts within the range of philosophic method ; and all this without sacrificing the technical acquirement which it is his immediate business to communicate.

In other words, the schoolmaster is forced to consider the *particular* method belonging to each particular subject of instruction in its relation to general method ; the particular *end* being the communication to the pupil of a certain power over a specified subject (whether it be reading, writing, or arithmetic) as opposed to the general and ultimate end of education. The particular method which the teacher is in search of is the most sure, sound, effectual, and therefore the most easy and rapid way of communicating the required power. Manifestly, the particular method which has reference to a specific subject, and the general method which has reference to education in the general sense, are not of equal authority in the eyes of the enlightened schoolmaster. Where they conflict, or, I should rather say, seem to conflict, the latter is paramount. But as the *general* purpose of education can be attained only by the active exercise of the intellectual and moral powers of the pupil in accordance with their natural laws of operation, so it will be found that the *particular* purpose of instructing him in some specific subject cannot possibly be attained in any way so sure, sound, easy, and rapid, as by that which is in accordance with the same laws. Thus, happily, the particular method which has reference to each separate subject of instruction, and the general method of education, which contemplates solely the development and discipline of the mind, will be found to be fundamentally one and the same. The truth of this will appear in the course of ascertaining and stating the best methods to be employed in teaching the various special technicalities of the primary-school curriculum.

OBJECTS AND METHOD OF TEACHING READING.

The particular end proposed in teaching Reading is, if rightly understood, an end much more comprehensive and involving much more than is generally supposed. I have already incidentally adverted to the large view which the schoolmaster ought to take of the three time-honoured foundations of primary-school work,—Reading, Writing, and Arithmetic. Reading especially admits of and demands a wide and liberal interpretation. To put it concisely and practically, the teaching of this art is the communicating of a power to read works which constitute ordinary literature, easily, intelligently, and intelligibly. To accomplish this object *thoroughly* is, as we shall find, to give, explicitly or implicitly, so large an amount of instruction and discipline as almost to effect the whole higher purpose of elementary education.

We have now to see how this special end—Reading —may be most surely and soundly reached, and to elicit the harmony that subsists between the particular technical end of instruction and the general purpose of education.

Initiation in the Art of Reading.

The Phonic, the "Look and Say," and the Alphabetic methods—Spelling.

To initiate a child into the art of Reading, is to give him the power of recognising the conventional symbols of words, and of uttering them accurately.

All words whatsoever are merely different groupings of a limited number of conventional signs, and the labour of learning to read is thus infinitely less than if every word had a distinct symbol written or drawn. Were we in the latter unhappy predicament, the primary teacher would be almost wholly occupied in teaching the ten or fifteen thousand different symbols necessary for the instruction of a child in the art of reading his Bible or the daily paper, and even after this was accomplished, the pupil would find that an immense number of word-signs were still to him a sealed book. By arresting words in the act of enunciation, and analysing their sounds into their individual parts, we find that the same sounds are continually recurring in different combinations, and that, while words seem infinite in number, the sounds which enter into them are few. In the English language, even including biliteral sounds, the total number probably does not exceed thirty. To these elementary simple sounds, we have only to attach written symbols, and the art of reading becomes simply the *act of recognising these sound-symbols and re-combining them into words.*

The first step in teaching to read, therefore, manifestly ought to be to give the child a knowledge of the elementary sounds and their corresponding symbols,— I say *sounds*, not the accidental *names* of the sounds; the second, to guide him in the attempt to group them into words of the most simple kind, but gradually increasing in difficulty. The first step is only a lesson in form, to be taught as lessons in form ought to be taught, and is purely an act of memory ; the second step is a lesson in the building up of parts into a whole, —bringing into play, in an arbitrary way certainly, those powers whereby the child has been acquiring all his knowledge up to the date of his entering school, namely, the powers of attention, comparison, analysis, and synthesis.

This, shortly summarized, is the method which is best adapted for giving a sound and rapid knowledge of reading and spelling ; for, while calling for continual acts of observation and memory, it also subserves the intellectual purpose of an easy, because unforced and natural, discipline. I forbear adverting here to the defects which are inseparable from this phonic method, till I have adverted to the two other modes adopted or advocated.

And, *first*, we have the "word and name," or " look and say" system, which teaches that complete words, such as 'I see a goat,' 'The maid milks a cow,' 'Tom is a boy,' are to be taught to the child in the first instance, just as they stand, and until he has acquired a certain facility in reading. This system is advocated on the ground of its affording more interest to the pupil, and so exciting his powers to more rapid acquisition. But the fact that the analysis into their simple elementary parts, of the sounds which enter into each word, is only postponed, and must be achieved sooner or later, is frequently lost sight of by the teacher, in the satisfaction which the manifest progress of the child in the knowledge of words yields.

This system is to be objected to because it reduces written language to a system of pictorial representations of words as *wholes*, and so compels the child to learn some three or four hundred different pictorial symbols before he begins to suspect that there is a shorter way of getting at the symbols of spoken language—a key for each and every word alike. What is the process which, under this system, goes on in the learner's mind ? It is this : after a few months' instruction, in which the memory alone is exercised, he begins to discover that the same simple forms or letters are constantly recurring in all words, and unconsciously to attach to each separate form its own specific phonic power. The teacher takes advantage of this dawning analysis, and improves it into a knowledge of all the elementary signs, with their corresponding names or sounds, or both. The teacher and pupil, in point of fact, retrace their steps in order to find the key which lay conspicuously enough at their feet when they started on their journey, in order that, having armed themselves with it, they may push on with fresh vigour to the easier conquest of all future verbal difficulties. The process of analysis and synthesis thus certainly comes at last, bearing with it its intellectual advantages, but it comes later than need be, and only after the superfluous difficulty of learning hundreds of different pictorial forms for complete words, has been thrown in the way of the child's early progress. The process of learning must, it seems to me, from the very nature of the case, be ultimately slower according to this method than according to those more generally practised, while the disciplinary benefits of learning to read are unnecessarily postponed. That the process of learning twenty or thirty words is both a pleasanter and more rapid one than that of learning twenty or thirty forms, with their corresponding names or sounds, must be at once admitted, for the simple reason, that symbols which have a meaning must be more cheerfully acquired and more easily remembered than symbols that have no meaning. But it is surely absurd to suppose that the learning of two or three hundred symbols for words, even with the suggestive aid of the meanings attached to them, is easier than the acquisition of the twenty or thirty elementary symbols which enter into all words. Moreover, it is a mistake to suppose that the learning of the elementary shapes in their unmeaning nakedness is a process insufferably tedious to the pupil. We must not judge children by ourselves. The symbolic forms are novelties to them, and interest them, deeply interest them, as *form-lessons*, and as such they present no peculiar difficulty.

The *second* method of teaching to read is that almost universally practised, and consists of giving the child a knowledge of the elementary forms (teaching him the alphabet, as it is called), attaching to these forms certain arbitrary *names*, and then proceeding to combine these forms and names into wholes (that is, into words) having no resemblance in sound, or a very remote resemblance to the names by which the individual forms making up the word have been designated. For example, the child is taught to say *em wi* is *my;* *aitch ō yew ess-ee* is *house;* *see ā tee* is *cat*. But inasmuch as *see ā tee* cannot *sound* the word *cat,* but only *stand for it,* the process of acquiring the word is manifestly a pure act of memory.

Now this, the "alphabetic" system (though bad), has several distinct advantages over the "look and say" system. It gives the child a quicker knowledge of words (after the alphabet has been learned), because, by directing his attention to the individual parts which make up the wholes, it facilitates his perception and remembrance of the grouping of the forms which make up the complete word. A child who sees a cart for the first time, and has his attention directed first to the wheels and axle, and then to the body and the shafts, and *finally* to the object as a whole, will afterwards more quickly distinguish a cart from every other sort of vehicle, than if he had looked at the object, first and last, only in its general outline as a unity. So with the written symbol for cart : the naming of *see ā ar tee,* cannot by any possibility suggest the sound *cart,* but it individualizes the pupil's attention on the various constituent elements of the general pictorial outline of the whole word, which consequently is more clearly and vividly depicted on his eye and in his memory. Again, in the act of enunciating the names of the different elements of the symbol, he spells it, and thus acquires a know

ledge of spelling simultaneously with that of reading.
Further, this breaking up of the word more quickly
suggests to him the conclusion which every mode
of teaching elementary reading has ultimately in
view, namely, that each separate sign plays a peculiar
part in making up the *sound* of the *whole*, and has a
certain and specific *phonic* value. Having acquired an
unconscious power of attaching to the various signs
and sign-names their peculiar phonic values, his enunciation of the names of the signs, when he comes to
a *new* word ("spelling it over," as it is called), before he pronounces it, is a real help to him; and why?
because it suggests the *sound* of the whole word. Let
not the teacher, however, imagine that a child so
taught receives any assistance from the *naming* of
the separate signs in making out the word, *until he
has unconsciously and gradually worked out for himself a complete phonic system.* This he *must* do.
There is thus thrown on the child the labour of finding out for himself the sounds or powers of each
separate sign which he is daily in the habit of *naming*,
and for a considerable period the facility which this
phonic knowledge gives in making out words, has
accordingly been wilfully sacrificed; and, along with
this facility, the intellectual exercise which the independent elaboration of fresh words out of given
materials would have yielded to him.

We are thus brought back to the method which was
introduced at the beginning of this chapter, as the

natural consequence of an analytic system of written language—that, namely, which takes the individual parts of the words, and gives them, from the first, the *sounds* which they actually have when grouped to form words ; shortly, the Phonic Method. Given the power of recognising these sign-elements, and a knowledge of their force in combination (in other words, given a knowledge of the sounds of the letters of the alphabet), it is manifest that the pupil is provided with the means of constructing words for himself. His teaching and learning have thus, from the very first, a significance which they derive from their direct and palpable bearing on the practical application of his knowledge of sounds to the making out of words and sentences.

It is a trivial objection to the phonic method that the sounds of the letters when they stand by themselves are not precisely the same as they are when in combination; for example, $b\breve{e}$ $\breve{a}$ $t\breve{e}$ does not, when rapidly pronounced, yield precisely *bat*, nor does $d\breve{e}$-$\breve{o}$-$g\breve{e}$ quite yield *dog*, when allowed to flow into a unity of pronunciation. But the answer to this simply is, that it *very nearly* yields it (especially if an effort is made to sink the vowel element in the sound), and that in a great number of words it *quite* yields it ; for example, s-$\breve{u}$-n yields *sun*, and so forth. Failing the possibility of getting the precise sound of the constituent elements of words, it is surely the next best thing to get something which approximates to this, instead of at once throwing up the task of sounding in despair, and plunging into an arbitrary *naming* of the elements,—a device which only remotely and indirectly contributes to facilitate the acquisition of the art of reading. According to the phonic system, the diphthongs *oi, ou, aw, ai, ae,* etc., are of course learned as distinct sounds along with the other letters of the alphabet.

The most serious objection to the system is the obstacle which the numerous irregularities of the English language oppose, causing words to assume sounds as a whole which cannot by any amount of contortion be shown to be derivable from the sounds of their individual parts. For example, the words *are* and *have* the child would naturally expect to find sounded with the *a* long, while *one, two, were, said,* and numerous others, present, almost at the outset of the child's career, seeming contradictions to the phonic lessons he is being taught. In reply, I have to point out the fact that the principle on which the method proceeds affords a key to nineteen-twentieths of the words in the language, and that the outstanding irregularities can be taught *as such*, on the "look and say" system, without any attempt to show that they are capable of phonic analysis. According to the present almost universal "alphabetic" system, *every* vocable is an irregularity, and has to be learnt as if no other words had been learnt before it, for the names of the letters can afford no direct help in finding out the sound of the word which they represent. It is surely a manifest gain to be able to furnish the child with a key to the great majority of words, and thereby to reduce stumbling-blocks to a minimum!

Moreover, in learning to read according to the phonic method, the child, in addition to possessing all the advantages of the method ordinarily adopted at present, is furnished with an instrument,—namely, *the sounds of the letters*,—which he can *himself* apply with a view to fresh acquisitions. He thereby has his love of power and discovery gratified, and in the pleasing act of word-elaboration, he finds an exercise of understanding, humble indeed in its object, but beneficial in its disciplinary effects. The mental act is in truth worthy of all respect and encouragement, as it in no essential respect differs from those higher but similar operations which we admire in the cultivated intellect of the scholar or the man of science.

Thus it is that the soundest and easiest way of teaching the technical art of reading, indirectly contributes, even in its initiatory stage, to that intellectual discipline which is one side of the great object of the primary school (formation of character) ; and further, that it tends to interest the child in his work while facilitating his progress. A question seemingly unimportant thus assumes proportions which make it worthy of the attention of all concerned in education, if it be once admitted that education has any principles at all.

In SPELLING we find further confirmation of the

practical superiority as well as the philosophic character of the phonic method of teaching to read. According to the ordinary method, spelling is an act of memory performed by the eye, which carries away an impression, more or less accurate, of the elementary forms entering into a word, and by the ear, which aids the eye by recalling the order in which the *names* of the letters were uttered, when spelling out the word with a view to the reading of it. According to the phonic method, spelling is all this and something more ; for it is an effort to disentangle into its separate parts a complex sound, resulting from the fusion of several elements into one whole ; and therefore it is an intellectual act. Bi-literal sounds are, of course, treated in the same way when spelling as when reading ; and when the child comes to name the letters he will do so in such a way as to show that these sounds are simple, though denoted by two letters. " Seek" will be spelled *s* double *e*, *k*, and "full," *f*, *u*, double *l*, not *l*, *l*, as is the too common practice. But it must be admitted that the mind of the child, as well as of the adult, has a tendency to run instinctively to the easiest way of overcoming a difficulty, and that spelling, consequently, becomes practically an act of eye-memory more than of intelligence. This being the case, it is remarkable that the habit of exercising infant classes in printing words on slates should have been of so recent introduction. If the eye is to remember, it can only do so by looking steadily and looking long ; and it is materially aided by accustoming the child to trace over on the black-board, and then to form on his own slate, the word a picture of which he is to keep in his mind for purposes of spelling. This exercise is equally helpful in teaching reading, nor is it a matter of great importance whether the child succeeds or not in delineating the forms before him. The benefit arises out of the attempt.

Notwithstanding the importance of a right method, even in the initiatory months of a child's education, it is to be admitted that the best results are, after all, invariably attained by moral means, even though these be brought into operation by a teacher regardless and unconscious of principle or plan. No one can have watched the vivacity, the playfulness, and the mental activity which some teachers can educe from their pupils, even in the apparently unsuggestive labour of alphabetic and monosyllabic instruction, without being convinced that where such qualifications can be found, all others may be dispensed with. Just as the moral purpose of the school takes precedence of every other, so does the moral vitality of the teacher supersede every other qualification, by enabling him to transfuse into the minds of his pupils a force similar to that which he himself exhibits, and which stirs and elevates the action of their understandings. Nor is this true only of the teaching of words and other initiatory knowledge ; it belongs to every subject and every stage of school life. The earnest, living interest of the master in the subjects and the objects of his work will not fail to be reflected in the minds of his pupils, and to be more fruitful in results than the most philosophical methods in the hands of the formal and half-hearted precisian.

The Juvenile Stage in teaching Reading.

Mental progress and Progress in Reading should be concurrent—Intelligent reading—To teach to read properly is to educate—The imagination and the moral and religious sensibilities of children—Intelligible reading.

The initiatory process, lasting for a year, or a year and a half, as the case may be, ends in giving the child a knowledge of reading, in the lowest technical sense. He can name, and, it may be hoped, sound the letters, and combine them into monosyllables, and into the simpler kind of dissyllables. He now knows that the groupings of forms which lie before him on a printed page are words and sentences; he knows also, in general, though within certain very narrow limits, what these words and sentences are. I have assumed that it is quite superfluous in these days to point out the necessity for a carefully graduated and well considered selection of reading-lessons, of the importance of giving the child words conveying a meaning, and only such sentences as faithfully represent, in a somewhat improved form, his own little thoughts and modes of speech. To dwell on such established points would be to waste time.

The stage of the child's progress in the art of reading, on which we next enter, is one which we

E

cannot approach with too much consideration, both of our specific aims and of our means of applying them. For what does progress here mean? It means giving to the child more difficult and more numerous words to decipher, longer and more complex sentences to grasp, consecutive narrative to follow and understand. To do this would be unmeaning and futile, did we not presume a mental growth in the child corresponding to the growth of his command over written words and sentences. We presume that his daily experience, stimulated and intensified by school discipline, prompts to the acquisition of new words suited to express in oral intercourse the constant accession of new facts and fresh generalizations which observation has been from day to day forcing upon him, and which have added to the material, and through this to the capacity and power, of his understanding. If such a progress has not been going on, the pages of his book will be to the child a series of hieroglyphics, which he may be laboriously taught to pronounce, but which he not only cannot interpret, but *cannot be taught* to interpret. The initiatory discipline involved in acquiring the rudiments of the art of reading has, it is presumed, consolidated and methodized both the words and the thought of the opening mind, and laid a firm basis for the future structure of knowledge. If the reading-lessons of the second stage anticipate, instead of simply meeting, or, at most, slightly preceding the growth of the child, the bond up to that moment subsisting between the lesson to be acquired and the mind acquiring is broken; the consentaneous and parallel movement of intellectual development and of progress in the technical art of reading gives place to a discord which is irreparable. The significance and interest which ought to accompany every act of knowledge disappear, and the child is doomed to a future school career essentially dreary and unprofitable. That which ought to have been at worst a labour becomes a toil. I do not say that the pupil will stop short permanently at the point at which he has been abruptly shunted off the intelligible into the unintelligible, and that all acquisition is thenceforth rendered impossible; but what he acquires will be an ineffectual knowledge of words and sentences uninspired by any meaning. One consequence of this will be that such discipline as he may receive will be so much at discord with the natural development of the mind, and made up so much of shreds and patches, that the trifling benefit which it does confer will not compensate for the aversion to all intellectual exercise which it is sure to engender.[1] By inverting the intellectual order, the teacher subverts the natural love of intellectual activity. This is the result of overleaping a stage in the pupil's life, and presenting him with reading-lessons which do not truly reflect his mental growing and growth.

But this, it may be said, is a purely intellectual

[1] Teachers should not ignore the fact that the proportion of the poorer classes who ever read, for the purpose of extending their information, anything save the weekly paper, is by no means large, and very far below the reasonable expectation of those who establish schools.

shortcoming ; it may be admitted that it bears directly on one of the presumed aims of the school—the formation of a good habit of the intelligence ; but this is of little consequence, inasmuch as we have already abjured such general theoretic aims, under the irresistible pressure of the *immediate* and practical requirements of the children of the poorer classes : our business is to teach them, as expeditiously as possible, to *read*. If by this be meant that the work in hand is to teach the child to utter, with accurate pronunciation and with fair attention to "stops," the sounds of the human voice represented by certain typographical drawings upon paper, the expensive machinery of popular education should be broken up at once, and we should leave to the old dame-schoolmistress the work which a few technical rules will enable her to do sufficiently well. It is not such service that the State or the Church requires of the schoolmaster, nor is it such service as this that the schoolmaster whom I contemplate would deign to render. He may aim at a merely technical end, but the end in his view is to teach to read easily, intelligently, and intelligibly, the more common current literature. And how shall a child learn to read *easily* if the acquired word is to him a dead thing ; if the sound of it recalls to his mind no living reality of his experience, and remains unsupported by any suggestive association ? How can he read *intelligently*, if he does not understand ? How can he read *intelligibly*, that is, in such a way as to be understood, if the sentences which he mechanically enunciates transcend his comprehension? Accordingly, the competent teacher finds that the process or method by which the technical end in its highest and only rational sense can be attained, must be determined by the intellectual growth and deeds of the pupil. Thus the general theoretic end and the special technical end of the schoolroom again in this, the second or juvenile stage of the child's progress, support and justify each other.

And to what practical conclusions does this fact compel the thoughtful schoolmaster? To these : *first*, that the reading-lessons of the child must, if the art of reading is to be properly acquired, be graduated in difficulty, considered as mere reading-lessons ; *secondly*, that they must be as *various* in their language and subjects as the pupil's own experience ; *thirdly*, that they must be abundant in respect of quantity, if the reading is afterwards to be easy; and, *fourthly*, that the subjects treated, and the style of treating them, must be graduated in accordance with the growth of mind, if the reading is to be intelligent and intelligible. Graduation in words and sentences, graduation in the thoughts and subjects of which these treat, variety, and quantity,—such, succinctly stated, must be the qualities of the reading-lessons to which the teacher should, in the juvenile stage, introduce his pupils. In other and more general words, the reading-lessons, if they are thoroughly to attain their merely technical end, are, in respect of quantity and variety, to reflect faithfully, but in a more perfect form, the full range of the child's intellectual experience, and in their graduation the *order of growth* of his understanding.

It would seem, then, that to teach a child reading effectually, it is necessary to adapt ourselves to the child's intellectual speed and capabilities. The question of the method of teaching reading, accordingly, passes into another and a higher and larger question,— the method of training, informing, and disciplining the young intelligence itself. The kind of reading which accomplishes this, will most effectually secure the technical end; while the possession of the technical power *so* acquired will be a guarantee that the child has been thus far *educated*, so far as the intellect is concerned.

Were the objects of our care possessed of physical desires and intellectual capacities only, the work of the teacher would be comparatively easy. Lessons, oral and read, on the visible *things* of his experience, on the forms, properties, and relations of these, and on bodily acts, would constitute the whole work of the school—work hard and dry, but in the hands of one who understood his craft not therefore uninteresting, toilsome, or unattractive But this direct discipline of the powers of observation, comparison, and inference, though essential to good reading, as well as to sound intellectual training, is only part of the work, and that the least difficult part. To teach reading effectually, and to educate in any sense worthy of the name, it is necessary to cover, with our lessons

JUVENILE STAGE IN THE ART OF READING. 71

and instructions, the *whole* field of the child's experience, and to meet *all* his mental wants. We have accordingly to recognise, interpret, assist, explain, and extend the experience of the child, as a being of Imagination and of moral and religious sensibilities, as well as of intellectual faculties. This is the most delicate part of our task, and requires delicate handling. Yet how constantly do we find the wondering germs of sentiment which arise in the young mind treated with a rough and masterful hand. The teacher seems to forget that, in such matters, he passes out of the region of mere knowledge and intellect into that of feeling and emotion; that he enters into the realm of the impalpable and invisible, and must not attempt to touch too rudely or see too clearly. To handle things which are in their essence mysterious and infinite, as if they were the parts of a house or a tree; to drag forth into the hard light of a schoolroom the silent emotions that attend the birth of imagination and piety, is to desecrate holy ground. A child must always be treated with respect; there are occasions when he should be treated with reverence. There are sacred precincts in the school which must be approached with preparation, or not approached at all.

The precise nature and function of the Imagination in children, as in men, it is neither my business nor my intention here to attempt to explain. In the child, speakingly roughly, I understand it to be that reproductive power which leads, or rather compels, him to build up fresh wholes out of the broken and scattered fragments of his experience, in complex combination with the dim instinctive suggestions of love, fear, hope, and wonder. Under this natural impulse the manifold and disconnected elements of his external observation, and the hidden workings of his sensibilities, are dwelt upon, compared, combined, connected as cause and effect, and woven into a kind of crude unity. This vital process, accordingly, is educative in the highest sense, because it is a self-education, and because it embraces within its sphere the whole of the conscious life of the child, and brings into easy and healthful play all his capacities. The result is an unreality; but to the child it is quite as real as external nature, simply because it is the product of his own spontaneous activity, and spun out of materials of his own. This instinct of the child is to be respected by the teacher, were it only because it is doing more for his pupil than the master can do. And it is to be respected, chiefly by being exempted from all didactic talk. The art of teaching in this matter is to dispense with the art altogether in its usual sense. Sympathy takes the place of art. The teacher will, therefore, read the imaginative lessons, whether in prose or verse, *to* the child, and *with* him, sharing his interest, evolving the stories, explaining away difficult words, and then passing on. He may ask for the repetition of the story in the words of the class; he may help the children in their efforts to reconstruct it, as a mother might, but he must not mar its simple unity by putting questions or suggesting explanations, nor defeat, by personal applications or dull discourse, the simple lesson which the tale or fable or poem teaches. All these precautions it is necessary to take if the nascent imagination is not to be repressed or misdirected, and if the reading-lessons which appeal to this faculty are not to be robbed of that charm which makes them attractive, and which stimulates the pupils to extend a technical power which has many such pleasing stores in reserve.

If this careful regard to the imagination of the young be obligatory on the instructors of children of all classes, how much more is it incumbent on the teacher of the children of the poor? Divorced as they are by poverty, and the want of sympathetic response in their elders, from the pictures, fables, poems, and narratives which surround, in lavish profusion, the children of the middle and upper classes, they have but the one chance which the day-school affords of obtaining food for their starved imaginations. Nor will the teacher err, if, departing from his book, which, if justice be done to other subjects, can yield but a limited supply of such material, he introduce tales into the schoolroom, to be read as rewards of good conduct. The time so occupied will assuredly not be wasted; for, apart from the indirect moral instruction which he will thus convey through the imagination, he will shed sunlight and warmth on the tender mind, without which a genial and healthy growth is impossible.

But if the dreams and wonderings of the young imagination demand such cautious and sympathetic treatment, with how gentle and tender a hand must we approach the vague and timid aspirings of the Religious instinct, and the small perplexities and keen sensibilities which belong to the infancy and childhood of the moral sentiments. Here too, unhappily, the school has to supplement, nay, too often to be a substitute for the moral and religious training which ought to be the work of the home. The influences of combined love and awe which accompany spiritual teaching in families more favourably situated, the careful consideration or the wise negligence, are denied to the great majority of primary-school children. It becomes, therefore, the special duty and privilege of the schoolmaster to supply this want : with paternal affection to dissociate morality and religion from harshness of manner and tyranny of will, to cast the light of divine love over the invisible, and to introduce the young *early* to the Gospel story, and its personal relation to them. This subject will be handled more fully hereafter. It is touched on here in order to give it its due place in the education of the growing child, and therefore in his Reading-lessons, which we presume to be co-extensive with his moral as well as his intellectual experience, to reproduce that experience in a more perfect form, and to satisfy in some degree the vague desires, and to complete the imperfect conceptions which it rouses into activity. In this way the child early, but insensibly, becomes alive to the fact that books contain a true reflection of himself, that they answer his questions and please his imagination, and are consequently among the best companions and friends of his life.

Thus we find that by liberally interpreting the Reading-instruction of the school we educate not only the understanding but the whole nature of the pupil. That is to say, we take up the raw material of the child's experience, giving it that shape and definiteness, development, and completion, which, unaided, it would never attain, save in the vigorous and powerful brain of the few. The result of this treatment is, that the young groping mind begins, under the wise guidance of its instructor, to feel its path less devious and perplexing: observation, the beginnings of knowledge, and the words which denote these, gradually take the orderly arrangement and solidity which afford a substructure for the future growth; hesitating questionings about the nature and causes of things receive the satisfaction befitting the pupil's age; the half-hidden, half-revealed dreams of the imagination receive a legitimate and healthful encouragement; the uncertain dawnings of the moral and religious sentiments emerge into a clearer light, though still clothed with mystery, as they must ever be. This is the process of elementary education, and this the work of the elementary teacher. In *such* an education he finds his best auxiliary in teaching to read, and by *rightly* teaching to read he implicitly educates.

The work of teaching to read is thus to be identified with that of training the young to a good habit of the moral nature (in the largest sense), as well as of the intellect. The materials of both the teaching and the training, and the methods of both, are the same. From first to last the seemingly mechanical process of instruction in a technical art is in truth a living and life-inspiring method, resting on a sound, and to that extent a scientific knowledge of the human mind. The reading-book is no longer the exclusive object of master and pupil, but merely the text-book of a higher aim—education. As such, it is not only the auxiliary of his method, but a kind of fixed typographical embodiment of that method. It represents in visible form that intercourse between the mature and immature mind, which is the educative process. This method of teaching Reading accordingly may be fitly distinguished from others as the *Educative Method*.

To conclude : the intelligent reading must also fulfil our requirement of being intelligible. To aim at æsthetic reading, except in those few fortunate primary schools which retain their pupils to the age of thirteen or fourteen, is futile ; but such reading as will convey to an auditor, with accuracy, distinct enunciation, and emphasis, the thoughts of the prose or poetical lesson of the day, is not only possible, but easy of attainment. The pupil who does this, does more than simply absorb the mental product of others. The spirit and colour, as well as the thought, of the lesson enter into him ; and in the act of reproducing these for the benefit of his audience, with suitable emphasis and intelligence, they in a special sense become his own. Not only are the sentences themselves a second time appropriated by the art of elocution, but the style and character of the piece, whether didactic, imaginative, humorous, or pathetic, are brought into relief, and exercise their peculiar power as fosterers of the germs of taste.

If intelligible reading of this kind is to be attained easily or at all, the teacher must give the key-note of the reading when the child is in the initiatory stage. The foundation must be laid at the base, not in the middle, of the building, and laid *by the teacher himself*. Good reading is the successful *imitation of a good model*, and it is a work of time. No one can leap into the art, or read well to order.

Subsidiary questions as to the means, the manner, and the expedients whereby the method of teaching reading is more or less successfully applied, fall to be considered in another portion of this Report, where I comment on the means most generally adopted in the schools visited.

OBJECTS AND METHOD OF TEACHING WRITING.

The practical purpose, namely, facility and distinctness, to be kept constantly in view—Letters to be turned to use as they are learned—The power to be applied to copying on slates—Writing from dictation.

The particular purpose at which the teacher ought to aim in teaching Writing is the power of writing from dictation the sentences of the reading-lesson, in script characters, with facility and distinctness. That this is the end will scarcely in these days be impugned, though few teachers have yet fully realized the fact. Caligraphy may be said still to hold a kind of traditionary possession of the schoolmaster's mind. The sooner this delusion is expelled the better for the pupil, if not for the æsthetics of penmanship. Caligraphy is to be spoken of with the respect which is its due, when we find it in its proper place ; but I cannot think that place to be the primary school, when I reflect on the hurtful effects which its intrusion there has produced. Page after page, book after book, of letters and words and preposterous sentences, are copied by the pupil, with a view to the formation of " a hand," and the sum-total of result at the age of ten or eleven is, except in the case of a few, a power of imitating, in somewhat crabbed style, a model set before them—a model which is to them merely a series of forms, which they are unable to interpret without assistance. Substitute for this the distinct and accurate writing of the sentences of the reading-lesson as the practical aim to be constantly striven for, and a new significance and increased importance at once attach themselves to the art, while at the same time an intelligent process supplants a merely imitative exercise in Form.

The ultimate purpose of teaching Writing is determined by no abstract consideration, but solely by the limitations under which the teacher works—the general bearing of which on the materials and methods of elementary education has been already discussed. These limitations demand that the pupil, at the age of ten or eleven, shall be able to accomplish something more available in practical life, and in his own future education, than the imitative reproduction of certain script characters.

Given the purpose, the method or path whereby it is to be reached will not be difficult to find. The final purpose is the schoolmaster's beacon, which not only marks the goal towards which he is moving, but throws a light on every step of the way.

As a preliminary of all writing method, we have to bear in mind two things—(1.) That the time is short and the art is long, and therefore we must begin betimes. A slate should be put into every infant's hands on the same day on which he receives his Primer, and the foundation of the art of writing laid by causing him to imitate the printed letters and words of his lessons. As soon as sufficient familiarity has been gained with the elements of Reading—about the end of the initiatory stage—he should begin to copy on his slate script letters written by the master on the black-board; (2.) That the letters which he forms should not be too large for the tensive power of the muscles of the little hand. With these preliminary remarks, we come to the question of method proper.

The method to be pursued is to introduce the pupil almost at once to letters, and to print alongside each letter its typographical equivalent. The letters should be given in the order of simplicity of formation, and *combined into words as soon as the letters given admit of it, without waiting till the whole alphabet has been acquired.* In this way, the letters acquired are revised at the same time that they are at once turned to their practical use. The perception of a result so early attained in a new art is pleasing to the pupil, because it is novel, while it invests with an unmistakable meaning what is usually a stupid and stupefying exercise. It does more, for it supplies a motive; and a child is quite as open to the influence of a motive, or a reason which appeals to his intelligence, as an adult. Children compare and reason, it is true, with a smaller stock of materials than men, with a misapprehension of the true proportions of things and with less mental vigour, but it is a great blunder to treat them as if they did not reason at all, and were inaccessible to rational motives of action. The power of immediately putting to use a new acquisition supplies a motive for progress. It also furnishes an incentive. No one can have given the most superficial attention to children, without having learnt that their most intense delight is to be found in construction. To make some fresh thing out of such materials as they may have is their highest ambition. The practical and philosophic method of teaching the first elements of Reading takes advantage of this, as has been shown, and through it gives unconscious discipline; the practical method of teaching Writing appeals to the same mental characteristic.

If the child be so taught as to be able to connect every fresh script-form with something already known in print, and to be able to construct words for himself by help of these forms, a lesson, which must always be *essentially* one of imitation, becomes also an exercise of intelligence. The writing out of printed letters and words, and of sentences from the reading-lesson, on a slate, sustains throughout the whole course of instruction in Writing the intellectual character of the art, and makes it something more than a mere manual trick.

The higher stage and final purpose of the art—Writing from Dictation—will be introduced early, and give a new interest to the lessons, by giving a new power and revealing a new utility. By calling on the power of attention to what the master dictates, as well as on the power of applying what has been learned, a certain amount of intellectual discipline is given—limited, it is true, but by no means despicable. The teaching of writing thus comprehends spelling, though it by no means supersedes oral practice in that exercise. It is scarcely necessary to point out, that according to this practical method the pupil acquires the power of reading script while learning to write it, and thus a fresh, though incidental, interest is given to his task.

Of course the pupil will be taught to make great exertions to reproduce the shapely forms of his models; he will know that there is good writing and bad writing as well as good reading and bad reading. But the main purpose will be steadily held before him, and determine every step in his progress, namely, the power of writing from dictation a clean, accurate, and distinct copy of his reading-lesson.[1] I shall be much surprised if the practical expedients adopted for securing this result do not also produce better writers, in respect of mere caligraphy, than we now have. Whether they do so or not, fine penmanship must be rigidly subordinated to facility and distinctness of writing, in order that, at an early period of his career, a child may find himself possessed of a substantial power, which he delights to use, and which will stand him in good stead in his after life, saving him from that sense of inferiority which the want of an indispensable art is always found to excite, and giving him a sound and firm basis for further progress.

It is very far from my intention to discourage beautiful writing and feats of penmanship. But such accomplishments have their fit place in the school curriculum only *after* the essential and necessary work is done, and ought to be postponed as a distinct aim till the age of eleven. They are to be gladly welcomed and applauded if they are attained by the pupil without his having been required to deviate from the direct path which leads towards a more solid and fruitful acquisition.

Thus the practical end has suggested a practical as well as practicable path, and the result is that, in the art of writing, as in that of reading, *particular* method

[1] Elementary composition belongs to a more advanced stage of writing, and involves grammar.

subserves the *general* method of education; for the formation of a good mental habit is manifestly promoted by substituting for a method and aim purely mechanical a method characterized by intelligence, promotive of discipline, and instinct with a solid purpose.

OBJECTS AND METHOD OF TEACHING ARITHMETIC.

Intellectual discipline of Arithmetic—School Arithmetic should be practical and economic—Method of teaching: the concrete method—Moral uses of School Arithmetic.

Were the teacher free from all limitations in the formation of his plans for attaining the ultimate end of primary education, he might possibly choose to eject reading and writing from the schoolroom, in so far as these arts are merely technical, and to substitute the intellectual and moral discipline which can be best effected through conversation and personal influence, assisted by the objects of external nature, and the lessons that might be drawn from the hourly occurrences of life. It is true that, in the initiatory stages of reading and writing, there is a right and a wrong method, contributing more or less to the discipline of the pupil, as well as to his facility and certainty of acquisition; but beyond those stages the educative purpose is really attained, we have seen, through the identification, as much as possible, of the arts taught with the objects for which they are taught, viz., instruction, discipline, and moral and æsthetic cultivation. It is otherwise with Arithmetic. The art of manipulating numbers with dexterity, and the rationale of the expedients whereby the processes are abbreviated and guaranteed, are merely the evolving and strengthening, in the most direct way, of a special intellectual power which exerts itself spontaneously in all men. Irrespectively, therefore, of the future necessities of the child, this power would, in its relation to the general and theoretic object of education alone, demand and amply reward cultivation. The combination of parts into wholes, the dissolution of wholes into parts, and of these parts themselves into lower unities, are exercises in the relation of particulars to generals, and of generals to particulars, of great value to the intellect in other applications of its powers. The visible, we may even say the palpable, effects of error, which renders nugatory the most strenuous efforts, if vitiated by the most trifling flaw, must exercise a wonderful influence in giving the habit of accuracy and caution in all exercises of comparison and inference. Indeed, so universally diffused is the discipline given by means of the science and art of numbers, that we are perhaps scarcely able to estimate fully the extent to which it contributes to the intelligence of the people, and above all, to a rapid and easy movement of the human understanding in the conduct of ordinary affairs.

Nor are the above the most important of the disciplinary effects of adding, multiplying, and dividing wholes and parts; for it is impossible, notwithstanding the numerous contrivances for saving excessive tension of mind which enter into the rules in obedience to which the pupils work, to elaborate a correct answer to the questions which a good arithmetical manual supplies, without a certain amount of conscious intellectual *concentration*. A habit of mind is thereby strengthened which more than any other constitutes the intellectual superiority of one man over another, and of man himself over the lower animals. In acquiring other subjects, the pupil may give or withdraw his attention almost at his will, and yet make sensible progress in the acquisition of knowledge. In arithmetic there is a certain amount of deliberate and sustained attention essential to even the most elementary processes. This discipline cannot be evaded without leaving the work undone. The conscious exertion of the will to keep certain powers of the understanding in operation on a special question until a certain result be reached, is not only valuable in relation to the acquisition of the subject which for the moment may engage the mind; but, in addition to this, it increases the force available for the study of every other subject. This *kind* of discipline belongs peculiarly to arithmetic, even when taught merely as an exercise in abstract figures.

All this is true of arithmetic, apart from its practical relations to life, on which alone ultimately rest its claims to enter into the curriculum of the primary school. A consideration of these practical relations yields us at once the final purpose towards the realization of which the teacher must direct all his efforts, the methods which he ought to follow, and a further insight into the educative nature of the art.

Arithmetic is the science and art of numbers: school-arithmetic must always be, more or less, the adaptation of the art to the future uses of the pupil. Those uses tell us that the purpose of teaching arithmetic in elementary schools, apart from its influence as a discipline, is attained when such a command has been given over numbers as enables a young man or woman to calculate with facility all those questions which arise in the ordinary course of life. This may be called Economic Arithmetic. It embraces the addition, subtraction, and division of money, proportion, and vulgar fractions. Beyond these subjects no elementary teacher ought to attempt to go if he desires to be impartial in his instructions and do justice to other subjects much more important than *advance* in arithmetic.[1] His aim should be thoroughness rather than extent of acquirement.

Economic or school arithmetic embraces the domestic, but also extends to the general out-of-door, relations of the head of the family. The relation of his wages to the size of his family, to the several heads of legitimate expenditure, such as food, clothing, insurance, sick-clubs, saving, gives full occupation for the application of his knowledge, and ought to be constantly present to his thoughts. "Tell me how a man

[1] Except in those schools in which pupils stay beyond the age of eleven or twelve.

spends his money, and I will tell you the character of the man," was a remark in a special sense true of the labouring man. Almost the whole range of the duties of benevolence and justice fall under the head of income and expenditure, and resolve themselves into questions of arithmetic, which cannot be encountered, much less solved, by a man unfamiliar with figures. People of the middle class are themselves so much accustomed to economic calculation that it does not occur to them how serious an obstacle a deficiency of arithmetical training is to a labouring man, still more to a labouring man's wife.

Schoolmasters are frequently to blame for the meagre practical issue of their arithmetical teaching in the operative class; and the cause of their failure is to be found in this, that having omitted to define to themselves clearly the ultimate object of their labours, they necessarily fail to find a true method, and thus expend much well-meant labour in vain. The *quantity* of instruction given is generally ample, but much of it is irrelevant.

By the word *Economic*, the purpose of arithmetical teaching in schools has been defined : the method follows from the purpose, and is called the Concrete Method. And here I come on ground so much beaten by theoretical educationists that though it is yet untrodden by the great majority of practical teachers, I shall omit those details of ways and means, which have been so frequently reiterated. It will be sufficient to summarize the method in the following practical rules:—

(1.) To initiate children in arithmetic by means of the ball-frame alone, thereby making their elementary instruction a simple extension of their own daily observation. (2.) Simultaneously with this, and after it, to exercise the pupils in mental arithmetic; and (3.) To carry forward the instruction on the basis of concrete questions arising out of the necessities or experiences of common life, domestic and general, and to give prominence, at every step of the progress, to mental arithmetic.

As matters stand, the exercises worked by the pupils have, for the most part, immediate or sole reference to the attainment of a certain familiarity with the relations of number in themselves, and with the rules under which the exercises happen to be ranged; they ought, on the contrary, to bear with the greatest stress on the relations of number to every-day affairs. School-arithmetic is not a playing with numbers, but a dealing with the things to which number is attached. If it be not a playing with numbers, much less is it an intricate game with figures. Two lessons the primary teacher will at once draw from these considerations—he will avoid *slate*-work in its initiatory stages, relying on the presentation of *objects* to be numbered. He will see that through *mental arithmetic alone* he can approach the child naturally, and without a sudden dislocation of the infant numerical habit of mind. To begin with pebbles or balls, and exercise the mind apart from the manual exercise of the slate, is to accept the foundation which nature has herself laid. For the teacher to despise this, and to endeavour to rear the edifice of knowledge "in a way of his own," is to display ignorant pedantry where he ought to exhibit a wise faith, and to throw mystery and complexity into mental operations which to the child may be easily made clear and simple. In this, as in other subjects, the true method is to be found by considering the ways of nature, and following and fostering her spontaneous efforts. Having familiarized the child with the adding, subtracting, and multiplying of numbers which can be taken in by the eye, and in *this way* comprehended by the understanding, he will only then proceed to show the child the use of the slate in aiding the intellect, and facilitating processes which, in numbers above a certain amount, would to the child or even to the boy be a painful if not an impossible effort. He will not have failed in the initiatory stage to mass his balls in tens, and so to accustom the child to regard the highest figures as groups of tens of lower and higher multiples, without of course having prematurely suggested to the young mind the future applications of this expedient. The gradual introduction of difficult questions, which cannot be solved mentally, will *first* call for the help of the slate ; and the immense facility in solving these questions which slate-work, under certain rules of procedure, gives, will not be lost on a child taught according to the method of nature. It will be a relief, a surprise, and an encouragement. Further progress will continue to be made with constant recurrence to the concrete and reference to the economic, and thus figures and processes will be brought down from their abstract relations to the humble and practical needs of the day or the hour.

In urging on the schoolmaster's attention the definite and "economic" purpose of school-arithmetic, and the concrete method of attaining that purpose, I have been guided to the opinions advocated solely by the consideration of the limitations as to time and "utility" under which the primary teacher must consent to do all his work. But so harmonious are the operations of nature, that we find (as we also found in the subjects of reading and writing) that in obeying the restrictions as to the end and means of instruction imposed by the necessities of life, the teacher not only secures for his pupils thorough possession of the art of arithmetic in its purely technical aspect, but also best promotes the disciplinary purpose of all elementary education. For even the pure arithmetician, setting aside the practical requirements of the schoolroom or of life, will concur in maintaining that the art of arithmetic is only *then* thoroughly and scientifically acquired in its elements when it is acquired in those concrete relations out of which it arose. He will assure us that, except in those rare cases of peculiar native aptitude for numbers, which overleap the ordinary processes of education, solidity of foundation and stability of structure can be secured in no way so well as by the faithful pursuit of the method of nature. With whatever sleight-of-intellect numbers and their relations may be handled by professional arithmeticians, the only sound basis for the ordinary arithmetic of practical life, even when viewed in its merely technical aspect, is a concrete basis. It is not too much to say that in the initiatory classes of an elementary school the realities to which numbers refer should even take precedence in the order of thought of the numbers themselves; the actual *things numbered*, rather than numerical quantities, should be constantly present to the pupil's mind. This is essential to the vitality and solidity of the substructure of arithmetical knowledge, however abstract may be the future superstructure.

But we have to point out a still more important purpose which the teaching of the relations of number as Economic Arithmetic subserves. Economic Arithmetic, properly taught, must rest mainly on that class of questions which concerns clothes, feeding, housing, and foresight. The constant reference of figures to the acts, facts, and dealings of everyday life, thus brings Number to bear on subjects which are, in truth, moral, inasmuch as they have to do with a man's relations to his household and his occupation. It is evident that the familiarizing of the mind with the important part which number plays in ordinary affairs will promote what may be called arithmetical prudence in the management of the personal and family getting and spending. The expenditure of the operative classes has, in the vast majority of cases, not the slightest regard to present or future responsibilities. If we can get a man to consider seriously how he can best extend the benefits of his earnings to those of his own household, the economic object of education is in him fully attained. But this deliberation is the one thing desiderated. If this be secured, he will quickly see that although saving is a duty, it does not mean hoarding, and that economy does not mean niggardliness. He will perceive that a regulation of expenditure with due regard to the income, and to the various *present* claims which a man has on himself or which others have on him, is economy, and it is more; it is also benevolence, honesty, justice, and sense : a regulation of expenditure with due regard to the certain or probable claims of the *future* is prospective benevolence, honesty, justice, and sense. Now, these things ought to be taught to the people, and they are scarcely ever taught. This subject has been already adverted to in general terms, and it will be spoken of again under the head of Direct Moral Instruction; but I wish specially to show in this place, that even a study apparently so abstract as arithmetic can be so taught as to reveal an intimate connexion with the conduct of life, and that *it is best so taught*. And further, that arithmetic ethically taught in this its *economic* sense, is moral teaching, and that, while it confessedly contributes very largely to the dis-

cipline of the intellect, it also to some extent aids
in the formation of a moral habit of mind. It thus
promotes the ultimate object of the primary school in
both its aspects.

The Secondary Subjects of the Parochial School.

Education an extensive as well as an intensive process—Order of importance of
secondary subjects.

We pass now from the three main subjects of the
primary school to the consideration of those parts of
the curriculum which merit a place in the teacher's
time-table and in this survey of school-work, only if
kept strictly subsidiary to those studies which are determined beyond question by the future necessities of
the pupil. It is quite common to find in a school two
daily lessons of fifteen minutes each in Reading (frequently only one), with Writing from Dictation assert-
ing its existence only once or twice a week, while Geography, Grammar, History, Music, Drawing, and even
something called Science, receive each a certain share of
daily attention. This is a well-meant misuse of time.
I do not underrate the educational value of these
subjects. By means of them alone it is easy to see
that the ultimate purpose of all primary education
might be attained. But it is of prime moment to
secure for those subjects which are indispensable
to the future life and self-education of the pupil that
priority and pre-eminence in school-work which is their
due. It is true that the cultivation of the subsidiary

branches of instruction, in proper subordination to the more essential, has a tendency, by giving variety, to communicate greater vivacity and intelligence to the whole of the school-work, and thereby materially to further the acquisition of the magistral subjects themselves. But the ground of complaint is, that these subsidiary subjects receive in Scotland more attention than they can fairly claim, and that they introduce into the elementary school that greatest of all modern educational heresies,—the teaching and learning of a little of many things, rather than much of a few things. This is to eject thoroughness and real proficiency from the school, and with these, as a matter of course, all discipline worthy of the name.

It is, at the same time, a narrow theory of education which teaches that mental discipline is possible only when we rigidly confine the intellect within a narrow groove of study. Education is an *extensive* as well as an *intensive* process. There is a mental cultivation as real in the broadening of the field of observation, in the mere incorporation, if assimilation be impossible, of different *classes* of names and things,—in other words, of different departments of knowledge,—as in the severest application of the mind to one or two intellectual objects. Where *quantity* in education is ignored, you will certainly, in the general case, have a narrow man, though the intense application of his mind within a circumscribed course may have given him clearness, precision, and vigour: —a man of power without ideas. Where, again, there is quantity without great intensity, you will generally have breadth, openness, fairness, adaptability of intellect ; but the intellect will be of inferior edge and of less decision, unless the wide and comprehensive education be accompanied by considerable native energy of character. Where this native energy is ready-made to our hands,[1] a wide comprehensiveness is probably preferable to a close intensiveness of discipline. It lays a broader foundation, it puts a youth in possession of the elements of a more various cultivation, it brings more facts within his intellectual vision as he passes through the education of business and life, and supplies him with larger elements of judgment. An impartial and judicious breadth which lives in the constant anticipation of clearer light, or of new objects coming within the range of apprehension and suggesting new truths, is a better thing (if there be any higher purpose or meaning in education at all) than that incisive keenness of vision which is generally the characteristic of a mind which builds up judgments by the help of foregone conclusions, limits possibilities by experience of the past, and casts all the fresh lessons of life in a prematurely formed or traditionary mould.

These remarks are made lest it should be supposed that I in any way slight the extension of the parochial schoolmaster's conception of his work. So far is this from being the case, that I have provided, in the method of teaching reading, for the cultivation of every side of the juvenile mind, for the

[1] As it is in Scotland.

satisfaction in legitimate forms of the inquiring intellect, as well as of the moral and imaginative instincts. It has been shown how, in the act of teaching reading, the teacher may and must take a large view of his processes, if he hopes to be carried to a successful result : and if he takes such a view, he will assuredly give a range and comprehensiveness to the subject-matter of the primary-school curriculum which, to say the truth, I have rarely been privileged to meet with even in schools which affect to be too much engrossed with the higher subjects to pay sufficient attention to homely requirements ; and he will do so without sacrificing other subjects. It is precisely because the three indispensable subjects of elementary study require to be handled with a larger and more liberal grasp, and in conformity with a broader method and a more practical purpose, that I have dwelt with so much emphasis on their special educational functions. And further, it is with a view to admit of the more comprehensive method and the higher and more strictly defined aim that so large a space is claimed for them in the school work, and that all other subjects save direct moral and religious instruction are relegated to a very subordinate place.

The subordinate subjects will be taken up in the order of importance assigned to them in the chapter on the teacher's limitations, namely, Music, Geography, Grammar with Composition, Drawing, History, presuming that, in the case of girls, needlework and cutting-out take precedence of all other subsidiary subjects.[1]

[1] *Vide* Second Part of this Report.

MUSIC IN THE PRIMARY SCHOOL.

General effect of Music on the school—Sympathy as an educative agent—Sympathy and simultaneity contrasted—(*The simultaneous system*).—Singing, a moral and religious agency—Effect on the children—Method of teaching singing.

Music is much more to the elementary school than the ornament is to the capital of a shaft. It has itself a substantial duty to perform in the structure of the edifice. Under its influence the disjointed fragments of education take compact and harmonious shape in the growing minds of the pupils.

Sympathy is far too important an agent in the elementary school to be omitted from the calculations of the teacher, when estimating the forces which he can bring into operation for the attainment of his ends. The multitude of his pupils, which at first is a source of so much perplexity and difficulty, itself gives birth to a remedy for the evil it causes; for, the perplexity and difficulty to which numbers give rise are more than counterbalanced by the compensation which sympathy yields,—a compensation sufficient, when turned to full account, to transform an apparent disadvantage into an auxiliary. The force with which a sentiment is felt increases by the help of numbers beyond our power to calculate: it seems to return to each individual justified by being shared, and intensified by being expressed. Hence both men and children readily respond either for good or evil to mass-management. The teacher, accordingly, cannot afford to ignore so potent an instrument of power. Even in purely intellectual matters, sympathy is a great auxiliary; but in all that concerns sentiment and emotion it is all-powerful. And precisely in the degree to which a teacher can import moral and emotional elements into his manner of giving intellectual lessons, will he be able in this department of his work to calculate on the co-operation of sympathy, his best ally.

The sympathetic teaching of intellectual subjects, such as reading, writing, geography, and arithmetic, runs to seed in what is called the "simultaneous method," which is no method at all, but merely a device or expedient facilitating the application of a method. This expedient is still popular in many districts of England, in the French army, and in America, but there is in Scotland too deep an understanding of the real purpose of education to admit of its ever obtaining a strong hold. It puts forward two pleas for adoption, and both plausible. It claims to excite the attention of all as one, and thus give every child in a class of twenty the benefit of twenty questionings, which, on any other plan, would reach him only once; and, secondly, it claims to diffuse the knowledge conveyed, by making all the pupils think and utter the same thing at the same time. Even if the first claim were well founded, it would be a confession of weakness on the part of the teacher. A good teacher has no difficulty in sustaining the attention of all the pupils of a class, without swamping the individuals that compose it. Should he occasionally, from temporary or accidental causes, fail in his efforts to command attention, he has at least the satisfaction of knowing that the expedients he employs do not hold out a continual inducement to his pupils to resign their intellectual independence, and to seem to know what they do not. To conduct a class in such a way that all shall benefit by what each says or does, is, certainly, the first essential of class-teaching ; to evade the difficulty by the use of an expedient which does not guarantee the end sought, is to admit incapacity and to indulge indolence. The greater exertion required from the teacher who encounters and overcomes the difficulty of fixing the minds of his class on a common object, is well rewarded by the results visible in his pupils, and above all by the knowledge that he is not sacrificing their mental discipline to his own ease, or to a fallacious semblance of efficiency. A good teacher knows that no discipline can be real which is not individual, and he declines to adopt expedients which throw a false glare of success over school-work, while defeating the true ends of education. The second claim made by the simultaneous device is based on a misunderstanding of the nature and operation of sympathy. Sympathy is really efficacious in the acquisition of intellectual subjects only in so far as it is a *moral* agency. The excitement and vivacity which a teacher can produce by conducting his class in a vivid and interesting manner, the desire to respond with intelligence, if not with knowledge, which he is able to awaken, are intensified by being shared, and unquestionably tend in a remarkable degree to quicken and invigorate the understandings of the pupils. In *this* direction the teacher calls for and expects the co-operation of sympathy in his earnest efforts to exercise the individual intellects before him. But the simultaneous utterance of a reply to a question is the very reverse of this sympathetic process. Sympathy, in fact, is an organic, simultaneity a mechanical act; and to the extent to which the latter is mechanical, does it tend to establish routine, and to degrade the whole work of the school, converting both pupils and master into machines.

Leaving this device, which perhaps scarcely merits serious consideration, we have only to pass from the intellectual in education to the moral to find simultaneity and sympathy almost convertible terms. The affections, the sentiments, and the emotions of children are most powerfully influenced when the teaching, addressed to all, receives a common and united response. The more skilfully the appeals made to the consciences and feelings of the young, call to their help the common conscience and the common feeling of all, the more deep and lasting will they be in their effect. Hence the moral and religious value of Music in the primary school.

It is on the fact that it is a direct moral and religious agency that Music (by which is meant mass and part-singing from notation), rests its claim to rank first among the subsidiary subjects of instruction. The united utterance of a common resolution of perseverance, heroism, love of truth and honesty, or of a common sentiment of worship, gratitude, or purity, in song suited to the capacities of children's minds and to the powers of children's voices, devotes the young hearts which pour forth the melody to the cause of morality and religion. The utterance of the song is, in some sense, a public vow of self-devotion to the idea which it expresses. The harmony of the singers falls back on the ear and seems to reiterate the sentiment with which the music has been associated, in accents pleasing and insinuating, not harsh and preceptive. The morality and religion of song thus drop gently, and without the parade of formal teaching, into the heart of the child, and in this form they are welcome.

But Music is not only in itself a direct moral agency, and a medium for direct moral teaching, it is also the best auxiliary to the other moral and religious instruction of the school, because it *repeats* what has been already conveyed in a dogmatic or illustrative form, and it does so with melodious and grateful associations, which suggest, if they do not reveal, the inner harmony of the spiritual life. Nay, more, does not the *musical* utterance of a sentiment suggest to the young mind the fundamental union of goodness, truth, and beauty,—a union dimly apprehended, it may be, but perhaps none the less deeply felt? If this be so, there are the beginnings of a true culture in school-music.

Nor are these the only claims of Music on the primary teacher : singing is natural to man, and while affording a healthy outlet to the emotions of childhood, it refreshes and invigorates the physical frame. In this way it becomes in the schoolroom an economizer of time and a supporter of discipline. It may be compared to an engine constructed with a view to charge the general body with fresh vitality and continually to restore the sympathetic bond, which has a constant tendency to dissolution.

We must not suppose that either the moral or the physical influence of Music on children is different in kind, though it may be less in degree, than its influence on the adult. That influence has been so aptly described by Bishop Beveridge, that I may not unfitly quote the words here :—

" That which I have found," he says, " the best recreation both to my mind and body, whensoever either of them stands in need of it, is music, which exercises at once both my body and soul, especially when I play myself ; for then, methinks, the same motion that my hand makes upon the instrument, the instrument makes upon my heart. It calls in my spirits, composes my thoughts, delights my ear, recreates my mind, and so not only fits me for after business, but fills my. heart at the present with pure and useful thoughts ; so that, when the music sounds the sweetliest in my ears, truth commonly flows the clearest in my mind. And hence it is that I find my soul is become more harmonious by being accustomed so much to harmony, and adverse to all manners of discord, so that the least jarring sounds, either in notes or words, seem very harsh and unpleasant to me."

On the *method* of teaching singing from notation, it is not necessary to say much, because success in this subject depends entirely on the spirit in which it is taught. In the earlier stages the child will, of course, be taught by imitation and without notes; in the more advanced, notation will be introduced, and ultimately part-singing. I think, however, every teacher should seriously ask himself this question with respect to method : Is not instruction based on the

ordinary notation more likely than any other to give
the pupil that *kind* of musical knowledge and capacity which will enable and induce him to carry the
power, which he may acquire, out of the schoolroom
into the family and the church, and thus lead him
to continue and propagate the elevating influence
under which he himself has been happily brought?
If so, the ordinary notation seems to me to be
preferable to the tonic sol-fa, and men of experience
say that it is not much more difficult of acquisition.
However this may be, it is certain that the teacher
who takes up this important instrument of discipline
and instruction with intelligence and cordiality, will
not go far astray, if he steadily subordinate his method
and his purpose to the moral and æsthetic ends which
the subject is intended to subserve.[1]

GEOGRAPHY, AND THE METHOD OF TEACHING IT.

Chief error in teaching Geography—Practical purpose of teaching Geography
—Theoretical purpose—The two harmonize—Indirect uses of Geography—
Method of teaching Geography.

When Geography is taught in an elementary school,
the most common error is attempting too much. Every
inspector of schools must have endured, with such
patience as he was endowed with, the exhibition of a
detailed knowledge of Russia, Germany, and Thibet,
side by side with utter ignorance of the course which

[1] On this subject, and indeed on every other connected with school-
keeping, I would refer the teacher to Currie's *Common School Education*,
a work which every teacher ought to have in his library.

a vessel would take on its way from London to Sydney, or of the character and products of our native country. This arises from no want of energy and assiduity in teacher and pupil, for it is often the superabundant supply of these qualities which runs into such grotesque forms. The reply to a mild suggestion that the children might be more profitably employed, generally is, that they have already "gone over" Great Britain and Europe, to which the rejoinder that they require to retrace the ground from which their footsteps have been so quickly obliterated, remains unanswered.

In this, as in other subjects, the error arises from the neglect to define the purpose, the limits, and the method of the subject to be taught.

The purpose of teaching Geography in the primary school is to give the pupil a general knowledge of the configuration of the earth, the leading nations which occupy it, their chief industrial products as these are determined by climate and physical conformation, and the relation in which Britain stands to the rest of the world in the matter of exports and imports. Our own country should be at once the starting-point and terminus of the whole geographical journey. A much fuller knowledge of Great Britain and her Colonies should consequently be given than of other regions; but to build on this special knowledge, and without the broad basis furnished by general geography, would be to exclude the pupil from the elements of comparison, to confirm him in his national prejudice, isolation, and stolidity, and to deprive geography of its peculiar educative power.

Theoretically viewed, the educative function of geography is the antithesis of arithmetic and grammar—being *extensive*, while the functions of the latter are *intensive*. It gives intellectual breadth, adds to the stock of facts in their relation to causes, expands the moral sympathies, and tends to moderate rash judgments. Accordingly, the effect of Geography, thus theoretically estimated, is both moral and intellectual, and contributes as directly, as mere information can, to the ultimate end of the schoolmaster's labours—the formation of character. It has also this peculiarity: it is the easiest of all exercises in the perception of the connexion of cause and effect; for both causes and effects are, in the region of geography, visible and palpable. Its lessons, moreover, are capable of daily application by the child to the phenomena by which he is surrounded, and are in this way fruitful of discipline outside the school. To substitute for this admirable exercise the names of the places in each country where men most congregate, and of the large mountains and streams, is to convert a subject of instruction which is a living organism into an examinate corpse. No process could be more ingeniously devised for eliminating the rubbish from an important study, and presenting that rubbish to the pupil in the abused name of the subject of which it is the mere accident. This is not "practical" teaching as opposed to "theoretical;" for by no method of teaching the science could it be more effectively exhausted of all practical elements. The real significance of geographical knowledge, in the case of the peasant and the operative, is its tendency to give breadth, to store the mind with those larger facts regarding the earth and man which, when learned, lie quietly in the mind, germinate there, and contribute to that unconscious growth to which every man owes more than to the conscious steps of his onward progress.

To attain the "practical" purpose of school geography, as I understand it, is to attain these very high results; and thus it is that in this as in other subjects of elementary instruction,— the theoretic and practical purposes of education become identical.

In elementary education the sphere of the intellectual and moral vision is so crowded with objects, and every separate subject is so overcharged with meaning and variety to the opening mind, and the temptation to dissipate the attention and thereby to subvert sound intellectual discipline, is so strong as to require that the teacher exercise constant vigilance. An infinite multiplicity of forms and facts besets the fresh young brain from morning till night, and makes its natural life fragmentary and ineffective. To correct this is a portion of the teacher's task. The work of the school, accordingly (and this applies to every stage of education), is an *artificial* work. It rests on the method of Nature and obeys it; but it is the intrusion of the hand of man for the purpose of making a wiser and a better and a more efficient man than would otherwise grow. Till the power of a sustained act of will directed towards some definite object is supposed to be developed, we rightly leave the child almost wholly to Nature, our training being negative rather than positive; but when the time comes for education proper (which is Discipline) to begin, our business is to direct his powers into fixed channels, with a view to fixed ends. Hence the great importance in education of narrowing the attention of pupils to the subject immediately and directly in hand, and of checking all discursive talk, under whatever specious guise it may be introduced. In teaching Geography, however, the teacher may find an outlet for the discursive tendency which also has an important part to play in education, and a legitimate occasion for giving "general information," and for exercising the general intelligence by being deliberately discursive and conversational.

Nor are the uses of Industrial Geography exhausted by the wide range which we have already given to the educative functions of this branch. For, this is the true characteristic of a right purpose pursued by a right method,—that it is fruitful in its disciplinary effects beyond our immediate capacity to perceive. And we have but to advert to the manifest support which Geography rightly taught gives to Economic Arithmetic, to an intelligent apprehension of the Reading-lessons, and to the economic moral teaching which falls to be considered in the sequel, to appreciate its educational value in the elementary school, and in promoting the intelligence of the pupil.

Method.—There is no school subject in which the end so clearly points out the way and means as it does in the case of Geography. The knowledge to be acquired is real as opposed to formal, and from the first step to the last of the process of acquisition, reality is the principal consideration. The first notions of Geography must not be given from a map, which is only the representation of a reality, and, from the necessity of the case, a singularly bad one, but from the solid earth itself. The schoolroom and the parish constitute the microcosm in which all geography is visible, and are for the child the measure of the world. In this, above all subjects, the teacher ought to start conversationally from the point which the child has himself unconsciously attained and from his circumscribed point of view. Indeed, this is one essential fact in the art of educating,—that a child or man can know a thing only in so far as the knowledge is a living growth out of what is already known. A learner may stock his memory to any extent with propositions disjointed, or even logically connected, but they can be to him nothing save a memory exercise, unless they have been successfully grafted into the main stock ; for education is an organic, not a mechanical process. The first lesson in Geography accordingly ought to be an analysis of the general and vague notion which the child has of his own parish. Its plains, hills, streams, its arable and pastoral soil, its mines, quarries, manufactures, if it have them, furnish an epitome of the whole round of industrial geography.

It would be melancholy, were it not amusing, to see a teacher labouring, with the help of a text-book and a map, to convey to the child the notion of a lake, a river, a gulf, and an island, when these are all to be seen outside the school-door, if not in good weather, at least in bad : just as I have seen a teacher striving drowsily to make a class of fifteen understand the morphology of a plant as explained by some unskilful hand in the reading-lesson, careless and unconscious of the convolvulus and fuchsia bending through the open window into the room.

An analysis of the parish and instruction in the cardinal points, the children making their own observations at noon, leads to the drawing of a rude map of the parish on the black-board, to be afterwards delightedly copied on the slates.

This done, the neighbouring parishes and the county lead by easy steps to the general (quite general) industrial geography of Britain.

The pupil is now to be told that big as Britain is to him, it is a mere corner of the earth. His imagination will expand until he begins to have some notion of the magnitude of the earth in which he lives, and of the multitude of its people.

A globe should then be set before him, the roundness of the planet taught, if not explained, and the ten great divisions of land and water, and their relative positions thoroughly acquired.

A wall-map of the world may then for the first time be unfolded, and the leading countries in the different quarters of the globe, a few of the principal mountain ranges and towns, and the staple industry of each country, with the name of the inhabitants, taught.

Then should follow an inquiry into the *causes* which determine the localization of the different industries, an exposition of the interdependence of nations, and much time should be spent over imaginary travelling with merchant-ships from one port to another. If Geography be not pushed into undue prominence in the school-work, I see in what I have sketched at least two and a half years' work.

Lastly should follow a more minute account of Britain and its industrial relation to other nations, especially to its own Colonies.[1] The practice of occasional map-drawing on the slate, however rude (for it is the attempt not the success that teaches), should accompany these instructions as an auxiliary to the general method. Thus every step of the process towards the limited and practical end of geographical teaching is itself thoroughly practical, and the map does not divert too much the attention of the pupil from that which it badly represents, or subvert the sense of the reality and substance of the things and places about which he learns.[2]

To sum up, with reference to much of the ground traversed in this Report, I would succinctly say,—The

---

[1] The particular geography of Palestine should be taught in connexion with Bible reading.

[2] The best way of testing the practical, and therefore the educative character of geographical teaching, is to take the *Times'* advertisements of sailings, and make the pupils follow the vessels to their destination, and explain why it is that they go to these places.

purpose of teaching Reading is to give the pupil the power of reading intelligently and intelligibly, and the right method may be signalized as the *Educative* method : the purpose of school Arithmetic is Economic, and the method the *Natural or Concrete* method : the purpose of Geographical teaching is Industrial Geography, and the method is the *Real* method.

ON DRAWING.

Drawing, in the elementary school, means, or ought to mean, the art of representing, from the round, common objects in outline. If the subject be kept in proper subordination, more than this is unattainable, save by the few pupils who, having a natural talent for form, prosecute the art for their own pleasure as well as possible profit. All such exhibitions of special inborn talent it is the teacher's duty to encourage, taking care, however, that he does not allow his satis- faction in the few to moderate his anxiety for the many. There is no artistic training in school-drawing, as above defined. That is possible only through the imitation of beautiful forms, which, moreover, are imi- tated *because they are beautiful.* To this a few may, in peculiarly favourable circumstances, almost reach ; but all attempts to introduce drawing into elementary schools, on the æsthetic footing, have been and will be futile, except under peculiarly favourable circum- stances. The limitations under which the teacher works, and the exigencies of the time-table, settle this point beyond all question. Art, as such, can find a place only by superseding some more important subject; and even then, it will generally cease to be art-training before it finds its way out of the fingers of the pupils. To draw on the slate mathematical figures, cups and saucers, then maps, and chairs and tables, and finally, and above all, leaves and flowers,—this sums up all that can be accomplished in the elementary school. This amount of instruction in drawing may always be attempted by a teacher possessing such rare powers of organization as to extract out of the lighter subjects of instruction relaxation for the pupil, thereby ultimately saving time, while bringing into play a new disciplinary agent. And a disciplinary agent of no mean significance Drawing is. For all our observation from infancy upwards is a continual process of outlining an object or part of an object from other objects or parts. The greater or less success with which this is done, indicates the greater or less accuracy of the observing powers, though not necessarily their activity. To bring these powers out into a more conscious exercise by encouraging attempts to reproduce external forms as outlined by the eye, is manifestly an exercise tending powerfully to cultivate clearness, precision, and truth of intellect.

The nature of the discipline which drawing affords fixes the time of its introduction into the school-work. It belongs to the infant and initiatory classes mainly, and only partially to the more advanced classes. Self-evident as this is, masters continually invert the order of its appearance on the school stage, and treat it as an "accomplishment."

Whether the teacher be able to introduce this important discipline into his school or not, he himself is certainly only half equipped for his task as an examiner and illustrator of lessons, if he has not the power of appealing to the understanding through the eye whenever the nature of the lesson makes this desirable.

THE HIGHER INTELLECTUAL INSTRUCTION OF THE PAROCHIAL SCHOOL.

Advanced Reading—Analysis of Sentences—Advanced Writing or Composition—Method of teaching Grammar and Composition.

The course of instruction and discipline sketched in the preceding chapters, affords full occupation for five or six years of school life, when we take into consideration the irregularity of attendance which is constantly interfering with the teacher's plans, and making the application of methods occasional and disjointed instead of continuous and consecutive. Where pupils remain to eleven years of age and upwards, the teacher may fairly extend the means of education, and bring fresh materials to his aid in giving effect to the ideal purpose of the school. The schools among which the Bequest of Mr. Dick is distributed belong to this higher class, and it is, moreover, part of the legal duty of the Trustees to apply that Bequest towards the special encouragement of the higher branches of instruction in the school, as well as of superior literary and scientific acquirement in the teachers. The means adopted for securing the latter object, and the extent to which the former is actually attained, will appear in the second part of this Report. My business now is to bring within the range of the general school-method those subjects which I consider to be properly "advanced."

It scarcely requires to be premised that a longer than the average attendance at school will first of all be taken advantage of by the schoolmaster for the confirming and further extending of the elementary subjects, and more especially of Reading, Writing, and Arithmetic in their larger sense. It is not necessary to insist with equal emphasis on the extension of subsidiary subjects, because at this particular stage their relative importance to the magistral subjects seems to lessen rather than to increase. If the teacher, in hastening to make the best use of the additional time allowed to him, follow the principles which have guided him in the earlier years of the pupil's education, he will throw his weight mainly on the legitimate and natural extension of the three essential subjects of the parochial school, not forgetting, of course, the always pre-eminent claims of direct moral and religious training.

The extension of the Reading means the perusal of more difficult lessons than any yet attempted, varied in the subjects of which they treat, and giving stronger food both to the intellect and the imagination of the pupil. Through these advanced lessons the boy will begin to make acquaintance with the untechnical, but scientific, treatment of the objects by which he is surrounded, and which hitherto have been handled in his reading-books more from the point of view of observation and experience than of law, cause, and effect. Extracts from prose and poetical literature will, even when only partially understood, call on his understanding and imagination to make a wholesome effort to master them, while they furnish him insensibly with a standard of thought and of the life of the mind which will never be quite effaced. As the language of a man is generally a fair measure of his intellectual cultivation, so the power fully to comprehend what he says or writes is a test of the recipient capacity of the person whom he addresses. The effort to understand a difficult lesson accordingly is an effort to take a step forward in intellectual life.

In every stage of his reading, the pupil has of course been taught to understand the words and thoughts presented to him. This is essential to the intelligence of the reading, as well as to its intelligibility. The same process is continued in the more difficult reading which he now encounters; but it will be desirable, if not necessary, in order fully to evolve the meaning of complex sentences, especially in poetry, to study them in detail, and separate them into their various limbs. Thus to show the mutual bearing of the clauses on each other, and on the principal clause, is to analyse in the grammatical sense. Reading in this, its advanced stage, is educative no longer solely through the contents of the lessons which are read, but also as being a formal discipline in the organism of language. It is true that the mere perusal, if intelligent, of any composition in prose or poetry brings with it, even in the most initiatory stages, a formal discipline of intellect, apart from the *real* discipline given by the subject-matter. The intellectual process by which a thought is elaborated into its linguistic form is revealed in the utterance of it, and it is therefore impossible for a child or man to understand the latter without an unconscious participation in the conceptions and reasonings of the mind which gave the thought expression.[1] Intelligent reading is thus itself a formal discipline of intellect. But in an advanced class this unconscious discipline becomes supplemented by the *conscious evolution* of the organic structure of language. This process, which is called Sentence-Analysis, or advanced Grammar, is a kind of applied logic, and as an intellectual discipline takes that precedence over every other which language takes over science.

Thus we find that advanced Reading seems naturally to call to its aid the study of Grammar and

[1] This fact shows the importance of putting before the child pure and well-constructed sentences. The lessons in many of the most popular reading-books are not even grammatically written. The standard of English in school-books, above all other publications, should be high.

Analysis. Unfortunately, this discipline in the analysis of language is very apt to degenerate into a hunting after shadowy distinctions, and into a fanciful application of abstract technicalities. Every subject of the school curriculum, however, is equally liable to abuse, and the remedy is to be found only in the steady contemplation of the special purpose of each study. The discipline which grammatical analysis is intended to give, accordingly, will be defeated, and the whole subject will run to waste if the teacher lose sight of its object, which is twofold— (1.) The facilitating of the understanding of complex language, with a view to secure to the higher reading its full disciplinary effect. (2.) The giving of greater precision and accuracy to the thought and expression of the pupil himself in composition exercises, oral and written. If these two eminently practical objects be kept constantly in view, the teacher will not deviate far from the right track. In giving effect to the *former* purpose, he will certainly find his progress hampered and complicated if he multiplies terms, and if, by insisting too much on technicalities, he disturbs the usual vocabulary of grammar. Analysis is to be admitted into the school only on the plea that it is grammar. Should the teacher find that it fails to deepen and extend sound grammatical knowledge in the pupil, he may be assured that he is pursuing a false method, and giving undue prominence to trivial subdivisions and a technical terminology. In giving effect to the *latter* purpose, he will not deviate far from the right path if he decline to follow analysis into distinctions which cannot be readily applied in the synthesis of composition.

In teaching Analysis, a master is apt to be betrayed by the charm of pseudo-science, with which technicalities invest a subject, into inverting the proper order of things. He forgets that the boy can analyse only in so far as he distinguishes the main proposition of the sentence, and apprehends the *meaning* of the various limbs in relation to it and to each other. The *understanding* of a sentence is a necessary and first condition of its analysis, and the analysis of it again gives greater completeness to the understanding. To comprehend a sentence is in fact to comprehend the living connexion of all its parts, and is itself an act of unconscious analysis. The object of conscious analysis is to bring out more distinctly the parts of the organism, to name them, and thereby to give the mind greater acuteness and capacity for the comprehension of difficult language generally. To comprehend and to analyse are essentially only two different sides of the same grammatical effort. They act and react on each other. So oblivious are teachers apt to become of the real practical significance and purpose of the subjects which they teach, that it is necessary thus to impress on them that it is only on the full comprehension of the sentence that sound grammatical teaching or knowledge can possibly rest.

So much for the intimate connexion of advanced reading with grammatical analysis, and the extent to which the latter can find a place in the parochial school.

It is true that it is quite possible, with the help of Logic and Latin, to give a minute grammatical account of every separate word and element of the longest sentence, in its relation to the organic whole of which it forms a part; but this is an exercise to be attempted only by boys of fourteen or fifteen years of age, after the practical purposes of the study have been substantially attained, and when they begin to follow out the subject as a pure exercise of grammatical and logical ingenuity. In this sense, therefore, analysis of sentences belongs to a stage of education with which I have, in this Report, nothing to do, and enters into competition with studies, instructive and disciplinary, among which it will, no doubt, soon find its proper level.

By advanced Writing, to which the teacher will at the same time direct his efforts, is to be understood the power of writing, in accurate English, letters and narratives; in other words, Elementary Composition. By Composition is meant the reproduction, in the pupil's own words, of the lessons which he reads, and also *précis*-writing. It is at once manifest that only by the help of grammatical analysis can this subject be efficiently taught. Analysis enables the learner to recognise the elements of a sentence, and to detect his errors of construction. It is fortunate that the specialties of advanced study in the primary school—Grammatical Analysis, and the opposite process, Composition—contribute directly to the completion of the two most important of the magistral subjects, and that their mutual helpfulness renders it possible to prosecute both concurrently.

Method.—The nature and aim of Grammar, as a discipline and an acquirement, contain implicitly the method of teaching it. A few explicit words on the steps of the process, however, will not be superfluous.

Grammar is of little utility in the school, I have said, except in so far as it is approached from the syntactical point of view, with distinct reference to the ultimate objects,—sentence-analysis and sentence-construction. The whole of grammar, accordingly, starts from the idea of the simple sentence—subject and predicate. Until the child is able to comprehend this, he can make little real progress in grammar. Copying from his lesson-book, reading, the habit of accurate speaking when answering questions, and dictation exercises, will meanwhile accustom his eye and ear and tongue to the difference between grammatical and ungrammatical expression. He will not be allowed to trespass beyond the limits of this imitative grammar into the field of analysis, until he is able to understand and apply the fundamental proposition of the whole science (if so it may be called), namely, "a simple thought as well as its corresponding proposition consists of a subject and a predicate." The predicates, which require an object for their completion, will be easily learned, and, with this, the opposition of subject and object, the fact of the subjective or nominative case, the agreement of the nominative and verb, and the government of the objective case by transitive predicates. This method is further justified by the fact that the analysis of the simple proposition lays the basis of Composition as well as of Grammar, and that it involves an amount of grammatical knowledge far exceeding what is usually attained in the whole present course of grammatical instruction in primary schools.

In taking this first and all-important step, the knowledge of the noun and verb, and of number, is inevitably acquired. A slight extension of the elements of the sentence,—for example, the extension of "*The dog eats his dinner*" into "*The black dog greedily eats his cold dinner*," and so forth, introduces the various parts of speech and the three persons, and thus gives the pupil a knowledge of the classification of individual words from the point of view of syntax, and of their organic connexion with other words. He sees that it is *this organic connexion* which determines their names and characters, and begins to comprehend grammar as the formal exposition of a sentence, and as furnishing the rules of sentence-making.

Sentence-making, or Composition, will then be begun

by the exercise of constructing simple sentences out of words supplied to the pupil; an exercise very valuable in its relations to grammar, because it furnishes constantly recurring examples of the right and wrong in speech and writing. This initiatory exercise having been sufficiently practised, the pupil cannot afford to ring many changes on the technicalities and ingenuities of sentence-building, but must plunge at once into the writing of short accounts of what he has seen or read or heard. The teacher will read to his pupils an anecdote or biography, or it may be the description of a country, an animal, or a mechanical process, and call on them to reproduce it grammatically on their slates in their own words. This exercise in *précis*-writing having been corrected, will be produced again on paper as a home exercise. Steady practice of the kind thus briefly indicated will, in a wonderfully short space of time, secure (as they have secured in a large number of the schools in the north) results which will astonish those who have never had experience of the capacity of boys in this direction when their intelligence has been already cultivated by means of sufficiently various, instructive, and disciplinary matter in the course of their reading-lessons, and when they have overcome those obstacles of writing and spelling which properly belong to an earlier period of school work.

History.

To the young man whose mind is already disciplined by severe scholastic pursuits, no subject will so readily yield all the elements of moral culture as History. To the schoolboy, on the other hand, it is of value only in so far as it brings to his knowledge wonderful deeds done in the discharge of patriotism and duty. In all other respects it is utterly barren of good results, and involves a futile expenditure of valuable school time. A dim outline of royal genealogies, of dates, the intervals of which are full of plottings and counterplottings, and of facts which however capable of interpretation by the matured capacity, are, to the raw experience of the child or the boy, little more than an exhibition of the worst passions that afflict humanity, and all these epitomized into small compass, and only partially and fragmentarily acquired—such is school history. It seems to me, therefore, that the reading of History in the parochial school is little better than an abuse of time. And when we further consider that this subject, so fruitless of good results, obtrudes itself into a region which ought to be sacred to the varied culture, literary and scientific, to which exercise in advanced reading and writing ought to be made subservient, it cannot be too much discouraged. The thing chiefly to be regretted is that teachers, otherwise intelligent and earnest in the discharge of their duty, should be led astray by the mere semblance of solid instruction which is yielded by bald historical records.

The proper place of History in the parochial school is in the school library. The children will require little encouragement to read it if it be written in a style to suit their age, and they will always welcome gladly a public reading of the narrative of some great event by the master himself, as an occasional reward of good conduct, or as a relief from the tedium of the day's routine.

Latin and Greek. (Middle Schools.)—Language versus *Science.*

There is always a certain proportion of the boys in attendance at the parochial schools in the three north-eastern counties, who, being the sons of small farmers, tradesmen, or ministers, may be expected to remain at school to the ages of fourteen, fifteen, or even sixteen years.[1] The proportion,—about seven per cent. on the average,—is sufficiently large to make it incumbent on the teacher to provide a training which does not fall within the proper range of advanced *primary* instruction, but rather of Middle-school work. The

[1] In some cases boys of seventeen, eighteen, and nineteen years of age are met with.

Scotch parochial school being thus called upon to discharge the function of a Middle or Grammar school, the teacher and managers have to determine what direction they shall give to the higher instruction. They have, in fact, the same question to solve, the solution of which in favour of the ancient classics in the middle and public schools of England has now been for forty years made matter of question, and at this moment may be even said to be under reconsideration by the supreme civil authority.

In discussing this subject the disputants on both sides have regarded it too much as a *school* question. It is essentially an University question ; and no district of Great Britain so forcibly illustrates this as the counties of Aberdeen, Banff, and Moray. That kind of discipline which we conclude to be the best for the undergraduate and for the future work of law-making, law-administration, the church, philosophy, and the higher walks of the medical profession, must, of course, find full recognition in the middle school, whose chief business it is to prepare boys for the university. By thus transferring the question from the middle to the higher education, we narrow and simplify the issue, and reduce it ultimately to a question of the intellectual benefits derivable from a knowledge of man as compared with those to be derived from a knowledge of external nature. To state the question as a training in the knowledge of the lifeless signs of speech and their relations, *versus* a training in a knowledge of living Nature and its manifold operations, is to misunderstand the real point at issue. In the university, and in the upper classes of the middle school, the dispute is *not* between the claims of Formal and of Real studies. Both studies present the realities of knowledge to the mind of the student—the one the realities of Man's nature, the other the realities of external Nature. Again, both Greek and physics exercise and discipline the formal powers of intellect, and both admit the student to an unconscious knowledge of the operation and the laws of intelligence. But that the purely Formal discipline of language (where we happen to have a highly developed language to work with), is more delicate and subtle, more deep and thorough, than that of physics, I shall endeavour to show when I speak of the claims of linguistic studies with exclusive reference to the middle school, presuming the education of the boy to end there. The further superiority of linguistic training over scientific consists in this, that in the former we have the generalizations of the wisest men on human life and human duty expressed in the most artistic forms; in the latter we have only generalizations on the facts and sequences of the visible world. The realities of moral experience, embodied in forms historical and dramatic, as these are impressed on the acquiring mind by the very effort implied in deciphering a difficult language, are of more value, both in themselves, and as giving solidity and power to the mental fabric, than a knowledge of the phenomena of heat and electricity. These moral generalizations of the wise are, in truth, an unsystematic philosophy of human nature, furnishing the learner not only with the experience of the past, but with instruction in the motives and purposes of life.

To become acquainted with the thoughts and imaginations of the past, through the medium of translation or when transfused through modern literatures, is to sacrifice the benefits which we derive from the study of a thought produced in circumstances not only different from, but even in some respects antagonistic to our own. It is to sacrifice also the artistic forms in which the thoughts are clothed—forms which are the most perfect in literature, and which the structure of the ancient languages forces even upon the negligent student. The peculiar value of the æsthetics of the intellect and of morality, as distinguished from the æsthetics of feeling and emotion, in promoting the discipline and cultivation of mind, and above all the opening mind of youth, has not, so far as I know, been adverted to by writers on Education, though it must have been experienced by all who have had the benefits of a classical training. It is not simply an æsthetic, but also an intellectual and moral cultivation, which flows from close contact with ideal and artistic forms of expression.

Such results in the growth of mind are, it is true, neither ponderable nor commensurable quantities, but they assuredly tend to produce a *quality* of mind rarely to be attained in any other way, save by men of native genius. Richter has well said, and probably without much exaggeration :—"The present ranks of humanity would sink irrecoverably if youth did not take its way through the silent temple of the mighty past into the busy market-place of after life."

To return, however, to what more immediately concerns Middle Education: it is necessary to clear away from the field of discussion all illusory imaginations as to the larger proportion of boys who would benefit by a middle-school system, based on real and scientific training, as compared with the number which now benefit by the discipline of the classical tongues. Severe mental work, having knowledge or other mental purposes exclusively in view, is naturally distasteful to the great majority of boys. We must not draw too large an inference from the inquisitiveness and love of knowledge which characterize childhood. The recipient stage of the child's life should be gently and wisely dealt with, and this it is the function of the primary school to do. But in the middle school, receptivity has given place in the boy to force, which seeks not to accept impressions but rather to make them. To break in upon the spontaneous and healthy career of this fresh boyish energy with Latin verses or classifications of birds and beasts, is, even in the most favourable circumstances, to traverse the natural and genial current of life, and to call for a painful and self-sacrificing exertion of will. Most boys will be found to make this exertion, when they do make it, not from love of the work itself, but from the moral considerations of respect for authority, of personal attachment, or a sense of duty. And of this we may be sure, that when inborn stupidity and rampant boyism have claimed their own, the residue of real intellectual workers, where there is no external motive to intellectual exertion, will always be found numerically disappointing. Nor will the substitution of Pneumatics, Physiology, or Chemistry, for Latin and Greek, draw out a larger amount of talent, or show better on the reckoning-day, when stock is taken of the quantity and quality of available knowledge and discipline really acquired. That by means of better books, and of methods based on a knowledge of human nature, a larger proportion of boys might be drawn within the circle of school-work is undeniable; but this points to the improvement of existing practice, not to the subversion of the existing system.

There are only two valid objections to the prevalent practice :—(1.) The almost entire exclusion from middle schools of elementary physics, which, if properly taught, can be made attractive as well as instructive, promoting rather than retarding the magistral classical studies. (2.) The non-provision of a course of study for those pupils who do not contemplate a university career, and who, though repelled by linguistic studies, might possibly be reached by those consecutive and methodical accounts of the external world which we call Science. If the study of Latin and Greek, as the leading subjects of middle-school work, renders once for all inevitable the total exclusion of all instruction regarding external nature and economic science, the cause of the classicists is, by the admission of this necessity, irretrievably weakened. As a matter of fact, however, there is no difficulty in prosecuting the study of the ancient languages concurrently with those subjects which every educated man may be reasonably expected to know in their general principles and purport. This amount of (so-called) *realistic* scientific knowledge is easy of attainment in middle schools, and as imperative as it is easy. Nor would any northern schoolmaster have a moment's hesitation on the subject. Such subjects as Natural History can be successfully treated only as diversions or recreations.

It is only after we have assumed *a certain amount* of realistic and scientific instruction to be given in grammar and public schools that we properly approach the question of Language *versus* Science as an educative instrument; and the question then becomes this : Is formal science, as such, or the classical tongues, when taught with average ability (for it is only on a mediocre teaching capacity that we ever can safely rely in estimating the value of subjects of instruction), more promotive of the ultimate end of the secondary school—the formation of those good intellectual and moral habits which we call, in the larger sense of the words, good Character ? As the way in which this question is viewed has a powerful retrospective effect on the whole significance, method, and tendency of primary education, and as, moreover, the parochial schools of the north discharge the function of "grammar schools," it may not be irrelevant to the purpose of this Report to try to state, in as few words as possible, the special and independent claims of Language to the prominent position which it has so long held.

As an intellectual discipline Language makes good its claim to preference on the following among other grounds :—

(1.) Words stand for things real or notional. Now it is only in so far as words denote the objects of external perception, that a training based on science can be said to have the advantage over linguistic. Even in this case, however, language is defined for the pupil only within the narrow limits of the department, or fragment of departments, which it is possible within a given time to teach, whereas linguistic training, by teaching the value of words, *as such*, to whatever department of human knowledge they may belong, educates the intellect to precision in the use of them generally. So true is this, that men trained only to a special department of science, but whose education is limited by it, fail to use the language even of their own department with that accuracy and consistency of signification, which would alone satisfy a mind trained on language or philosophy. In the only sense, then, in which physical science, to *the extent to which it can be taught to boys*, can affect to do the work of linguistic training, it does not succeed.

Even if it succeeded, how small the ground it would cover! The language of a single department of science or fragments of a few sciences, which, because of their fragmentary nature, fail to yield discipline, would represent the whole range of the vocabulary taught. All those words which are daily in our mouths, as denoting the realities which are constantly influencing our lives in our social and moral relations, would be left outside the range of the scientific teaching. It would be superfluous here to dwell either on the pre-eminent importance of this aspect of man's daily existence, or on the immense value of a right understanding of words, and a wise use of them. Every successive inquirer into human nature has descanted on the error, misunderstanding, and consequent misery, into which an abuse of words is constantly betraying mankind. It seems to me that if a linguistic training had no other result than to teach us that words were our servants and not our masters, and that we must question, define, weigh, and estimate them, it would require little other defence of its claim to the traditionary prominence in the middle school which it inherits.

(2.) When we pass from the consideration of the discipline of language in teaching us the exact use of single terms, to the employment of these in the expression of our thoughts under the necessary operation of mental laws, we find in language a just, though imperfect, reflection of intellectual processes. In this view the study of language is the informal study of the laws of thought. We may assume that few will be prepared to require from boys that reflective grasp of intellectual laws, that effort after a conscious realization of abstract processes which is implied in any study of logic or psychology worthy of the name. At the same time, all will recognise the paramount importance of exercising the formal powers of mind, and by a careful method giving practice in the art, while avoiding the scientific terminology and formulæ, of logic. Now, it is precisely in this relation that the distinctive characteristic of language-training reveals itself. For language being the body of thought, the student of it is studying concrete mind. While dealing with objective things—with vocables, which are audible and visible, and which, therefore, do not evade his grasp,—he is at the same time unconsciously tracing the operations of intellect in others, and learning the right use of his own faculties; in other words, he is a student of logic, in the widest sense of that term, without being aware of it.

Nor is this position a vague affirmation; it is capable of illustration in detail.

In the first place, the similarity of inflection in the simple sentence leads the pupil to the clear perception of the concord and partial identity in thought of subject and attribute, whether the attributive appears as an adjective or as a predicative verb. The distinct forms by which inflected languages indicate this mental concord, must necessarily give the pupil a clearer notion of what a judgment and an affirmation really are. I do not here speak of the use which might be made of this part of linguistic discipline by a teacher who was himself conscious of the course of logic which his instructions in language were scarcely veiling, but of the *inevitable* discipline which the average boy receives from the average teacher. And it is not only in simple sentences that the pupil is thus exercised in the concord of thought as expressed in attribution, but he is also led by the help of the same mutual good understanding among the inflections to trace a connexion between clauses, and to detect the fact that complete assertions, no less than individual words, may be attributive of each other. The tracing out and perception of this unity of thought between affirmations is a valuable intellectual exercise.

I pass over the clearness which must be given to the pupil's perception of time and of government by the resembling, yet differing, terminations of verbs and nouns, to point out the training in syllogistic logic which he necessarily receives when he enters on the analysis of an involved complex sentence. The varying inflections of the words before him necessarily lead him to the discrimination of an assertion from its grounds, and an act from its causes, motives, or purposes. The forms set apart to denote these qualities of propositions compel his attention, detain it, and thus fix the distinctions in his mind. Again, those qualities of propositions which we express by the words hypothesis and probability, and even so fine a distinction as that between probability and possibility, are forced upon the understanding of the learner, however unconscious the teacher may be of the full meaning and value of the instrument he is using, and however ignorant the pupil of the generalizations of propositions and the names by which these generalizations are known. What higher discipline of intellect can be proposed for a boy whom we desire to discipline severely, but whose self-consciousness we do not yet wish to draw, or to force, into activity, than to lay before him a mass of words, apparently dead and disjointed signs, and to require that, from a steady consideration of these, the living organism of speech shall be built up—an organism into which all the formal elements of intellect run, and which calls for the discrimination, not only of the various relations in thought of the propositions before him, but of the precise force of many and various vocables, possessing it may be a wide and various connotation?

(3.) To the reply that the intellectual discipline of which we speak can be equally well obtained from subjects more immediately useful than Latin or Greek, such as Natural History or Physics, two objections present themselves:—

The instruction of boys, in all subjects in which the material (as opposed to the formal) is, from the nature of the case, of primary importance, is necessarily dogmatic. Even the statement of principles is received by the pupils as dogma: to suppose any thing else is to deceive ourselves. Though they may be occasionally startled into the conscious perception of rational relations under the influence of a teacher of original mind, they do not and can not in any adequate or appreciable sense realize the reasoning process by which scientific conclusions are reached. Hence, while in the study of Natural Philosophy, or any branch of it, they are taught not only facts, but classifications, laws, and causes in relation to their effects, these are not, and in almost all cases can not be, elaborated by the pupil himself. The teaching of them, accordingly, degenerates into a statement of fact, and the learning of them into an act of memory. It is to be at once conceded, that were pupils led by an intelligent and rarely endowed master in an inquiry into nature, with a view to re establish, for himself, results already known, a training would be given by this means unequalled as a discipline; but such a method of instruction is on a large scale quite impracticable, and, even if practicable, it would be premature in its demands on the pupil's powers. Those educationists who are not mere theorists feel the necessity of finding instruments which do not make mannikins of boys, and which can work fairly in the hands of no very cunning workmen. Where Natural Philosophy is that instrument, the method which looks so well in theory must degenerate in actual practice into the most ordinary and vulgar *cram*. Differences, generalizations, laws and causes will not be truly apprehended *as such*, but will be arranged in the pupil's mind by virtue of association alone, however glibly they may be enunciated at call in their proper places and sequences. It is only the select few, even of those who fairly master the subject taught, that are fully conscious of the reasoning process involved, and do not simply trust to faithful memory and association.

It is no doubt true that, a few years later, the boy who has been well taught may reflect on the results of that teaching, and in this way these results may fructify into a kind of retrospective discipline ; the relation of cause and effect, differences, likenesses, and the grounds of generalization, may be seen, and the intellectual ends of education be thereby attained. But even the production of this winter fruit assumes particularly good teaching, a good memory, and habits of mind which are *naturally* more than usually reflective. In Language, on the contrary, the intellectual processes of differentiation, generalization, and reasoning are not only much more fully, delicately, and variously represented than in Physics, but they have the signal advantage of not being offered to the learner as scientific *results* which are capable of being tabulated and acquired by the memory as so many co-ordinated facts. On the contrary, they have in every successive sentence to be sought out and brought to light *anew*, and this as the very condition of making a single progressive step. In every successive sentence the boy has to construct a living organism out of a seemingly chaotic aggregation of dead symbols, and in · the construction of this he brings into play all his intellectual faculties whether he will or not. The discipline is thus obtained *independently of the teacher*, and we might almost say independently of the will of the pupil also. Of no other subject can this be said. The boy either does the work before him or he does not: if he does it, he cannot, if he would, avoid obtaining the discipline which the work affords, whereas in elementary Science, the power of memory facilitates the acquisition of a semblance of knowledge which may pass muster, but which is comparatively useless as a discipline of any faculties save those of memory and association.

Accordingly, as in the training to a perception of the force of vocables, so also in the disciplining of the formal and intellectual powers, there seem to be sufficient grounds for maintaining that Science, *as it can be alone taught to boys between twelve and sixteen years of age*, is a feeble instrument as compared with Language.

The kind of discipline above claimed as the almost exclusive property of Language in the field of secondary instruction, cannot be obtained through the modern tongues, except in those cases (on which it would be vain to calculate), in which the rare excellence and general philological cultivation of the master supplement the inherent defects of his instruments. It is the contrast of the Latin and Greek tongues to our native mode of casting thought, no less than their own perfection of structure, that makes them so valuable as a discipline. The conspicuous device, moreover, whereby, in these tongues, grammatical, and therefore thought-relations are indicated, reveal even to the careless pupil of the most ordinary teacher the logical structure of Language. The organic character of Thought is thereby more completely exhibited, the relations of its elements more delicately indicated, and the whole riveted more firmly into a compact living body in the classical tongues than in any other.[1]

If limitation of time makes it necessary to choose between Latin and Greek, the former presents paramount claims to preference. Being the storehouse of a large portion of our own tongue, it yields in quite a peculiar degree an exercise in the history and force of words. And when we add to this the fact that it is the basis of the Romance languages, and smoothes the way to an acquaintance with these, we add the weight of utility to an already adequate ground of preference. Hence, perhaps, the prominence given to Latin over Greek in Scotch education, and its almost universal adoption in the parochial schools of the North, when pupils are likely to remain beyond their twelfth year.

[1] The literary and æsthetic arguments in favour of basing education on the classical tongues do not fall properly within our range here: they exercise their peculiar influence only after the boy has left the middle school (at least in Scotland).

On the Method of Teaching Latin and Greek.

It is not necessary to enter into any detailed statement of the method of teaching Latin and Greek in schools, because the method employed is generally unobjectionable. The errors made in teaching the ancient languages have been in the past caused by the defects of the school-books used rather than by the deficiencies of the masters. Except in a few schools where the inveteracy of habit and tradition obscures the common sense of the masters, we do not find boys of eight or nine required to learn rules before they have an opportunity of applying them, or initiated in translation by means of sentences the moral purport of which even the experience of the teachers can barely interpret. It is admitted on every side that the learning of rules and the practice of them should begin concurrently; in other words, that the boy should see in a concrete form what he is expected to remember as an abstract and generalized statement. It is also admitted that the subject-matter of the earlier years of classical instruction should be adapted as much as possible to the capacity of the learner. To attain these two objects, good school-books are manifestly indispensable, and they are now, thanks in the first instance to German scholars, amply provided. The facts of inflection and of syntax are worked into the boy gradually by means of easy sentences,—sentences easy not only in their structure but also in their signification. Familiar Latin narrative leads up to Cæsar, Livy, and Virgil, and the path of the boy is as much smoothed as it admits of being, or as it is desirable that it should be. Exercises in Latin and Greek composition, graduated on a similar principle, lead to a much more general practice of this exercise than used to be found anywhere in Scotland, save in the schools of the district which benefit by the Dick Bequest, where the prominence it receives perhaps diverts the attention too much from the more important exercise of translation into English.

The methods which ought to be employed in teaching the higher classics do not concern us here. But it is not travelling beyond the proper limits of this Report to advert to that mode of teaching the elements of Latin and Greek which carries the *rational* method to excess. Memory and rules must, it seems to me, in the initiatory and juvenile stages of acquiring a foreign tongue, take precedence of reason and reasoning. It does not follow that rules are to supersede *intelligence*, or that intelligence should ever be absent from any part of the process of learning Latin or any other subject. But the substitution of Comparative Philology for the simple statement and thorough committing to memory of the facts of inflection and the rules of syntax as they stand, is less wise than philosophic. This method rests on a confounding of the philosophy of the subject taught with the philosophy of teaching. It involves the immature mind in reasoning for dogmatic rules, and of the surprises of the discursive entanglements of the history of words and forms, and, which is worse, in the rational grounds which lie at the basis of syntactical rules. It is, of course, discreditable to the intelligent teacher to ignore the advances of Comparative Grammar and to hesitate to re-classify word-inflections on the basis of philological science, or to modify the rules of construction so as to bring them into closer accordance with the laws of General Syntax and of Psychology. This is due to the learner, in order that artificial difficulties may be removed from his path, and that he may at a future period enter on the study of Comparative Philology without having to unlearn much that he has painfully acquired, and being compelled almost to reconstruct his conceptions of Grammar. But to do more than this is an educational blunder. It tends to produce what Goethe speaks of as "a mature judgment in an immature mind." As in general education, so in teaching the special department of Language, our first care should be to avoid over-estimating the intellectual capacity of boys and anticipating their growth. An enfeebled brain, with its accompanying poverty of physique, and a pedantic intellect, are not improbable fruits of mistimed demands on reflective power.

Nor is it necessary to introduce prematurely into the classical school the "reasons of things." For, as has been already pointed out, one of the great claims, if not the greatest, which Latin and Greek can put forward to be the magistral subjects of secondary education, is this, that they are a means of giving an *unconscious* discipline to the reasoning powers. But if we substitute the vagueness of analysis for the precision of isolated facts, or linguistic reasonings for syntactical dogmas, we can do so effectually only by causing the boy to contemplate Language as the articulate expression of mind and its processes. Now, to call on a boy to make any such self-analytic effort, whether the subject-matter be Language, Science, Morals, Æsthetics, or Religion, is quite to misunderstand the theory of secondary education, and to forestall the university. The governing principle of the middle-school, both in the intellectual and moral sphere, is law, as that of the primary school is sympathy, and that of the university is freedom. Rules and the accurate application of rules, laws and the willing obedience to laws,—these must dominate in the management of boys. That rules shall be intelligent and capable of intelligent application, that laws shall be wholesome and promotive of moral discipline, sound method demands. That such obstructions shall be removed as convert labour into a toil for the intelligent, and quite stop the way for the average boy; and further, that work should be made as attractive as possible, either in itself or by connecting it with pleasing associations, is also demanded. But if we do more than this, and allow our fervour rather than our judgment to guide us, hastening to make the pupil see through the master's eyes, and with the master's grasp of principles, we do him a permanent injury. Minds of finer quality respond freely, but only by bringing into premature activity those powers of reflection on mental operations, and of wide generalization, which it is the exclusive business of the university to exercise. Minds, again, of ordinary capacity do not admit the poison into their intellects at all, but learn to repeat and produce on demand *reasonings* just as they do *rules*, and with the same amount of benefit. There may be exceptional cases among pupils, just as there are among masters men of original powers and rare sympathetic endowment; but, speaking on *a priori* grounds as well as from the results of experience, we may, as a general rule, depend on this, that teaching which has constant reference to the ultimate reasons of things, and necessitates self-analysis in the boy-learner, fosters a crude and premature development, which may have the glitter but which has not the substance of gold. In matters that concern the Intellect, such teaching adds to the bulk at the expense of the organic growth; in matters that concern Morals, it manufactures either a morbid sentimentalist or an insufferable prig.

Mathematics.

In the upper department of the parochial schools of Scotland, Mathematics means Mensuration, Algebra as far as quadratic equations (this only in the most advanced parochial schools), and a few books of Euclid. The discipline in school-mathematics comes from Geometry. The precision of the definitions, the necessity of constantly referring to them, and the purity of the exercise in syllogistic reasoning, are of great benefit to the intellect. But alone, and unsupported by the higher linguistic training, it would be an unsatisfactory discipline in even mere syllogistic logic. The subject-matter of the reasoning is confined within too narrow limits, and the landmarks of the ratiocinative process are too clearly defined to admit of geometry ever affording by itself a liberal culture. Both the subject and the discipline which it gives are alike too monotonous and inflexible.

The method of initiating boys in geometry has engaged the attention of writers on Education; but I think they have frequently lost sight of the fact that although in geometry, as in other subjects, there is a right method and a wrong, the age at which boys begin the study makes them less dependent on the method pursued by their teacher. They have already acquired the power of forming and understanding abstract notions. More *thoroughness* in the teaching of the elements is required rather than new methods.

We return now to the Parochial School in its general aspects :—

ORGANIZATION.

Classification—Time-Tables.

To teach, on the average, four subjects to each of sixty or eighty children, of different ages and of different stages of progress, within five hours, is a task which, at the first glance, seems to be almost impracticable and is always difficult. It is necessary to devise expedients for overcoming the difficulty. To apply these expedients is to organize. It is as a means of getting through his *own* share of daily school-work that the teacher first finds himself compelled to betake himself to organization ; and all the most serious errors still prevalent in the organizing of schools flow from the pertinacity with which the teacher persists in looking at organization from this his first point of view. The true object of organization is to secure that the pupils get through *their* work, not that the teacher gets through *his*. The subject in its details must be looked at from first to last in its relation to the pupil's necessity, not the master's.[1] Each child of the sixty has a certain amount of reading, writing, arithmetic, etc., to acquire before the hour of dismissal. In acquiring it he will of course receive the help of the master, who has already determined the nature and extent of the work

[1] See Historical and Statistical portion of this Report under Organization, p. 287.

to be done; but it is the pupil who has to *acquire* it, not the master who has to *instil* it. The teacher must, it is true, during the day come into direct personal contact with every pupil on each subject of study, test his work, clear up his difficulties, confirm his knowledge, and, above all, open up the way to the next step of his progress. This it is his duty to do: it constitutes his *direct* teaching. But direct teaching is a small part of his work in respect of quantity, though it is presumed to be the highest in respect of quality. The *indirect* personal teaching which is effected through organization, by means of which he arranges and directs the independent activity of the children in the attainment of the day's task, is a matter of perhaps more importance than the quality of the direct teaching, to the success of the school.

Questions of organization constantly tend to become questions of Discipline, which, however, is a distinct and higher agency. The objects of organization are attained when the arrangements for the working of the whole school as one class or one pupil are completed. The machine being thus finished in all its parts, the discovery and application of the motive power has next to be considered.

The first step in organization is to reduce the number of the individuals to be operated upon, by grouping them into homogeneous masses,—in other words, to classify. The theoretical perfection of classification is the arrangement of the pupils into groups, each individual of which is precisely at the same stage of mental development and acquired knowledge. As this, however, is impracticable, and as an equal amount of acquisition in respect of certain technical accomplishments, such as reading, writing, and arithmetic, is indispensable—and this irrespectively of the general capacity of the pupil,—acquired knowledge necessarily becomes the sole basis of classification. Nor is acquired knowledge altogether an inadequate test of the development of the pupil's mental power. In the rough, it may be said that boys having a similar knowledge of reading are at a similar stage of development. Reading, accordingly, affords on the whole the best basis of classification.

A master will generally find that where the children do not exceed eleven years of age, five groups, the lowest being subdivided, will suffice. Each of these five classes has to learn and to be taught a portion of four subjects, on the average, within five hours. Now, what the master has in the first place to arrange is the order and times of learning. Having divided the time of the whole school into sections of fifteen minutes each, his next duty is to provide for the occupation of each group during every successive section of the time with such a succession of work as shall, by its variety, prevent too continuous a strain on the pupil's mind. To do this is to construct a Time-table. This must be constructed by the master from the point of view that he is the director of a machine rather than a teacher. He must know what each portion of his machine is capable of doing, what it ought to do, and he must arrange for its doing it. If a teacher cannot tell what each group, and each pupil in the group, ought to be doing at any one point of time in the course of the school-day, and if he cannot tell at the end of the day how much or how little has been done, his school is not thoroughly taught. Let him keep in mind that it is the arranging of the work and the directing of the powers *of his pupils* which is his first and main duty. Effective instruction and discipline are possible only when the pupil does by far the larger share of the work.

The machine being thus constructed and set in motion, the school is organized. The chaotic materials which lay to the teacher's hand are built up into a harmonious whole, having a meaning and a purpose. I have called the organized school a machine : it ought rather to be called a living body, the various limbs of which are inspired by one central purpose, and dependent on one regulating head.

The words " Classification" and " Time-table" sum up the whole of organization. The extent to which each group is brought into immediate personal contact with the teacher depends on the relation which the numbers taught bear to the teaching power, and on the master's skill in multiplying his presence. An average attendance of seventy gives quite as large a school as ought to be attempted single-handed. The further duty of the teacher, as distinct from an organizer and the originator of an organization, falls to be considered under the head of School Discipline.

SCHOOL DISCIPLINE.

Indirect Moral Teaching—Rewards and Punishments.

The living machine being constructed and set in motion, its just and true action will depend on two things: the method according to which each limb is made to work, and the means taken for securing that the work is really done. The former subject has been already sufficiently considered under the general head of Methods: the consideration of the latter embraces what is somewhat vaguely called School Discipline.

School-discipline is, in the first instance, instituted for the purpose of insuring the attainment of the ends of organization, viz., a certain quantity of appreciable work. After it has been instituted, however, it becomes at once and directly subservient to a higher end, the ultimate end of the school itself,—the formation of good habits. Not efficient *work*, but efficient *working*, is the immediate, as well as the final purpose of discipline as such. In other words, discipline, quickly losing sight of its original object, contemplates chiefly the *manner* of working, and is so intent on this that it can afford almost to disregard the results of teaching in respect of quantity of work accomplished. The *manner* of working is a wide and important question. It embraces obedience to school-rules as to time, place, circumstance, and style : it implies, moreover, the exercise of diligence, and the practice of accuracy and honesty. Discipline is therefore pre-eminently a moral question, and may be said to be the moral teaching of the school, as it is embodied in the hourly *practice* of each member of it.

The mere obedience to school-rules however trivial, simply because they are rules and proceed from a recognised authority, is in itself a moral act ; while the practice of diligence, accuracy, and honesty contributes directly to the formation of the habit of perseverance in duty, and of that intellectual conscientiousness which contributes so largely to general integrity of mind. The formation of habit is the chief moral purpose of education ; the instilling of sound opinions, the clearing away of error, and the correcting of occasional perversity of judgment or of will, being all merely subsidiary to the constant insistence on the doing of certain duties in a certain way, with a view to the formation of a good mental habit. When those individual acts, which were originally conscious efforts of will, have been so frequently repeated that they are the result of unconscious tendency, habit is formed. And, as discipline has for its direct object the individual acts of every boy composing the school, it may be regarded as covering the whole field of moral training, as distinguished from moral teaching.

Not only so: without the practice of obedience and the other duties above enumerated, the subordinate result of a certain quantity of knowledge attained in the various school studies is manifestly beyond the reach of teacher or pupil. It would seem, therefore, that the whole of the work of the organized school starts from discipline as its first condition, proceeds according to discipline, and finds its proper consummation in the mental effects of discipline. The technical results,—that is to say, the acquisition of a certain quantity of knowledge,—are not overlooked; nay, they are reached only in so far as discipline is effective.

I have endeavoured in previous chapters to show that procedure according to a right method of teaching and learning each subject, while it contributes to the training of the intellectual powers, is, at the same time, the most effective way of securing the largest result in respect of positive knowledge. It now appears that even sound methods will fail, if unsupported by effective discipline, and that, therefore, the cultivation of the practical morality of the school is not merely the indispensable handmaid of method, but the surest path even to technical results, while it directly promotes the ultimate aim of the school.

To treat of school-rules for the conduct of study,

and of the best means of making the pupil diligent, accurate, and honest in his work, would be foreign to the purpose of this Report, the object of which is to define the legitimate aims of the parochial school, and to indicate methods and aims in principle rather than in detail.

Moreover, to do so would be superfluous. The teacher who understands the nature and purpose of discipline is never at a loss for ways and means. These are indeed numberless. To the teacher, on the other hand, who cannot see wherein discipline really consists, and what it aims at, ways and means, expedients and devices, become mere tricks, destitute of all moral significance and purpose. Two points of of detail, however,—preliminaries rather than elements of discipline,—even the wisest disciplinarian requires to be reminded of: *First*, The limitation of each successive subject of study within narrow limits as to quantity and duration. If sustained attention is to be expected from children, the continuous strain of the same subject ought to be limited to fifteen minutes, except in circumstances of peculiar interest. The intervals of entire relaxation, again, ought to be frequent however short. *Secondly*, In matters of morality he must avoid making demands on the powers and obedience of the young greater than they can easily respond to.

But the clearest comprehension by the teacher of the nature and purposes of discipline, the wisest elaboration of the subordinate ways and means whereby the pupils' efforts after obedience, diligence, accuracy, and honesty are to be guided and supported, may break down. Anarchy of the will and dissipation of the intellectual powers may be the sole fruits visible in the schoolroom, even where there are the best intentions and the most assiduous labour. The teacher, in other words, may fail as a disciplinarian. How is this failure to be avoided and the reign of discipline established? By supplying motives to the pupil. Even the rare boy who likes study for its own sake is not always disposed to study. His powers are not under such perfect control as always to submit cheerfully to the rules of time and place. Fitful exertion is the habit of the yet undisciplined mind, however well disposed for knowledge. The majority of the minds in a school have not even this disposition : at best, they study with a view to the conquest of a difficulty or the performance of a duty, both motives being generally associated. On such motives a teacher must rely, and his first duty is to facilitate the operation of them. The path must be so smoothed that the difficulty to be overcome may not be insuperable to the intellect, and the duty required may not be too great a strain on the moral power of the pupil. But the most potent of all motives, and one essential to the sustained and regular working of all others, is the love of the master's approbation. To facilitate the operation of this motive in a consistent way, and irrespectively of the master's changing moods, certain fixed and public means (such as marks, which result ultimately in slight privileges or rewards) must be taken for testing and noting the successes of the pupils. The schoolmaster, however, must beware of committing the vulgar error of using the word *successes* to indicate that difficulties have been overcome. He has to do with discipline, and this has to do both primarily and ultimately with moral training, not intellectual attainment. The consciences of children are much injured, and their desire to labour in the discharge of their school duty weakened, if not utterly extinguished, by the rough and ready style of estimating moral qualities according to their measurable results in intellectual acquisition. That man is a clumsy manipulator of the tender mind who does not scrupulously and anxiously distinguish between the gain in intellectual and moral habit and the coarse and more palpable profit in respect of mere knowledge. The whole purpose of this Report is to insist on the former as the ultimate aim of the parochial school, and to illustrate its favourable influence on merely technical acquirement, with a view to vindicate its claim to constant, if not exclusive consideration. To test the moral qualities by the amount of intellectual ground traversed, is as unjust as it is beside the whole higher object of education. The master, then, in distributing the great motive influence of the school,—his approbation for rules obeyed, diligence exercised, accuracy and honesty attained, must have regard to the working, not the work. Each child whom he can ascertain to have laudably striven, must receive the meed of approbation which is his due. If a doubt exist as to there having been a *bonâ fide* effort, it is safer to give the pupil the benefit of it. Justice must lean to mercy's side. The master must not cover his want of time or ability to sift the moral elements of a question by assuming the aspect and manner of supernatural penetration and sternness. Under mercy there lies a kind of large justice which, in the schoolroom, is rich in moral return. The school conscience will more easily recover from undue leniency than forget groundless severity.

Many teachers seem, even in these days, to imagine that good discipline and severity of manner and language are inseparable, whereas, on the contrary, severity defeats every object of discipline. Where the painful silence of awe pervades a school, all the technical results, however high, ought, in my opinion, to be rigidly discounted by the inspector. What amount of acquaintance with words and things can compensate for the loss of a freely-working conscience? Silence and slavish obedience do not constitute moral order. Teachers sometimes require to be reminded that there is such a thing as anarchical order.

But what if a teacher finds that the motives usually successful in schools fail in his particular case to move the wills by which he is surrounded, even when aided by an organization which makes duty plain and easy, and by methods of instruction which harmonize with the natural operations of the pupils' intellects? His rules are fair, but the pupils will not obey them; his demands on their intellects and wills are reasonable, but they decline to respond to the demand; he is ready to distribute approval and disapproval justly, but they do not care for his approbation. The answer is easy: the master is deficient in moral power, and must at once take himself out of the school into some other more congenial sphere of work. For, the praise and censure of the teacher constitute the keystone of the whole edifice of the school; and if we withdraw from these their legitimate power, discipline dissolves and organization crumbles to pieces. The adult yields, whether he will or not, to the dispensing authority with which the visible pre-eminence of goodness or of strength invests a man: the child is a still more willing slave. For *his* subjection the mere semblance of moral superiority is enough. But it must be the moral superiority of real or apparent *strength*. To goodness and love the child responds with affection; but affection does not always prompt obedience in the undisciplined mind: on the contrary, we find affection and systematic disobedience to be not uncommonly conjoined, where no other influence supervenes. The young are not yet a law to themselves; and, so constituted is the moral nature of man that children are happier when an extraneous law supplies the defect inherent in their tender age. They instinctively welcome the strength which claims their allegiance. That teacher consequently must be a very weak (though he may be a very good) man who cannot, even with the help thus amply given by the children themselves, become the source of right and wrong to his pupils,—the external and visible exponent of duty. He must be destitute of the first requisites in a teacher, namely, a sense of law dominating his own life, and an impulse, conscious or unconscious, to communicate this sense of law to others. Law must be conspicuous in his words and acts, manifesting itself in self-control and anxious subjection to the spirit of the rules which he imposes on others; and this is the same thing as saying that he must himself have, and *visibly* have, a good habit of will. How can we expect that a man destitute of force of character should be capable of forming the character of others? Character is, in truth, as we have before said, the first necessity in the teacher; the second is, that in his efforts to bring others under the influence of law, he shall exhibit in his dealings the characteristics of law, namely, clearness, vigour, dogmatism, imperativeness, and consistency. Given a teacher so endowed, or striving, nay, only *seeming* to strive, after such endowment, and the difficulties of discipline vanish, except in so far as they are the adventitious results of faulty organization or blundering methods.

It has been said, some pages back, that the

intellectual and moral strength which each child draws from his neighbour, in other words, co-operation and sympathy, far more than counterbalance the apparently insuperable difficulties which numbers present to the teacher, when he, for the first time, enters his school: organization turns the scale in his favour as against the tutor of one or few. Still more efficacious are numbers in the maintenance of discipline, and this because of its moral and therefore emotional character. The complicated machinery of the school is so interlaced and interdependent, that the moral movement of any one part tends to move the rest; and where the majority of hearts move, the minority almost involuntarily fall in with the movement, which thus becomes general.

The primary object of discipline, we have seen, is to guarantee the objects of organization, but as this has to do with the *manner* of working, discipline becomes a moral question. It involves, in fact, the whole subject of moral training, in so far as it relates to the intellectual work of the school. Further consideration of the subject shows that discipline has even a wider sweep, and that it may be defined as the means resorted to for giving practical effect to the whole of the moral as well as the intellectual instruction contemplated by the master. It thus opens up questions the most various and delicate, and is co-extensive with the subject of Education itself in its higher sense. The conduct of the pupils towards each other, and towards their teacher personally, falls within its range, and this is a department of discipline which perhaps tells more largely on the formation of a good moral habit of mind than even the thorough and conscientious discharge of the day's work. The regulation of mutual intercourse, moreover, affords the only means available for correcting the evils which prevail in the homes of children, for cultivating truthfulness, and for subjecting unregulated wills to the operation of humane and Christian feeling. These and other aims of *direct* moral teaching I shall speak of in the sequel. The best way of *enforcing* moral instruction, so as to convert precept into habit, is what we have specially to consider under the head of Discipline. This has been already partially indicated, and it is further illustrated in what follows.

Rewards and Punishments.

Even the schoolmaster who is powerful enough to centre the discipline of the school in his approving or disapproving word, can ill afford to dispense with the assistance which a system of rewards and punishments gives. There are some men who, having stopped short at the first step of moral analysis, set up, both in the family and the school, the calm ungenial approval, or stern disapproval, of conscience or authority as exhaustive of all legitimate motives of conduct. It is unnecessary to combat this theory in so far as it has reference to the matured mind, because our business here is only with the young. In their case assuredly, the natural tendency which all men feel to follow up their approval by communicating to the person approved some pleasure over and above the moral satisfaction which is the inner reward of having deserved well, should be generously yielded to. Liberality in approval generates liberality in the service of obedience. By carrying out the approval of the right act into consequences which are in themselves pleasing, the rightness of the act is established in the mind of the young in association with the agreeable. An adventitious but perfectly legitimate support is thereby provided for the yet unfashioned will.

If approval may be so signalized, it follows that disapproval also fairly claims to be supported and enforced by adventitious associations of pain. In itself disapproval is punishment, if there exist in the mind of the child regard or respect for the authority which disapproves. In such a case the sense of a link of attachment or reverence rudely snapped is often painful in the extreme—more painful than any kind of adventitious punishment. Nay, physical chastisement sometimes lessens the moral suffering in such cases, and is hailed by the culprit as a relief. Adventitious punishments consist in the further association of pain to body or mind over and above that which the act of disapprobation causes; but, like rewards, they are to be regarded simply as accessaries in the maintenance of discipline. They deepen the impression which disapproval makes on a hard or low type of mind, and thereby aid in the development of conscience: they give unmistakable and vivid expression to the authoritative moral dispensations of the master, and are valuable, if not indispensable, even to the morally strong.

But let it be observed that adventitious punishments are *only* auxiliaries. If they are allowed to become the principals instead of the subordinates in moral discipline, and to supplant the expression of disapproval, of which they are only the accidental consequences, they usurp a sovereignty which does not belong to them. As the moral power of the teacher or parent decreases, adventitious punishments always increase, and *vice versâ*. Of this fact there can be no doubt, and the teacher may safely and profitably measure himself by it. A reliance on adventitious punishment invariably reveals the inherent weakness of the teacher. This reliance is avenged; for it is only by a cumulative intensity of punishments that the teacher can in such circumstances continue to maintain his supremacy, and effect even the technical objects of school-keeping. Ere long a school so governed becomes a spectacle of one rude material force, predominating, or striving to predominate, over other and lesser forces, amid the silence of rebellious fear or the confused murmurs of just resistance. A melancholy contrast this to the school governed by the scarcely conscious power of a lofty purpose and a disciplined and earnest will!

A collection of all possible punishments which attained the ends of discipline, without bearing too hard on the mind or body of the child, would be a valuable guide to the teacher and the parent. Such a collection would help to check the sin of over-severity, which will be found only as the offspring of passion,—a state of mind forbidden to the teacher by every moral consideration. That a teacher or parent should constantly exhibit judicial calmness in the presence of the wrongdoing of children is neither desirable nor necessary. Such affected superiority to natural and legitimate emotions is artificial, and, while failing of its aim in respect of the pupils, it exhausts the teacher. So long as anger is under the control of the will, it is as effective in the discipline of the school as it is natural in the ordinary relations of life. Its effectiveness, however, is in proportion to the rareness of its manifestation. It must not be expended on peccadilloes or errors, but reserved for serious and deliberate faults.

Worse than occasional passion is chronic crossness or peevishness, the most unhappy mental state of all. Peevishness is, in fact, the continuous passion of petty souls, and much more detrimental to the moral life of the school than occasional outbursts of violent wrath. It exhibits itself in a continued series of small acts of injustice. It is itself a continual act of injustice towards all within its range. Where it exists there can, of course, be no such thing as discipline, the sole object of the pupils being to avoid the fractious word, and evade the task for which there is no reward.

As over-severity is much more frequently the result of passion than of errors of judgment, the teacher has only to control his temper in order to be just in his punishments. This precaution having been taken, there is a wide field of petty inflictions open to the observant and ingenious mind. The general rule which ought to regulate punishments is that they shall be as nearly as possible the natural consequences of the transgression. A boy who comes late is fitly punished by reproval, and being left in the school room while the other boys are at play. A boy who forgets to bring his reading-book to school is justly punished by being excluded from the lesson, receiving bad marks as if for non-preparation, and being required to prosecute some isolated and disagreeable task as a substitute for the reading : a boy who tells a lie is rightly punished by being forbidden to speak ; and so on.

But as many cases arise both in the family and in the school which are transgressions not in themselves, but only *because they are disobediences,* and which have therefore no *natural* consequences except the disapproval of the parent or teacher, and for which this disapproval is not a sufficient punishment, it becomes necessary to attach certain artificial penalties to such wrongdoings. And here the just and judicious teacher is often the victim of much conscientious perplexity. It is very difficult to write a catalogue of punishments suited for various cases, but some assistance may be given if we point out the general heads under which penalties may be classified. It will be found that they all fall under the two heads of Deprivation and Infliction. Punishments of deprivation have two advantages over punishments of infliction. They do not afford so easy a channel for the passion of the teacher; and they are constantly fresh. Boys grow callous to frequent inflictions, whether of pœnas or the rod, but there is a perennial and ever fresh aggravation connected with deprivation of time, or pleasures, or privileges. Punishments of infliction are either mental or corporal, according as they touch the mind or body first: but fundamentally there is no broad distinction; for the affections of the body pain the mind, because of their association with censure, while the toil and harassment of the mind are often more painful to the body than corporal chastisement. Bad marks, ending in public disgraces, pœnas, exclusion from the current routine of the school, especially when supplemented by punishments of deprivation, ought, if the teacher be competent for his task, to be sufficient for all purposes of discipline without having recourse to flagellation. Pœnas, however, or additional work, should not consist of the repetition or extension of the usual lessons, because this associates legitimate work with the hatefulness of a penalty.

There are occasions, however, on which the cane must be resorted to. I have no sympathy with objections to flogging (if done in cold blood) on the score of cruelty or indignity. It is much more merciful to castigate a boy than to wear his nerves to exhaustion by appeals to sentiment, affection, or duty, which minister to the vanity of the hard, and the morbidness of the gentle and sensitive. Nor is pœna-giving less severe in the physical pain it often causes than the application of the taws or rod, while, when carried to extremities, as is common among masters of inexperience or of shallow moral endowment, it has the further vice of making both pupil and teacher dwell too long on an offence. Punishments should be prompt, sharp, decisive, and there end; the object being not to inflict pain but to deter from future offences, and to restore the moral equilibrium of the offender and of the offended school-conscience. This object once attained—the more expeditiously it is attained the better—no more should be heard of either offence or punishment. A teacher or parent should never bear grudges. The young interpret such exhibitions as sulkiness and injustice, and do not fail to learn the lesson for themselves. A boy should be allowed to start afresh after punishment, and without stain. There should be no dregs for a culprit to drain. For these reasons, corporal chastisement has a distinct advantage over many others which seem more merciful.

The objection that a flogging hurts a boy's self-respect is true only in this sense, that he feels that he is being treated as a person on whom physical coercion only can have any influence. The fact that it is always associated with this indignity furnishes the only sound reason for the total expulsion of the practice from the school and the family. The substitution of physical compulsion for moral authority, tends to lower all boys of good dispositions, and weakens the sense of *free* responsibility. And, inasmuch as the object of moral discipline is to develop the conscience of a freeman, not of a slave, it is *primâ facie* degrading to both the punished and the punisher to treat a child or a man as if he had forfeited his humanity, and could be brought to see and do the right only by having bodily pain presented as the alternative. As a *system* of discipline it will be found to rest on an ultra-materialistic theory of Ethics. If, therefore, the master find it necessary to call to his aid corporal penalties, he has good reason to pause and to question himself. If his self-examination leaves the blame of resorting to the last extremity on the head of the offender, he has no alternative but to make the solemn example of a rational being driven like a brute, because he is accessible only to brutal motives. Only the parlour educationist will deny that boys (and men) exist, possessed of moral hides too indurated to be sensitive to purely moral appeals.

As corporal chastisement, however, is to be regarded as an extreme measure, and as standing apart from all other adventitious aids to discipline, this peculiarity should be conspicuously brought out by the teacher, and in every school, accordingly, there should be a chastisable and unchastisable class. A certain number of wilful offences, revealing a conscience too callous to be influenced by ordinary motives, should bring with it the disgrace of being reduced to the class of boys punishable with the rod. The descent to this school purgatory, however, should be difficult and slow ; the ascent and return to the light of responsibility and moral freedom plain and easy.

There is a flagellation of the mind worse than any castigation of the body. The masters who resort to it call it satire ; but the impartial spectator detects that it is simply uncontrolled passion finding an outlet under the thin delusive veil of irony. Sarcasm and ridicule make the courageous feel callous and revengeful, and the sensitive oppressed and abused. It is an unmanly use of superior strength so to lacerate the feelings of the defenceless. It is also dishonest and disloyal; for this engine of punishment finds no recognised place in the school code. It is therefore unconstitutional, and justifies rebellion. Infliction, not affliction, marks the limit of legitimate punishment.

It would seem that we are as yet only on the threshold of the large subject of Discipline. Rules, obedience, diligence, accuracy, and honesty, have necessarily led me to speak of the moral training of the school in general, as well as in its special relation to the merely intellectual daily work which each member of it has to do, and of the natural and artificial supports of discipline. But I have adverted only to principles of action : the whole field of detail is still untrodden. To enter upon it would be to write a school manual, for which there is neither space nor need. The master who brings to his work a habit of will which is itself an example to others and a guide to himself will fill up the details of a general outline with ease. Even the average teacher, if in earnest, will evolve from general principles his own details, which will have the additional advantage of being his own, and therefore vital and efficacious.

A few additional words, however, for the help of beginners who feel they need it, may be serviceable, even though put in a curt form, and disjoined from their connexion with the educative aims and principles of the subject as a whole. And *first* of all, let the young teacher give heed to the admonition and the example which come down to him through nearly two thousand years, from the Pagan philosopher and the Saviour of the world—Reverence childhood. The task he has to do requires a delicate and respectful as well as a strong hand. *Secondly*, Let his rules be just, and *easily obeyed*. *Thirdly*, Let him not expect the will of a man where there is the heart of the child or the boy. *Fourthly*, Let him not strain too far the power of application. *Fifthly*, Where there has been assiduity, let him accept a little well done, and discountenance quantity and display. *Sixthly*, Let him trust the honesty of his pupils, but remove all occasions of stumbling. *Seventhly*, Let him be vigilant, but let him disdain inquisitorial prying or deputed espionage. *Eighthly*, When he doubts in the matter of truth-telling, the fulfilment of obedience, or the propriety of punishing, let him always give the pupil the benefit of the doubt. *Ninthly*, Let him so act that the school will feel that it is regard for the moral law rather than for his personal authority that regulates his praise and blame, his rewards and punishments. And, *finally*, and above all, let him do unto others, *even to children*, as he would that others should do unto him.[1]

The difficulties which both parents and schoolmasters experience in the regulation of punishment, leads me to add to my own remarks on the subject certain extracts from the writings of one of the most eminent educationists of this century :—

"If the word be always suited to the action, and every gradation on the side of merit and demerit be candidly and distinctly characterized by the terms employed, and by the tone and look with which they are delivered, such an ascendency may be gained over the minds of youth, that a word or significant gesture will have more weight, and make a deeper impression, than an angry expostulation or heavy blows. Praise and blame, when sparingly and judiciously dealt out, are engines of incalculable power. But, on the other hand, if a master, for some trifling misdemeanour, pour forth a volley of abusive epithets, he has

---

[1] The subject of Drill, as an aid to moral discipline, as well as to the development of a healthy *physique*, belongs perhaps more to the detail of a school manual than to a general statement of principles and methods.

nothing, of course, in reserve for heinous offences but flagellation; and if, on the other hand, he be either extravagant or partial in his commendation, it will have little or no value.

"I would push the economy of praise and reproof so far as to pitch the tone of both a note or two below the natural scale. This is a useful rule in commending, because it enhances the value of a strong expression. But it is in reprimand and punishment that its importance is best seen; though, I fear I must add, in practice least understood. There prevails among schoolmasters such a dread of relaxing wholesome discipline, that, when a public example is to be made, even the most temperate and conscientious think themselves called upon to colour the offence a little highly, and to express even more indignation against the culprit than they actually feel. This I conceive to be a capital blunder. The very reverse of it is a great secret in the management of youth. No infliction can benefit the sufferer, or serve as a warning to others, which is not felt and acknowledged to be just by the great body of his school-fellows. The moment it exceeds the measure which the impartial spectator can sympathize with, it generates compassion for the offender, and dislike of the punisher. . . .

"On the other hand, there is nothing that so completely disarms the bad and unsocial passions of a boy as kindliness; nothing so popular as stopping short of the severity which strict justice might award. Nor will such forbearance, if it appear to flow from enlightened principle and affection, ever tempt to a repetition of the offence. . . .

". . . To dispense with corporal punishment in all minor school-offences, and to reserve it for cases of moral delinquency or turpitude. . . . Of the latter kind were deliberate lying, dishonesty, wanton cruelty, indecency in word or deed; of the former, neglect of preparation, failing to answer questions, or to say by heart, coming late, being inattentive, or talking in school time, teasing a school-fellow, etc.

". . . If a boy was reported by the monitor to be unprepared on the lesson, the gentlest interference on my part was to call him out of the division and admonish him privately. If he could assign no reason for his failure, he was dismissed with a word of advice, and a hope that this negligence would not occur again; but at the same time, with an assurance that if it did, I should feel it incumbent on me to reprove him in presence of his division. This had never, probably, occurred to him as an aggravation of his disgrace, but the very mention of it was sufficient to make him think so, and he returned to his place resolved to avoid it, and not perhaps without a sentiment of thankfulness for the attention to his feelings implied by this preliminary warning. . . .

"The next step in increase of severity was to reprimand before the whole division, care being taken, in this as in all other cases, that reproof should be administered more in sorrow than in anger. This mode of reprehending was that most frequently practised, because it gave an opportunity of instructing and warning others, though it was often exchanged for the gentler mode of giving the boy an audience apart, when I read in his eye that he had a private reason to assign, which he was unwilling to impart to any ear but mine.

" For minds of less sensibility, or greater tendency to go wrong, there remained a reproof before the assembled class, mild or sharp, as suited the character addressed. Occasion for this reproof was taken by calling such boys to say in the class, as soon as the divisions broke up. . . .

"But as there must, of course, be many in a numerous class either too sluggish or too thoughtless and playful to be permanently or uniformly affected by any of these motives, the last resort was to what was technically called a *pœna*, or written imposition. . . . Nothing can be more equitable, than that a boy who fails to prepare a lesson at home, or give attention to the construing in the class-room, should be obliged to write it out, and be curtailed of his play. It was an improving exercise, too, and thus accomplished the most desirable ends of punishment, —correction and warning. . . .

" . . . For a considerable time after these methods had completely superseded corporal punishment in all that regarded the lessons, it was still had recourse to now and then, as the appropriate means of deterring from grave acts of immorality. . . .

" . . . The great secret in this, as in the instance of minor misdemeanours, is to estimate fairly the gravity of the offence, so long as it is spoken of in the abstract, and to fix its place correctly in the scale of demerit; while, at the same time, the individual culprit is allowed the benefit of all the circumstances which can be honestly urged in extenuation. When the master seems to take pleasure in dwelling on these, the punishment he does inflict will appear to be extorted from him, as it really is, by the demands of justice, and will create no feeling in the breast either of the sufferer or the spectator which is not friendly to virtue. Precept thus enforced by example is the most impressive of all moral lessons.

" But so regularly did the dread of corporal chastisement increase in proportion to its mildness and rarity, that, during the latter half of my rectorship, it was entirely discontinued; partly, and chiefly, in consequence of the manifest improvement in the morality of the boys; partly, because the feeling of honour had become so nice as to make it too severe an infliction for any school offence that could be committed. The solemnity and the lecture were still continued when occasion offered. . . .

" Among the various substitutes for corporal punishment, I have made no mention of one which was and is in very common use: that of turning a boy down in his class, often by ten or twenty places at a time, in consequence, not of the better saying of those below him, but by the *fiat* of the master. To him this mode of deterring and punishing recommends itself by the tempting facility of applying it. It is generally used in cases of talking or trifling in the class-room, or being late. For the former it is admissible, if preceded by a demand for the next word, or an order to repeat the clause last construed. As to being late, a fault to which boys are so liable, that it must be sharply dealt with, it was checked not by loss of place, but more effectually by stationing the the general censor outside the door, to collect the names of the late as they arrived, and note them for a *pœna*, to be delivered next morning. Forfeiture of place, for such offences, is both unjust and inexpedient."- *From Professor Pillans' Contributions to the Cause of Education*, p. 340.

MORAL INSTRUCTION.

*Initiatory stage—Direct moral teaching and suggestive moral teaching—
Juvenile stage (Laws of Health, etc.)*

Moral instruction, as distinguished from the moral training which Discipline affords, means the inculcation of moral duties in a preceptive form. It is a kind of colloquial preaching on the part of the teacher, the more colloquial the better.

Initiatory Stage.—When the mind is sufficiently matured to apprehend a principle of conduct, to adopt it, and to give it effect by the power of a sustained purpose, preceptive teaching is of unquestionable value. In proportion, however, to the weakness of the power of exerting a continuous and conscious effort of will, in other words, in proportion to the youth of the pupil, precept is, at the time of its inculcation, inefficacious. The moral principle if not the moral sentiment of the very young is most effectually reached through the moral habit, and the moral habit can be formed only by ordering the child *to do* certain things in a certain way, giving him the help of the example of his teacher and fellows while doing them, and taking means to make sure that they are done. But this, as we have seen, is to discipline. Discipline signifies the enforcing of the *doing* of the moral law by means of motives, which motives are supported by rewards and punishments.

I have said that by the doing of moral acts alone, in other words, by means of discipline, moral sentiments and principles thoroughly enter into the mind of a child as intelligible and living guides of conduct. The form of words is, however, by no means altogether useless. To throw into a preceptive form the moral *acts* which the teacher is continually insisting on is of value, *as subsidiary to the practice of them*. Precept serves as a guide and a standard of measure to the child, the significance of which gradually dawns on him. Especially after reward for right-doing, or punishment for wrong-doing, a gently-urged precept will be dropt into a prepared soil and will take root.

There are two kinds of preceptive teaching— the Suggestive and the Direct. The suggestive is the more efficacious, because it is associated with a concrete example. In the doing of right acts, the child is presumed to be supported by the example of his teacher and fellows. By sharing the moral life exhibited daily in the school he gradually becomes a constituent part of it: it is the *example* of those around him that points both the moral and the way. This is true of the *indirect* moral instruction of discipline: it is equally necessary that the *direct* moral instruction of the school, in so far as it is conveyed by books or conversation, should be in the earlier years as much as possible the instruction which the example of others gives, that is to say, the instruction of biography, fable, and anecdote. The lessons of fair play and peaceableness, for example, almost defy abstract preceptive teaching in the case of the very young, but enter vividly and graphically into the mind through the story of the two boys and the nut, which ends in the arbiter eating the kernel and liberally dispensing half a shell to each of the little disputants. Next to seeing a good example before us is imagining that we see it, and this we do when we read or hear of it.

Direct Precept, if less important than the Suggestive, has yet a useful part to play. It is true that all moral precepts are laws of conduct generalized from particular acts and their consequences, and therefore that to demand of a child that he shall strain his intellect to grasp fully a moral generalization is to demand an impossibility. Even such seemingly simple generalizations, as "To steal is wrong," "All must be just in their dealings;" "Generosity is a duty," "Truthfulness must be observed," and so forth, although committed to memory and produced when required, are understood by the child only in so far as they are illustrated by *particular acts* coming within his personal cognisance. If the teacher says, "Do not take your neighbour's pencil as I saw you do this morning, for that is to steal, and to steal is wrong," he is intelligible. A certain number of acts thus from time to time become known to the child as stealing, from which he infers the wickedness of other acts which have a common characteristic with them, and in this way he extends his moral knowledge with his moral experience, until at last there flashes upon him in its full force and meaning the generalized precept, "Thou shalt not steal." This is the process by which the understanding of moral principles is reached by the growing mind. But, true as this is, the moral generalization is not wholly valueless to the child, although not fully intelligible, at the time of its being imparted. He himself is, by the very instincts of his nature and the necessities of his external condition, groping his way to some such general statement of duty which will bring harmony into the chaos of his moral life by bringing law. To furnish him at the outset of his journey in search of duty with the conclusion to which the wisdom of the past has come, is like giving the young builder a plan of the house we require him to build. It is only a semblance, but it facilitates and expedites the attainment of the reality.

The theory of education, which, so far from regarding direct preceptive teaching as a help, considers it to be an overlaying and overburdening of the child's mind, and which would lead him on in his moral perceptions step by step, and, at a certain moment of his development, and not till then, give the generalized truth which, if earlier given, would be in its full scope unintelligible, is, I suspect, shallow, sentimental, and impracticable. Even if a teacher had full control over the first sixteen years of his pupil's life, and were carefully to macadamize and bridge his path in accordance with this theory, he might, perhaps, reach the end which he proposed to himself, but only to find that it had changed its character. He would be vanquished in the moment of victory. The pupil would probably reach the goal of a clear comprehension of principle in its practical significance, exhausted by the facilities and monotony of his too easy route, while his comrade who had reached the same point across country, unaided, and after many difficulties, obstructions, and stumblings, would come in later it might be, but exhilarated by difficulty and braced for fresh exertion. The teacher must bear in mind that life from first to last is a progress and a struggle, and that the purpose of education is not to give possession of a certain quantity of facts of the understanding, or even of principles of morality, but of powers; not the conferring of attainment, but the qualifying for pursuit. The only essential equipment for every man is the weapons of the chase, an object to pursue, and vigour of faculty. The School does its work best when it makes the mode of acquiring the weapons, whether they be moral or intellectual, itself the means of training the faculties of pursuit.

Although, therefore, the early storing of the memory with generalized moralities serves an important purpose,—and this, by suggesting difficulty, compelling intellectual effort, and giving the consciousness of self-effected progress when light at last is seen,—such direct preceptive teaching is to be admitted into the initiatory classes of a school only as distinctly subsidiary to *particular* instruction as to the qualities of individual acts by means of reading, conversation, and above all, discipline. The particular instruction and the disciplinary training constitute substantially the whole moral education during the initiatory stage, to which all else is only an accessary. It is necessary to insist on this, lest teachers should imagine that they have acquitted themselves of their duty when they have inculcated fine sentiments and right principles. This is not teaching, but preaching. It is through the doing of a thing only, as has been already said, that principles of conduct can take living root in a child's mind. A schoolmaster discharges his duty, not by enunciating or inculcating the right, though this is both necessary and desirable, but by watchful noting of the acts of his pupils towards each other, as well as towards himself, by explaining the nature of wrong acts individually, and by causing the right *act* to be done instead of the wrong. The forms which stealing, lying, injustice, cruelty, malice, and envy take are difficult to number, even among adults, but among children they are infinite in their petty variety. In the reading-lessons, in the incidents of the school, and in the events of the parish, will be found further material for the exemplification, illustration, and personal application of the various virtues and vices, both in their patent and their insidious forms. Individual acts will be on these occasions referred to their proper preceptive head, and the command, whether it be prohibitive, "Do not bear false witness," or hortatory, "Love thy father and thy mother," will be thus apprehended as a vital fact, not as a dead phrase. Through all the teacher must constantly bear in mind that it is only in their petty exhibitions that the child can know even the greatest vices or virtues, and it is with these petty things consequently, and the precepts which they suggest, not with abstract and large utterances, that the teacher has mainly to do. The thousand trivialities of daily life constitute the moralities of children. They are so numerous, it is true, and so ever-changing, as to baffle the teacher's attempt to know them, much more to anticipate them. But, fortunately for him, as well as for his pupil, the rule of conduct which covers all other minor precepts, and suits all possible cases, is given to us in a form at once the most widely general, the most closely individual, and the most easy of application. "Do unto others as you would that others should do unto you," is a command which should be kept constantly before the children, and persistently introduced as the measure of all their little acts. It will help the teacher as well as the child.

Where the tone and system of the school are good, the correction of petty immoralities is quick and easy. A glance, an upraised finger, or a single word, is generally sufficient. But even if it should cost time to correct them, the time must be given. The very purpose of the teacher's professional existence is the formation of character; and of the two elements of character, a good habit of the will claims his supreme attention. Nor, indeed, is any time wasted even for intellectual purposes which is devoted to the formation of a habit of will in harmony with the sentiments and imperative laws of right conduct.

I have dwelt on the seeming trivialities of moral instruction, because I have a strong conviction, that it can be effectual in the primary school, especially in the initiatory classes, only when conveyed in a particular and disciplinary, rather than in a general and preceptive, form, and because it is beyond doubt that moral training, in all its comprehensiveness and importance, has not so prominent a place in the minds of parochial schoolmasters and in the scheme of school duty, as it unquestionably ought to have. The master has a tendency to think chiefly of certain intellectual results, and in matters of morality to consider himself absolved from all other and loftier aims if he merely enjoins a certain number of imperative moral laws, inflicts occasional punishment, and keeps outward order.

Juvenile stage.—When the pupil passes out of the Initiatory into the Juvenile stage, that is to say, when he reaches his tenth year, his power of realizing the practical detail which precepts indicate and sum up increases : he begins consciously to adopt them, and when he errs, to err less through ignorance or weakness than through wilfulness. Even at this stage, however, and long after it has begun, the short biography, the fable, and the parable are still the best instructors in moral duties. Nevertheless, as precept in its abstract form becomes intelligible and capable of easy explanation and illustration, it may now enter formally and with more effect into the daily work. The principles which are to regulate his conduct towards his fellows and his master are already pretty well known to the boy in their particular forms, and are consequently now easily made intelligible in their general and summarized expression.

Accordingly, as precepts and the grounds of them are now comprehensible to the pupil, and there fore really operative in the formation of good habits, it is the duty of the teacher, while confirming the moral lessons and practices of the initiatory stage, to prepare for himself a scheme of preceptive teaching, to some extent adapted to the circumstances of his pupils. As, in regulating, refining, and elevating the character of the petty acts of the school, the master is presumed to have had in view the counteraction of the too prevalent evils of home influence, so now, in inculcating the precepts which are to guide the boy's future, he must have regard to those errors to which the class to which he belongs is most prone. I have, in a previous part of this Report, when speaking of the limitations and conditions under which the primary teacher works, adverted to the kind of preceptive teaching most imperatively demanded at this stage. It is easy to imagine a lad to have learned the general duties of justice, honesty, truthfulness, generosity, and even to be honestly striving after the practical realization of the Golden Rule of conduct, and yet utterly to fail in doing the just and right act. And why is this? His intellect has not been instructed on the final issue of many of the acts which he considers to be harmless, or, if wrong, venial; especially those numerous acts which he imagines to terminate in himself alone. In the regulating of his body, for example, he has not been taught that he owes a duty to himself as an intellectual and moral being, and to the Creator who endowed him with his physical frame. Least of all has he learned to follow out into their evil effects *on others*, the consequences of his own infringement of the physiological laws under which he lives, and to find in wilful self-neglect, or self-injury, the causes of pain and injustice to his fellow-men. In all these respects there is the inner habit of conscience, which suggests that there is a right, but it is an uninstructed conscience which cannot see wherein the right consists. The intimate connexion of mental and bodily health, and the *moral obligation* of maintaining the latter, requires, it seems to me, to be directly and carefully taught. Above all, the illusion under which young men live, that their body is their own, with which they may do as they please, and that men of irregular habits are, as the saying is, only "their own worst enemies," has to be anxiously dispelled. That every man owes his body to his family, to the State, and to the God who made it and placed it here, is a part of the moral law. It is a part, however, the abstract statement of which is utterly useless. It requires to be evolved in connexion with a knowledge of the special laws under which we breathe, eat, digest, and labour, if it is to enter into the reason and not merely into the memory of the pupil. Our purpose in the school should be to make such things as familiar as the knowledge that to take another's property is theft, and punishable by law. The necessity and the *duty* of ventilation for himself and others, of regard to the preparation of food, of attention to cleanliness and exercise and of temperance, are all easy of explanation in connexion with the grounds on which they rest. They must be worked into the mind as part of its ordinary moral stock. Without the principles on which they rest, such teaching would be manifestly useless. Be just to your body that you may discharge your other duties efficiently, and that you may be just to others dependent on you and derived from you, is an abstract generalizing of the duty, which is as useless as other abstractions which cannot be readily translated into the numberless particular acts to which they refer. The very object of school teaching of morality is to give, not only the *what* but the *how* and the *why* of duty—to guide, not to make, the conscientious mind.

The next most important translation of the rule of justice into the duties of common life, is the inculcation of frugality and providence. The relation of sick societies, annuities, and life-insurance, to the self-respect and independence of a man, and to the proper discharge of the barest duties which he owes to his family, should be slowly, carefully, and frequently explained and illustrated. In the course of doing so, the connexion of providence with the other virtues, the motive which it gives to the control of the lower appetites and passions, the sense of moral freedom and self-respect which it engenders, forces itself into view, and furnishes the means of re-impressing the great moral laws under a fresh aspect and in new relations.

Such rational preceptive teachings as these, adapted of course to the age of the pupils who receive them, are not only an important, but an essential part, of any parochial-school moral education worthy of the name. The thing to be regretted is, not that there is any serious obstacle in the way of finding a place for them in the school-scheme of a thoughtful teacher, but that even thoughtful teachers seldom deliberately set before themselves the direct systematic teaching of practical morality.

The buying and selling of labour, and the many moral and social questions which depend on the right understanding of this, belong rather to the Evening or Continuation-School, where boys of from thirteen to seventeen years of age assemble to resume and carry forward the instruction of their boyhood.

The moral relations of the sexes also belong to the Evening school, and ought to be handled with the delicacy of perfect openness. It is a subject in connexion with which arguments and facts superabound; arguments based on the sacredness of the family, and on considerations of self-respect, morality, courage, generosity, justice, chivalry, and religion. No moral subject admits so readily of being invested with purity and dignity of treatment. In Scotland, at least, it is surely worth while to make the attempt. It is probable that the hope of the country in this respect lies in the improvement of the manners, the refinement of the habits, and an increase in the modesty of the young women, rather than in the better education of the men. However this may be, it is a matter for the grave consideration of school-managers, that the counties which boast, and truly boast, the highest parochial education in the world, are also distinguished (if we may believe statistics) by eminence in a vice which is not only bad in itself, but indicates the existence of much irregularity of conduct, prevalent disregard of the weak, and a degraded view of social relations.

MINOR MORALS OF THE SCHOOL.

Courtesy between boys and girls—Influence of female schools—Politeness—
Order—Cleanliness, etc.—Personal habits of teacher.

The subject to which the consideration of moral teaching led me in concluding the last chapter, leads not unnaturally to the subject of the present. There is a close connexion in mixed schools, as (practically) all Scotch parochial schools are, between the petty moralities of daily life, and the growth of proper mutual relations between the male and female pupils. It is in these petty moralities indeed that, as regards the special vice already adverted to, the teacher's chief power and chief duty lie. It belongs to a higher instructor, at a later stage, to elaborate principle out of the groundwork of propriety of sentiment and decency of external deportment. There is no reason to believe that the mixing of boys and girls together, *under proper supervision*, tends to lessen the respect of the one and the modesty of the other. Shyness in mutual intercourse is certainly quite eradicated by this means; but in the rooting up of this species of tare, the wheat of real modesty is not necessarily pulled up with it. I guard myself, however, by presuming *proper supervision* and good school discipline. Where these are absent the consequences are lamentable. Respect is broken down entirely, and the feebler sex is regarded by the stronger as merely fair game for what is in truth insult. And a worse result than this follows: the feebler sex itself half accepts as legitimate fun what it ought to resent as rudeness and insolence, and the sense of shame and vexation too soon gives place to the mock modesty of the averted giggle. That teacher or inspector must be blind indeed (probably with the blindness which familiarity causes) who, even without wishing to see, has not had such results of lax discipline in mixed schools forced upon his notice. On the other hand, the well-disciplined mixed school affords opportunities of regulating the conduct of boys and girls towards each other, and so giving a natural and healthy direction to sentiments which must in any case spring up. The morbid and wondering suspicion of each other, which is apt to be the result of entire separation or jealous vigilance, is in itself a vice—or the anticipation of a vice,—the immediate forerunner of the very evils which it is our object to prevent. Such feelings cannot exist where boys and girls are allowed to consort together, and to look each other frankly in the face as friends. There ought to be no difficulty, where this custom is once established, in insisting on courtesy and propriety from the one sex, and gentleness and decency on the other, thereby accustoming both to the recognition of a difference which is not intended by nature to be an antagonism. At the same time, while the actual facts of the case, so far as I have observed them, acquit the mixed-school system of being the positive cause of one of the prevalent vices of Scotland, it is, if it may be so put, a negative cause. To the improved demeanour, and to the elevation of the more purely womanly characteristics of the girls, we must look for the amelioration of the relations between the rustic youth of both sexes in Scotland; and this cannot be thoroughly attained without surrounding the girl with gentler and softer influences than those to which she is subject when sharing with boys an education expressly arranged with a view to the special need of the latter. It is necessary that girls should breathe the purer and gentler atmosphere of the female school, if the more womanly virtues are to live and grow. It is gratifying and encouraging to see the readiness with which the tender sensibilities of girls, who at first sight are very unpromising, respond to the gentle influence of the female school, where one has been instituted. It is impossible to shut our eyes to the unexpected moral results of exclusively female training, or refuse the conviction which such facts force on us, namely, that the extension of girls' schools, under properly-trained mistresses, is one of the most powerful moral agencies at present within our reach. The deficiencies of "mistress's grammar" are far more than counterbalanced by the prominence given to industrial skill,—itself both a womanly accomplishment, and exercising a feminine influence on the learners.[1]

This subject is a large and important one, worthy of much fuller treatment than can be given to it here; but before leaving it, I shall quote from Mr. Brookfield's Report for 1860 a few concise and felicitous words, which sum up the argument. After admitting the intellectual inferiority of schools in England taught by mistresses, he says:—

[1] The specially feminine portions of instruction stand very much in need of organization in Scotland. Mr. Birley, on p. 30 of the Privy Council Blue-Book for 1865, sketches a very good course of industrial instruction. On the Influence of Female Schools, see Report by Rev. J. P. Norris (Privy Council Blue-Book for 1861-2, pp. 85-9).

"But though figures are inflexible, and a remorseless average discards the modifying influence of chivalry, it must be remembered that, after all, this average itself confesses that in every hundred girls' schools there are fifteen which indicate the ablest, the most suitable, and the most judicious management, and forty which are by no means to be complained of, and which, according to the prevailing standard, must be considered no less than fairly satisfactory; while of all the hundred (with very rare, surprisingly rare, exceptions) the cleanly appearance, the quiet propriety of demeanour, the modesty of speech and manner, and, so far as I can learn, the moral rectitude by which they are characterized, give evidence of their being placed under an habitual influence, incalculably more important than any intellectual qualifications, and entitle our schoolmistresses to be pronounced one of the most praiseworthy and valuable classes of the community."

A consideration of the feelings and the outward behaviour which should regulate the intercourse of boys and girls in a mixed school, will reveal the defects of the present system of training, or rather of disregard of training, in little things, where boys only are concerned. The teacher's business is, while avoiding everything that is inquisitorial, and discouraging reports brought by others, to exercise such a general supervision as will enable him to know the spirit which pervades the school, and to guide and correct its exhibitions when necessary. He must make the school feel unmistakably that his weight is thrown on the side of weakness and gentleness, and against the rude assumptions of physical strength. It is not enough that he take the opportunities which will be abundantly afforded him of reproving deceit and falsehood, of correcting injustice, and of contemning meanness; he must convince the rough boys under his charge that the younger and less able of their fellows demand more than ordinary consideration from them. The strong man owes more, as a mere act of equity, to the weak than he owes to his equal in strength. Mutual consideration among schoolboys becomes the more important the lower the stratum of the population from which the children are drawn.

Mutual consideration involves much; not merely substantial justice and truthfulness, but kindliness, pity, helpfulness, gentleness, and also civility and politeness. By politeness is meant the forms of civility, civility again meaning that *feeling* of respect for others, and of what is due to them, which exists more or less in every mind which has emerged from the unadulterated self-assertion of barbarism. To insist upon the forms of this feeling even where the reality does not exist, is not to be condemned as we condemn the requiring of the outward show of love when it has no root in the heart. To *require* a child to love is to lay the foundation of a false nature. But, while we admit the radical error of exacting love, we must not carry too far the principle which leads us to condemn all forms of feeling. The attitude and the words of prayer, for example, should be always demanded whether the pious emotion be active or dormant, because, in requiring these, we only insist on what it is possible to give *at will*, namely, submission and reverence to our Creator and Preserver. As it is perfectly legitimate in the region of religious sentiment to order what can be responded to by an effort of will, so also in matters of mutual courtesy of deeds and words. Further, where by skilful treatment the finer sentiments can actually be stirred into activity in the young heart, to insist on their natural expression is so far from encouraging hypocrisy, that it is welcome to the child.

Teachers should also bear in mind that all formal expression of sentiment, is like the expression of struggling thought in words. It gives it clearness, definiteness, and substance. It reacts on the mental state, and confirms it. Hence the utility of mere forms of civility. In requiring the form, the teacher either helps the pupil over the awkwardness of showing what he feels, or he reminds him that the feeling is wanting and ought to be supplied. In either case he has conferred a moral benefit on the pupil. The repetition of those formal acts of politeness for which the school affords scope, tends, by constantly suggesting the corresponding sentiments, to establish civility (which is only a kind of refinement of justice) as a habit of will. So great is the effect of due attention to the petty moralities of the school-room. It is scarcely necessary to add, that apart from direct instruction and *his own example*, the only way in which the teacher can attain the results at which I point in matters of propriety and courtesy is by detecting the wrong-doer, and causing him to do *over again and rightly*, the act which in his haste or his selfishness he has done wrong.

Passing from those minor morals of the schoolroom which concern the conduct of the pupils towards each other or their master, we come to those which immediately concern the pupil himself. Lounging in class with hands in pockets should be interpreted by the master as a mark of disrespect to himself as well as of inattention to the lessons. Personal cleanliness, entering and leaving the schoolroom as a boy of decent manners is expected to enter and to leave a private house, quiet formation of classes without jostling, are all of importance in creating that habit of mind of which good manners is the fruit. It is in Scotch schools especially that all these little-great things are neglected. Very many of our teachers seem to have quite lost all delicacy of perception on such matters, and they consequently submit to practices which, to the unaccustomed visitor, are intolerable. It is by no means so uncommon as it ought to be to find boys standing in class order, or rather disorder, at irregular intervals, with hands in pockets, and from time to time spitting on the floor. It is always best to find some one notion, the possession of which removes from the mind all difficulties in the way of applying principles. The notion which facilitates the solution of all difficulties in the matters of which I am now speaking, is this, that the schoolroom is the master's house, and that no manners or practices can be suffered in the one which would be discountenanced in the other.

The general rule given above has the further advantage of throwing light on those minor moralities of the school, which depend on the example of the teacher himself. The courtesies and the personal habits which he inculcates he must practise; and he will find no safer guide whereby to regulate his personal demeanour towards all around him than the reflection that he is in the position of the master of a house receiving guests—guests under somewhat special conditions certainly, but still, in all essential respects, guests. He will scarcely venture to discharge the duty of host dirty, unshaven and in slippers; nor will he dare to take unfair advantage of the fact that his pupils are compulsory guests, to speak to them in a style which would empty the room were they free to leave. He cannot in any case expect his pupils to behave better than himself.

The last department of petty morals concerns the arrangements of the schoolroom itself. These all fall under the heads of cleanliness, order, light, and ventilation. A dirty floor, and dirtier walls and windows, untidy arrangement of little things,—such as ink-wells, copybooks, pens,—the accumulations on the master's desk, the uncleaned black-board, the absent chalk and towel, the dusty maps and globes, the slovenly hearth and absent fender—what must be the moral effect of such wilful renunciation of everything in the furnishing of daily life that makes civilisation better than barbarism? With such surroundings as these it is absurd for the teacher to talk of school ideals, or indeed of education in any lofty or refined sense. To teach attention to the laws of health in the midst of dirt and in an unventilated room, and to require activity of brain in the midst of a tainted atmosphere, are mockeries. The existence of such contravention of the very first conditions of education seems in these days almost incredible, and yet are there twenty 'per cent. of Scotch schools in which cleanliness and ventilation are systematically and properly attended to ? I should say not.

But to enumerate all the petty moralities of the schoolroom would be to depart from the general objects of this Report and to write a school-manual —a useless labour, even if it were practicable, here. Let a man cultivate the personal habits and cheap necessities of a gentleman, and carry these into the schoolroom with him, and, in the matter of the minor moralities, nothing more will remain to be done.[1]

THE TEACHING OF RELIGION.

In the inculcation of moral duties, whether this be done by the direct instruction of precept and example, or by the indirect and more efficacious instruction of discipline, the teacher must employ the sanctions of Religion. He must early associate the authority of God

[1] The bearing of school-gardens on the minor morals of a school would merit consideration here did space permit.

with the imperativeness of the Moral Law. Divine revelation is not necessary to the discovery, nor the Divine sanction to the obligations of morality, but both are means of re-establishing and sanctifying what nature and reason teach. Nay, more, such is the frailty of man, and such the inherent tendency to wrong, that morality requires all the support which it can draw from the constant impression on the growing mind that it has its first source and ultimate sanction in the Divine reason. To teach morality in its infinite ramifications, with all the aids which the arguments of personal wellbeing and social utility yield, with constant reference to the God who created us and in whose hands our destinies are, and to the revelations which He has made of Himself and His purposes, is the highest duty of the schoolmaster, and is that part of his national function which gives it dignity, and secures for it the respect of the thoughtful.

But this kind of teaching presupposes that the child has first been taught that there is a God, and that He is "a Spirit, eternal and unchangeable in his being, wisdom, power, holiness, justice, goodness, and truth." And it is precisely in this, the first and greatest lesson which the child can learn, that scholastic methods intervene and insist on being obeyed. The subject is too momentous to be left to the rude handling of those who seem to think that the fact itself is all in all, and the mode of presenting it nothing. The earliest impressions are the strongest, and in matters connected with our emotional nature this is in a special sense true. The teacher must pause, therefore, and consider as he approaches the deepest recesses of the young mind. . He goes there to give right shape to the confused sense of an all-pervading, unknown power, on which foundation must rest the idea of God. This idea, let us remember, formed under the influence of Christian doctrine, is to be to the child the basis of his future religious life.

How, then, shall we introduce the child to that which must, whether he will or not, be at once the ground-plan and the foundation of any religious edifice which may be afterwards reared in his mind ? This assuredly is a solemn question, and to the teacher full of great responsibilities. The parent and not the schoolmaster, it is true, should lay this foundation ; but even where the latter finds it laid, his religious teaching must have constant reference to the idea which has been sown, and must tend to foster, retard, or modify its growth.[1]

In Religion, as in everything else, a child can know a new thing only as it stands related to things already known. It has also to be remembered that

---

[1] It is scarcely necessary to point out that neither here nor in the corresponding chapter in the second part of this Report, have I to do with the subject-matter of the religious instruction in the schools. I shall be understood to have reference to the *order* of the instruction given, and to the method pursued by the master. If I seem to dwell longer on the mere initiation into religion, than on the more advanced doctrinal instruction, I do so because it is in the initiatory stages of teaching all subjects that method is of greatest importance, and also because systematized initiatory religious instruction does not receive sufficient attention in the majority of parochial schools.

things abstract have to the child or the boy no significance whatsoever : it is only in a concrete form that anything can enter into his intelligence. Even in very palpable moral duties, to speak to a child or a very young boy about being just, true, merciful, and honest, is, we have found, to speak to the winds : it is a comparatively useless process, so far as the pupil is concerned, and at the same time it interposes between him and his natural guide and instructor a multitude of unmeaning words, thus cutting him off, by the intervention of the barrier of the unintelligible, from that candid and confiding moral relationship which is his greatest (though unconscious) happiness, and the essential condition of moral influence in the teacher or parent. That he is not to do this or that *particular act* because the person he loves or respects disapproves of it and because it is unkind and wrong, he can understand ; but it is long before he can generalize these various individual acts under their proper terms, and guide his conduct by the generalization. If this be true in morals, how much more necessary in a matter so delicate and difficult as early religious teaching, to connect the truth we give with concrete forms, and with other things already known, by which its meaning may be interpreted.

Happily, the Faith which has to be taught in our schools furnishes us with the great fundamental truth of the religious life in a form which fulfils all the requirements of the most exacting method. That the great unseen Power, of which the vague surmisings fitfully pass through the hearts of children, is a Father—loving them and wishing to do them good —this first truth, if *faithfully* taught, explains the Unknown in the spirit of love, and gives from the first a Christian direction to the feelings and thoughts regarding the Unseen, those premonitions of knowledge and faith, which observation and reading from time to time inevitably stir up in the minds of the young. If this simple and gentle thought of God—the thought which the Saviour of mankind revealed to us—be honestly and fully impressed on the tender mind, I think we can almost afford, so far as *method* is concerned, to let all future religious teaching take the direction which the teacher's idiosyncrasies may give it ; insisting only on one condition, that the abstract statement of systematic truth be postponed to the biographical and concrete forms in which Divine wisdom has seen fit to embody that truth.

The teacher must be careful in his teaching. He must not first instil into the unfolding mind the God of law and judgment, rectifying and exalting that idea afterwards by the true doctrine of Christ. This is to assume that the revelation of Christ regarding God, and man's relation to Him, is merely a *supplement* to the notion of a God of law and judgment, whereas it is a *superseding* of that imperfect notion by means of a higher—the notion of Fatherhood and love. This new idea must be made to lie *at the root* of the idea of God in the minds of the young, His character of Lawgiver and Judge being shown to arise out of and to harmonize with the higher conception. When afterwards enforcing religious doctrines and duties, the teacher must anxiously keep in view this the Fatherly character of God. For a child may obey what he believes to be the commands of God; he may fear God and have Him often in his thoughts; but to love God is in the very nature of things an impossibility, except in so far as he apprehends clearly that God first loved him, and that the chief and ruling attribute of the Divine Being is love.

The teacher's next duty is to present Christian doctrine in the richly coloured but simple language of the New Testament, interesting the child personally in the story of love which is the foundation of the Christian faith, causing him to feel that it is to him personally and truly a message of good-will.

It is evident, however, that a method, however admirable, may be nullified by the *mode* of applying it. If we convert the life of Christ into a series of school lessons, failing to make any pause when we approach holy ground, whereby to distinguish the Religious lesson from others, we shall certainly do our best to weaken the effect of the Gospel teaching. The ancient custom of using the Bible as a reading lesson-book originated at a time when no other manual was to be had, and is now continued merely through the force of habit. I can

imagine nothing which could bring more genuine
satisfaction to a teacher in earnest about laying sure
and strong foundations of the spiritual life in his
pupils, than the discovery that he might dispense with
the Bible as a task-book, and give it a distinct place of
its own in the schoolroom. Some progress has already
been made in this withdrawal of the Bible from the
category of lesson-books. It is no longer employed for
purposes of grammar and spelling. It is to be hoped
that the use of it as a reading lesson-book will also
gradually give way before a clearer apprehension of the
objects and methods of religious teaching. The Bible
should be approached with solemnity, handled with
reverence, and daily read by master and pupils together rather as a relaxation from ordinary tasks than
as itself a task. In the one subject of Religion, if in
no other, it seems to me that the teacher might advan-
tageously assume the attitude of a fellow-learner with
his pupils, and lay aside the magisterial airs of assumed
infallibility and hard superiority, which too often ac
company the Bible lesson. How else can Christianity
preserve in the school its distinguishing characteristic
as an exhibition of Divine good-will stirring the heart
to love, or retain those elements of mystery, infinitude,
and awe, which feed reverence and call forth worship?

The third stage of religious teaching is the catechetical or dogmatic. This kind of teaching is frequently
introduced at a wrong time. It is not a matter of
indifference that the Gospel story be first received into

the mind of the child in all the native purity, power, and charm of the form in which it has been given. Even St. Paul gives the difficult food of generalized and theoretic doctrine only to those who had already heard him deliver, in language suited to their previous habits of thought, the glad tidings of great joy, peace on earth, good-will towards men. Let us follow this example, and as far as possible postpone abstract dogmatic teaching until the concrete dogmatic teaching of the Gospels has become a possession. The age at which abstract catechetical instruction should be begun, however, is a question that cannot unfortunately be solely determined by the previous training and preparation of the pupil. The early removal of children from school imposes on the teacher the obligation of giving them premature mastery over the form of words which embodies their faith. We have at least the consolation of thinking that this practice is not so irrational and indefensible as some educationists assume. The teacher, in the primary, secondary, and university schools alike, is constantly outrunning his pupils. The conscious or unconscious exertion of mind to grasp something beyond its present powers is itself a discipline. Not only so, the form of sound words, whether they summarize intellectual, moral, or religious truths, is itself a valuable acquisition. It provides a kind of mould into which the growing experience shapes itself, until at last the form is vitally apprehended by the mind as the true and fit expression of the inner fact. It does not retard, though it may not hasten, growth and maturity. Thus far the unfortunate necessity of premature instruction may be fairly defended on rational grounds.

No less important than the substance and order of religious teaching is fitness of *manner* in the teacher when conducting the instruction of a class. What is desiderated in every subject is truth of manner, but this, above all, in handling religious topics. That is to say, the teacher must be seen himself to believe in the value of the lesson he gives. If there be this belief, the outward expression of it in the eye and the unconscious gestures will be true to the character of the subject which is before the class. The hard, dictatorial, and undevotional style in which masters are too often wont to give religious instruction, and their awkward, unjoyous mode of conducting songs and hymns, have led me gradually to the conviction that the education of *very young* children should be confided solely to mistresses. The man, when entering on the religious lesson (if lesson it ought to be called), seems to be less capable than the woman of feeling the delicacy as well as the greatness of the subject, and of adapting his mind to these conceptions. He more readily forgets that he is dealing with the emotions of his pupils—and these the deepest and purest emotions of which human nature is susceptible—and that his own mental attitude should be that of calm, solemnity, and reverence. It is the manifestation by the teacher himself of these appropriate feelings which can alone excite in the pupils a sympathetic response, and secure a ready ear and heart for the truths which they herald. This emotional response secured, the work of the teacher is more than half done : until it be secured, his work is not even begun, however frequent and elaborate his didactic utterances, or however exacting his demands. It is grievous to think how seldom it is secured, when we reflect on the readiness with which the infant mind responds to everything which touches the imagination or the emotions. The golden opportunities of childhood are wasted, and as years advance the heart becomes less accessible.

END OF PART FIRST.

REPORT TO THE TRUSTEES OF THE DICK BEQUEST.

PART SECOND.

HISTORICAL AND STATISTICAL.

PART SECOND.

HISTORICAL AND STATISTICAL.

CHAPTER I.

ORIGIN AND AMOUNT OF THE BEQUEST.

Mr. James Dick—Professor Allan Menzies—Trustees and Office-Bearers—Terms
of Bequest from Mr. Dick's Will.

THE founder of the Dick Bequest was JAMES DICK, Esq., of Finsbury Square, London. He was born of respectable parents, in the burgh of Forres, Morayshire, upon 14th November 1743. No authentic particulars of his early years have been obtained; but he is said to have received an excellent education. At the age of nineteen he went to the West Indies, and entered a mercantile house at Kingston, Jamaica, where his talents and industry soon gained for him a share in his employer's business. After twenty years he returned to England with a considerable fortune, to which, by judicious speculation, he made large additions.

Mr. Dick died on 24th May 1828, bequeathing nearly his whole fortune to the maintenance and assistance of "the Country Parochial Schoolmasters" in his native county of Elgin or Moray, and in the neighbouring counties of Banff and Aberdeen.

The Bequest amounted, in 1833, to a capital sum of £113,147, 4s. 7d., which was afterwards increased to £118,787, 11s. The annual income fluctuates with the rise and fall of the rate of interest upon Land Securities in Scotland, and the free annual revenue, after deducting all expenses of management, has varied since 1835 from £5489, 6s. 10d., to £3326, 17s. 3d. The amount divided among the schoolmasters in 1864 was £4344, 13s. 9d.

The passage of Mr. Dick's will containing the Bequest, with the conditions attached to it, is appended to this chapter. He revoked the nomination of persons through whom it was his original purpose to administer the Trust; but in all other respects the settlement remained entire, and was carried into effect. The proceedings in Chancery, by which the selection of Trustees was regulated, were explained in the first Report, published in 1835. The result was to vest the administration of the Bequest in the Keeper and Deputy-Keeper of the Signet, the Treasurer of the Society of Writers to the Signet, Edinburgh, and eight Commissioners chosen by and from among the Commissioners of the Signet, in terms of a Deed of Declaration of Trust, containing various provisions regarding the management of the Fund, which was executed by the Trustees in 1832.

The original office-bearers of the Trust consisted of a Treasurer and a Clerk, the duty of the latter being not only to administer the Bequest but to inspect the schools and to report on them to the Trustees. The Clerk was understood to complete a tour of inspection within three years. After the Treasurer's death in 1853, the experience which the Trustees had acquired led them to unite the duties of Treasurer with those of Clerk, and to resolve to appoint a gentleman to the office of Visitor, requiring him to visit the schools and report on them once in *two* years. The Clerk, Professor Allan Menzies, by whom the details of the administration of the Trust were to a great extent originated, and to whose firmness, sagacity, and elevation of character it owed the high estimation in which it was held, not only in the north of Scotland but through the whole country, continued to act as Visitor (being generally accompanied by Professor Kelland of Edinburgh University) until his death, in February 1856.

The death of Professor Menzies, who had acted as Clerk and Visitor to the Trustees from the commencement of their operations, was severely felt by all interested in the education of the three counties. To him more than to any other was due the initiation of the administrative rules under which the Trustees have so successfully applied the Bequest; and the more the elaborate machinery which he was the chief agent in constructing is examined, the stronger will be the disposition to admire its adaptation to effect, in the largest sense, the real objects of the testator. Professor Menzies's sincere and profound interest in the cause of popular education stimulated his naturally robust intellect to devise the best measures for promoting it, and sustained him in applying them, in the face of considerable opposition and frequent misconception. An educational bequest so peculiar in its provisions as that of Mr. Dick, manifestly required for its successful administration a mind capable of grasping general principles, and, at the same time, of comprehending and appreciating the minutest details. In Professor Menzies the Trustees happily found the requisite combination. The characteristics which have made the Dick Bequest stand alone in the history of popular education are, in truth, a reflection of the mind of the first administrator. But educational zeal sustaining a naturally vigorous intellect would not have sufficed for carrying out into practice measures in themselves novel, and unavoidably exposed to much suspicious criticism. It was the firmness of purpose, the sound judgment, the strong sense of equity, the unswerving integrity, so conspicuous in Professor Menzies, which made it possible to work out these measures successfully. To those who marked the progress of the Bequest from the outside these were the qualities in the administrator which secured for the Trustees respect and confidence. But to those who have perused Professor Menzies's Reports, and who had opportunities of conversing with him on the work which lay so near to his heart, it is well known that the source of all his strength and hopefulness, and persistence in the discharge of duty, was his ardent desire to promote the religious teaching of the schools, and, while training the intelligence of the young, above all to establish them firmly in Christian principles. To communicate to others his own strong faith and high convictions was the great object of that portion of his life which was devoted to the cause of education, with results so signally beneficial.

The following is the Minute in which the Trustees expressed the sense of their loss :—

"The Deputy-Keeper said he felt it to be his duty, on this their first meeting since the death of their late Clerk, to bring before the Trustees that fact officially. The meeting would, he knew, think it right, before proceeding with the regular business, to express in their Minutes the sense of the deep feeling which the Trustees entertained of the severe loss which they had sustained.

"The meeting wish, then, to express that feeling. Their expressions are not merely commonplace or conventional expressions, but those of sincere and heartfelt grief for the loss which has fallen on them personally by the death of Mr. Menzies, and on the trust which is committed to their charge. The loss may almost, and for no short time indeed literally, be said to be irreparable.

"Mr. Menzies had been Clerk to the Trust since its commencement, and had, to the ordinary duties of Clerk, added those of Visitor and Inspector. He was enabled to perform these varied duties by such a union of rare talents and acquirements as the Trustees cannot again hope to find in one individual. In Mr. Menzies they were directed also and guided by an untiring and conscientious energy, ever aiming at the good of the very important Trust committed to those under and with whom he acted. His views and suggestions were thus ever found by the Trustees to be worthy of that entire confidence with which they were ever received and acted on ; and for the results, the Trustees feel that they may fearlessly appeal to the good which they have been enabled to do to the cause of education in the schools under their charge. That good is certainly mainly to be attributed to the exertions of

Mr. Menzies, and the Trustees desired to record their sense of the value of those exertions, and of the loss which the Trust has sustained by being thus suddenly deprived of them." . . .

The Clerkship and Treasurership were then conferred on Robert Blair Maconochie, Esq., W.S., while the office of Visitor was conferred on your reporter. I mention these facts in order that the history of the Bequest may not be lost sight of by those who may be in future called on to act as its administrators, either in the capacity of trustees or of salaried officials. For the same reason I record here the names of the Commissioners of Signet who at present act as Trustees of the Bequest, and of others connected with the administration :—

Trustees.

RIGHT HON. SIR WILLIAM GIBSON-CRAIG, BART., KEEPER OF HER MAJESTY'S SIGNET.
JAS. HOPE, DEPUTY-KEEPER.
J. GIBSON, JUN., TREASURER.

Commissioners.

JAMES MACKENZIE.	A. CAMPBELL.
JOHN ELDER.	GEO. T. STODART.
JAS. M. MELVILLE.	JOHN ORD MACKENZIE.
HENRY CHEYNE.	JOHN WRIGHT.

Clerk and Treasurer.
ROBERT BLAIR MACONOCHIE, W.S.

Visitor of Schools.
SIMON S. LAURIE, A.M.

Examiners of Candidates for Participation in the Bequest.

THE REV. PHILIP KELLAND, F.R.S., PROFESSOR OF MATHEMATICS IN THE UNIVERSITY OF EDINBURGH.
THE VERY REV. JOHN TULLOCH, D.D., PRINCIPAL AND PRIMARIUS PROFESSOR OF DIVINITY, ST. MARY'S COLLEGE, ST. ANDREWS.
THE REV. WILLIAM P. DICKSON, D.D., PROFESSOR OF DIVINITY AND BIBLICAL CRITICISM IN THE UNIVERSITY OF GLASGOW.

Terms of the Bequest, from Mr. Dick's last Will and Testament, dated 18*th May* 1827.

"And it is my will, that the said Principals and Professors [1] shall pay the interest, dividends, and annual produce of such securities, from time to time, as the same shall become due, to the Professors of the Faculties of Arts and Divinity in the said Colleges for the time being, to be by them applied in manner, and subject to the regulations hereinafter mentioned, to the maintenance and assistance of the Country Parochial Schoolmasters, as by law established, in the three counties of Aberdeen, Banff, and Moray, excluding the royal burghs; it being my wish to form a fund for the benefit of that neglected, though useful class of men, and to add to their present very trifling salaries: And with regard to the distribution of the income arising from the said fund, and to the selection of the objects to be benefited thereby, I wish the following rules to be observed :—*First*, That the Country Parochial Schoolmasters, by law established, in the three counties of Aberdeen, Banff, and Moray, exclusive of the royal burghs, shall alone be entitled to the benefit of the said fund ;—*Secondly*, That the income thereof be applied in such manner, as not in any manner to relieve the Heritors, or other persons, from their legal obligations to support Parochial Schoolmasters, or to diminish the extent of such support, and so as not to interfere with the rights or power of Heritors and Presbyteries over Schoolmasters, or the schools intrusted to their care, as the same rights or powers are by law insured to them ;—*Thirdly*, That the said Professors for the time being shall have full power to pay and distribute the income of the said fund, from time to time, to or among all or such one or more of the Parochial Schoolmasters aforesaid, in such proportions, and, generally, to dispose of the said income among them, in such manner as to such Professors shall seem most likely to encourage active Schoolmasters, and gradually to elevate the literary character of the Parochial Schoolmasters and Schools aforesaid ; and, for these purposes, to increase, diminish, or

---

[1] This nomination having been revoked by Mr. Dick, the selection of Trustees was settled by proceedings in Chancery after his death.

altogether to discontinue, the salary or allowance to be from time to time made to all or any of such Schoolmasters, without being accountable for so doing : And I particularly recommend the said Professors to pay great attention to the qualifications and diligence of the several Parochial Schoolmasters, for and in superintending the education of Students in the said Colleges, during the intervals between the sessions thereof, and for and in preparing youths for the said Colleges,—taking care, at the same time, that the common branches of education are properly attended to at the said Parochial Schools ; and in order to enable the said Professors to perform the several trusts aforesaid more easily, I authorize them to appoint a proper person, from time to time, as they shall see fit, to act as their Clerk, who shall be properly qualified, and fully competent to such office, and to allow such Clerk such a salary as the said Professors shall think fit, and with power to them to remove any such Clerk, whenever they think proper : And I empower the said Professors for the time being to manage and dispose of the funds to be paid to them generally, in such way as shall seem to them best calculated to effect the purposes aforesaid."

CHAPTER II.

CHARACTER OF THE BEQUEST, AND OF ITS ADMINISTRATION.

The Bequest not a Charity—Historical sketch of Parochial School system—Outline of the principles of administration.

IT was contended by many in the North that the Trustees ought to make an equal division of the annual free proceeds of Mr. Dick's endowment, withholding the benefit of it only from such teachers as notoriously failed to discharge their duty. This would have been to convert the Bequest into a *charity*. The Trustees have always maintained that the money which they distribute annually is not a charitable or eleemosynary endowment, but a reward for good scholarship and efficient teaching. That they are right in taking this view of the Bequest is clearly shown by the terms of Mr. Dick's testament, in which the Trustees are empowered to pay the income to "such one or more [of the schoolmasters] in such proportions, and generally to dispose of the said income among them in such manner as to the Trustees shall seem most likely to encourage active schoolmasters, and gradually to elevate the literary character of the parochial schoolmasters and schools;" and further "to increase, diminish, or altogether to discontinue the salary or allowance to be from time to time made to all or any." The Trustees accordingly were not only authorized, but required to apply the Bequest to the encouragement of literary attainment in the teachers of the three counties, to the promotion of efficiency in teaching, and to the literary advancement of the schools. These three objects the Trustees have kept steadily in view throughout. The details of administration, whereby they have given effect to this interpretation of their Trust, I will shortly explain, for the information of those who may be curious regarding this portion of the history of Scotch education, and for the instruction of those who may in future be personally connected with the Bequest as beneficiaries.

But before doing so it is necessary to state shortly the nature of the Scotch school organization to which the Trustees had to adapt their rules. Without some such statement the rules of the Trustees would be unintelligible.

The Act of Parliament of 1696 definitely constituted the Parochial School system of Scotland.

Prior to 1696 we find an enactment of the Scotch Government, as early as 1494, enacting that all barons and freeholders of substance "should put their eldest sons and heirs to the schools from the age of eight or nine years; to remain at the grammar-school till they be competently founded, and have perfect Latin; and thereafter that they remain three years at the Schools of Art (Arts) and Jurisprudence, so that they may have knowledge and understanding of the laws; through the which justice may reign universally through all the realm, so that they that are sheriffs or judges ordinary under the King's highness may have knowledge to do justice, that the poor people may have no need to seek an audience of the sove reign lords for every small injury." There was a compulsory clause in this enactment, inflicting a pecuniary penalty of £20 on those who should neglect its in junctions. The very existence of such a law, with its compulsory clause, presupposes a large number of schools so situated as to be generally accessible.

At the time of the Reformation, the "Book of Discipline" contemplated, and indeed enjoined, the attaching of schools to the churches throughout the land. This book, however, was solely of ecclesiastical origin and validity, and though signed by the Church and the leading men in the country it did not become law. It, notwithstanding, laid the foundation of a national system of education. At this time, and up to 1616, there was great activity in the cause of popular education. The powers which the Church had happily assumed in the work of instituting and superintending schools, and even of compelling parents to send their children for instruction, "dryving them to seik after vertue," had been fully recognised by

the State in Acts passed in 1567, 1581, and 1592. They were further extended and consolidated by a Privy Council order of 10th December 1616, ordaining "that a school be established in every parish," and empowering the "bishops, with a majority of the parishioners, to assess the lands for their establishment and maintenance." An Act of Parliament was passed in 1633 ratifying and confirming the Privy Council order. The Church continued to exert itself to give effect to this Act, and to the various resolutions and injunctions which had proceeded from itself. A few years after the passing of the Act of 1633, we find the General Assembly instructing Presbyteries to take heed that its provisions were complied with, and at the same time indicating the course of elementary school instruction to be "reading, writing, and the grounds of religion." In 1642 this injunction was more explicitly renewed, and the visitation of schools and reporting on them was pressed on the attention of ministers. To the Church, indeed, the popular education of the country owed not only its origin, but supervision and protection.

Schools continued to multiply, although under great local difficulties, till the passing of the Act of 1696, which has been already referred to. This Act provided that a school should be settled in every parish by the heritors (proprietors of land) and minister; that the heritors should build a commodious schoolhouse, and provide a salary, not above 200 nor under 100 merks (£5, 11s. 1½d.); and that if the heritors when assembled could not agree, the Presbytery should apply to the Commissioners of Supply for the county, who, or any five of them, should have power to establish a school, assessing the heritors in proportion to their valued rent.

The next Parliamentary Act was passed in 1803. It entered much more minutely into the subject, and while increasing the schoolmasters' stipends, and making them payable by the heritors[1] as heretofore, it provided for the revision of the money payment once in twenty-five years. The average price of the chalder of oatmeal for the twenty-five preceding years was to be struck by the Sheriff of the county, and the salary of the schoolmasters fixed according to this average by the heritors and minister. The money-value of a chalder of oatmeal in 1803 was 200 merks, or £11, 2s. 2⅔d. The Act ordered that the minimum payment to the schoolmaster should thenceforth be the value of a chalder and a half, or £16, 13s. 5d., and the maximum the value of two chalders, or £22, 4s. 5d. The parish minister of the Established Church was appointed superintendent of the parochial school,[2] but the real power was vested in the Presbytery within whose bounds the school was situated. Not only had the teacher elected by the heritors and minister to compear before the Presby-

---

[1] Both the Act of 1696 and that of 1803 gave the heritors relief from their tenants to the amount of one-half their proportion of the school-tax, but, as a matter of fact, it is believed that the majority of heritors have not taken advantage of this source of relief.

[2] Clause XIX.

tery (after having taken the oath to the Sovereign before a Justice of Peace), and be examined by the members of it as to the "sufficiency for his office, in respect of morality and religion, and of such branches of literature as by the majority of heritors and minister [were] deemed most necessary and important for the parish;" but on a complaint being made to them against the teacher by the heritors, the minister, and the elder, of immoral conduct, neglect of duty, or cruelty, they could, after satisfactory proof, censure, suspend, or dismiss the schoolmaster. The Presbytery had also the power of fixing the hours of teaching and the length of the annual vacation, it being left to the minister and heritors to determine the rate of fee to be charged. Religion was one of the subjects required by the heritors and minister to be taught, and the orthodoxy of the teacher was secured by his being required to sign the Confession of Faith and Formula of the Church of Scotland. The Presbytery had, of course, a right of visitation.

The next Act of Parliament of any importance is dated 1861. It increased the salaries of the schoolmasters to a minimum of £35 and a maximum of £70, and substituted for the religious and ecclesiastical test a general declaration by the teacher-elect that he would never endeavour, directly or indirectly, to teach or inculcate any opinions opposed to the Divine authority of the Holy Scriptures, or to the doctrines contained in the Shorter Catechism, and that he would faithfully conform thereto in his teaching. Further, that he would

SKETCH OF PAROCHIAL SCHOOL SYSTEM. 221

not exercise the functions of his office to the prejudice or subversion of the Church of Scotland as by law established, or the doctrines and privileges thereof.

The examination of schoolmasters-elect was by the same Act transferred from Presbyteries to Boards of Examiners appointed by the Court of each of the four Universities.

The censure, suspension, or dismissal of a schoolmaster for neglect of duty was transferred to the heritors and minister of each parish, on the report of one of Her Majesty's Inspectors of Schools, if concurred in by the Presbytery of the bounds.

The power of censure, suspension, or dismissal for immoral conduct or cruelty was transferred to the Sheriff of the county.

The power of censure, suspension, or dismissal of the master for religious teaching in contravention of his declaration, was transferred from the Presbytery to a Commission to be appointed in each case of complaint by a Secretary of State, their judgment taking effect only after receiving the Secretary's approval.

The heritors have always been empowered to assess themselves for more than one school. By the Act of 1861 they may also assess for a female school, but in no case can the parochial assessment exceed £110 in all for educational purposes.

The remaining alterations and amendments of previous legislation it is not necessary to detail in this place. It is only necessary further to add that the powers of visitation by the Presbytery were not repealed, and that Clauses XIII. and XIX. of the Act would manifestly remain permanently inoperative if the right of Presbyterial visitation were not presumed by Parliament to exist and to be exercised by the Presbyteries.

The above is a short outline of the history of the Scotch Parochial School system, to which the Dick Bequest Trustees had to adapt themselves, without, on the one hand, rousing the jealousy of the various parties interested in the management of the schools (the teacher, the heritors and minister, and the Presbytery); or, on the other hand, failing to give effect to the testator's wishes and to secure the co-operation of all connected with the parochial schools in promoting their advancement and elevation. The manner in which they adapted their administration to the attainment of these ends, forms the subject of the next chapter. It will, however, contribute to the comprehension of what follows, as well as suffice for the purposes of those not professionally concerned with the subject, if the general course followed be here succinctly summarized :—

To insure the literary elevation of the schoolmaster, the Trustees instituted an examination in Literature and Science, and they exclude all teachers entering on the charge of schools from participation in the Bequest until they have passed this examination.

To insure the confidence of the minister of each parish, it has been the practice of the Trustees to communicate to him a copy of all correspondence with the teacher, which is of any importance.

To insure the co-operation of Presbyteries and remove their objections to the intrusion of an alien authority between them and the schools of which they had legal superintendence, they were asked to report annually on each school in detail ; this Report being accepted by the Trustees as an element in forming their judgment.

To insure the literary elevation and the "activity" or efficiency of the schoolmaster and the school, the Trustees attached a certain money value to instruction in the higher branches (by which were meant Geography, English Grammar, Latin, Greek, French, and Mathematics), and they further directed their Visitor to report on the manner in which these and all other subjects were taught, assigning to each teacher such a number (bearing a pecuniary value) under the head of "Merit in Teaching" as he seemed to the Visitor to deserve, under certain restrictions (see p. 231).

These various principles of administration I shall now speak of in greater detail.

CHAPTER III.

PRINCIPLES OF DICK BEQUEST ADMINISTRATION.

The Teacher—The Heritors and Minister and Presbytery—Plan of distributing the Fund—Assistant-Substitutes.

(1.) *The Teacher.*

To state historically the growth of the various requirements and regulations of the Trust, and to vindicate the justice and expediency of them, would be to go over ground already thoroughly traversed by Professor Menzies in the Reports of 1844 and 1854. I shall confine myself to a succinct statement of things as they stand, specially alluding only to such changes as have been introduced since the last general Report was issued eleven years ago.

The subjects in which the teachers, who desire to be admitted to participation, are required to pass, are Latin, Greek, English Grammar and Literature, History (including the outlines of Ancient and Modern History and Bible History), Geography Mathematical and Physical, Elements of Physics, Arithmetic, Geometry, Algebra, and Trigonometry. The rules of the examination, and a specimen of the examination papers, with accompanying circular letter of instructions, will be found in Appendix I.

To those unacquainted with Scotch education it may seem that this is too high a demand to make on teachers of parochial schools. But if we bear in mind that, in consequence of the inadequate development of the Middle School system in Scotland, the parochial schools have from their first institution been required to prepare pupils for the Universities, and that an university education is accessible on easy terms to almost all the northern youth of Scotland who give signs of promise, the Trustees will not be considered to have interpreted in too elevated a sense Mr. Dick's desire to raise the literary character of the parochial schoolmasters. The enumeration of subjects in an examination programme is, I am aware, no indication of the qualifications of those who pass the examination. The quality of the answers, not the pitch or quantity of the questions, can alone indicate this. That the standard of " pass " in the Dick Bequest examination is sufficiently high, is testified by the facts that graduates of Aberdeen are frequently cast in their first attempts, and that marks of distinction have scarcely ever been obtained by any save those who had been already favourably known at their University for eminence in more than one department of study. Another means of measuring the quality of work required by the Trustees will be found in the Appendix to the Report of 1854, where may be found the answers of a candidate who earned the mark of distinction. This mark is given only to those candidates who pass the whole examination at

P

one sitting, and whose papers as a whole are above average. The term FAIR is used by the Examiners to denote that amount of attainment which, while it is considered sufficient, is not deserving of special commendation. From this central point proceed in either direction two steps, those of the ascending scale being *Good* and *Very Good*, those of the descending, *Deficient* and *Very Deficient*.

The examination is held annually in September; and candidates are required to complete the examination not later than the third opportunity after the date of their appointment. Should they fail to do so, their whole papers, with the exception of those which have been characterized as *Good* or *Very Good*, are cancelled, and they must begin *de novo*.

When the whole examination has been satisfactorily completed, the teacher is paid such a proportion of the annual allowances reserved for him from the date of his entry on his duties as the statistics of his school, the report of the Visitor, and the character of his examination seem to entitle him to. Those who pass with distinction are further credited with a certain number of marks for scholarship, which tell favourably on the amount payable to them during their whole future tenure of office; and, in addition to this, unusually high proficiency obtains an immediate pecuniary reward.

The effect of scholarship on all future annual payments to the teacher brings me naturally to explain next the rules of allocation; but before doing so I would refer the reader to the examination statistics of the ten years ending Martinmas 1862, and which will be found in the Appendix (II.)

From this table it appears that, during these ten years, 8 have received pecuniary rewards for unusually high proficiency ; that, in addition to these, 8 have received the mark of distinction which adds permanently to all future allowances; and that 12 teachers and 7 substitutes failed from various causes to complete their examination.[1]

As it is interesting to note to what extent scholarship and efficient school-keeping are found in conjunction, I have examined the "Scheme of Division" as it stands at this date, and find that of those who have marks assigned to them for distinction in scholarship, 11 stand in the first class as practical teachers, 3 in the second class, and 5 are average, while only 2 are decidedly inferior. This result, I think, substantiates what my observation of schools has long led me to conclude, that superior scholarship is only an exhibition, in a specific direction, of superior qualities of the intellectual and moral nature as a whole, and that the powers and conscientiousness exhibited in the attainment of knowledge will, as a general rule, be found available in the practical work of life, whatever that may be.

[1] On the arithmetical knowledge of the teachers, see Professor Kelland's letter in the chapter on the arithmetic as found in the schools, p. 274.

(2.) *The Heritors and Minister, and Presbyterial Superintendence.*

The Trustees have two distinct duties to discharge with reference to the Local Committee, in whose hands rests the appointment of parochial teachers, namely, to avoid all interference with the superintending power of the Minister and Presbyteries, and, in terms of Mr. Dick's testament, to check any disposition that may be shown by heritors to take advantage of the Bequest in order to relieve themselves of a portion of what would otherwise have been a just assessment.

They have been successful in securing the confidence of the Minister and Presbyteries, by making the former cognisant of all important correspondence between themselves and the teacher, and by taking the annual report of the Presbytery into consideration when allocating the proportion of the Bequest to be paid to each teacher. A copy of the schedule (with a specimen of the answers) which they receive from the Presbyteries will be found in Appendix III. While leaving their own judgment perfectly free, and taking measures, by means of their Visitor, to become personally acquainted with every school eligible to the benefits of the Bequest, the Trustees have earnestly endeavoured to give their apparent intrusion the character of candid but independent co-operation.

Nor will it be said that they have anywhere failed in their efforts.

By their resolution to allow the amount of statutory assessment for education in each parish to determine to some extent their own distribution—their grant being reduced where the heritors fix a small permanent salary, and growing with their liberality—they withdrew the temptation to convert the Bequest into a fund for relieving proprietors of statutory obligations. It cannot be said, however, that the liberal salaries paid under the Act of 1861 to the parochial teachers of the three beneficiary counties, have been to any appreciable extent determined by the influence of this principle of distribution. In so far as the liberal arrangements then made are due to the Bequest, they are not to be ascribed to any direct influence, but to its general operation as an elevating educational agency throughout the districts to which it is applicable,—elevating not only in respect of the character and qualifications, but also in respect of the status, of parochial teachers. To such men as the Bequest has been one of the chief means of securing for the service of the parochial schools, heritors could not hesitate (and to their honour be it said, have not hesitated) to give liberally, and without any grudging calculations as to other sources of school emolument.

(3.) *Plan of Distributing the Fund.*

The preceding remarks on the general nature of the Bequest and the general principles of administration, will make intelligible the following statement of the mode of allocating the annual free revenue.[1]

A certain number of marks is credited to each teacher after his appointment, under the various heads of *Attendance throughout the year, Number in attendance for six months, Number learning the higher branches* (*i.e.*, Grammar, Geography, Mathematics, Latin, Greek, and French), *Salary paid by Heritors, Amount of fees, Number of scholars taught gratuitously,* and *Scholarship* as determined by the examination of the teacher. These elements of computation, as ascertained from returns obtained from the schoolmasters themselves, are called the statistical elements. The numerical sum-total represents the proportion of the teacher's claim on the fund. The amount of that claim is reserved for the teachers from the date of their appointment to that of their passing their examination. The proportion, however, of the sum so reserved, which is actually paid on their passing, is fixed by the Trustees after a due consideration of their literary qualifications and of the report of the Visitor on their schools (*Vide* p. 226).

As soon as a teacher has passed, he is admitted thenceforward to full participation, that is to say, he

[1] The total amount distributed last year (1864) was £4344, 13s. 9d.

is allowed the entire amount indicated by the sum of the statistical elements, if the Trustees, on considering the report of the Visitor, are of opinion that he is discharging his duty satisfactorily. Should the teacher be reported by him as surpassing the average of efficiency, he is allowed by the Trustees an additional sum under the head of *Merit in Teaching*. The precise amount of this addition is practically left to the discretion of the Visitor, and may increase the sum allocated on statistical grounds by 10, 20, 50, or even 60 per cent., according to the grade of merit to which the teacher may be assigned.[1] On the other hand, should the Visitor's Report indicate deficiencies in the practical work of teaching, arising either from incapacity or negligence, the Trustees, on considering the case, are in use to mark their disapproval, either, in the first instance, by censure, or, where deemed necessary, by restricting the teacher's allowance to the extent of one-fourth, one-third, or a half. In aggravated cases they wholly cancel it. In the case of young and inexperienced teachers, whose deficiencies seem to the Trustees to arise from want of skill rather than from carelessness, it is the practice, when first admitting them to participation, to reduce the statistical claim of the teacher by a fourth, a third, a half, thus putting them on what is called "The Preparatory Scale."

The amount allocated to each teacher is thus made

[1] The *aggregate* number of marks allowable for Merit in Teaching is restricted to one-sixth part of the whole divisible fund.

ultimately dependent on his efficiency in the discharge of his daily duty as a schoolmaster. The mode of visitation, and the grounds on which the Visitor forms his judgment, will be stated in the sequel.

It may be confidently affirmed now, as in 1854, and after an added experience of eleven years, that upon a careful retrospect " there appears to be every reason to believe that the above mode of distribution continues to exercise a salutary influence, by making the teacher's allowance depend upon the advancement of his school in *everything* which contributes to its prosperity, and upon his own proficiency in literature, and in professional skill.

" The distinguishing characteristic of the management, it will be observed, is the unequal distribution ; and looking at the effects, there is no cause to regret the adoption of that principle, but rather increasing occasion to value and adhere to it. This is what gives life to the operation of the Bequest, and prevents Mr. Dick's bounty from descending upon its objects with an influence which, under an equal distribution, would enervate while it enriched. The principle adopted supplies a motive to exertion, by securing to faithful labour and skill the grateful acknowledgment of a reward, which proves that they have been recognised and appreciated. Nor is the effect confined to the schoolmaster. The schools, and through them the whole body of the people in the three counties, participate in the results of Mr. Dick's benevolence, for the exertion which it promotes is bestowed upon them, whereas, if the boon were given unconditionally, the same motive to exertion would not be felt, and the bounty in many cases would prove to be an evil instead of a blessing."[1]

(4.) *Assistant-Substitutes.*

The Trustees, as has been fully explained in previous Reports, encourage the retirement from active duty of aged schoolmasters in connexion with the Bequest, without requiring them to resign their official position as parochial schoolmaster, and they admit to the benefit of the Bequest Assistants appointed to act for the principal teacher, on the understanding that they shall be, in the fullest sense of the word, *Substitutes.* The importance of this provision is manifest.

If the acquirements and qualifications of the assistant-substitute are satisfactory, it is considered unnecessary to inquire how he is appointed; but in every case in which it has fallen to the Trustees to suggest the mode of appointment, they have recommended that the selection should be made by the minister and heritors, who are the legal electors of the principal schoolmaster.

The pecuniary arrangement is that the substitute teacher receives the school-fees and the ordinary allowance from the Bequest, together with a minimum

[1] Professor Menzies' Report of 1854, p. 32.

salary from the heritors of £35, in parishes where there is only one parochial school, and of £25 in parishes where there are two or more schools,—the incumbent retaining the former salary paid by the heritors, and receiving also an extra allowance, at the rate of £12 a year, from the Bequest. The average amount of the provision for the substitute, from the sources specified, is £91, 14s. 3d. per annum, in parishes where there is only one school, and £81, 14s. 3d. in parishes where there are two. In addition to this the Trustees now require that the substitute shall have the exclusive occupation of the house and garden. The retired incumbent's income is in money about £41, exclusive of emoluments from other sources, of which the average is £5, 3s. 2d. per annum.

It is contrary to the implied understanding between the Trustees and the principal teacher that there should be any agreement between the incumbent and his substitute, imposing upon the latter, as regards his position and remuneration, any other conditions than are distinctly expressed in the arrangement as contracted with the Trustees. When it has turned out, therefore, that by private compact different terms have been settled, the allowance has been retained until the latent agreement was cancelled.

Except in the qualification of age, and the non-reservation of their allowances prior to their passing the examination, assistant-substitutes are subject generally to the same regulations as schoolmasters in full possession of the office of parochial teacher, with this exception, that if incompetent as teachers they are not put on restricted allowance, but at once required to resign.

When the state of the schoolmaster's health prevents him from personally making an arrangement, the Trustees are enabled to obtain an effectual contract for the employment of a substitute, by the judicial appointment of a guardian, empowered to act on behalf of the incumbent.[1]

An abstract of the regulations applicable to principal masters, to assistant-substitutes, as well as to temporary substitutes (acting for teachers during temporary absence at College), will be found in Appendix IV. To enter more minutely into these points of detail in the body of this Report would be wholly superfluous, after the exhaustive treatment of them in the Report of 1854.

For a similar reason I avoid enumerating and vindicating the regulations regarding the occupation of teachers with duties outside their proper school work; merely mentioning, that while the Trustees offer no objection to the occasional discharge of pulpit duties by those teachers who are licentiates of the Church (as the great majority are), they stringently enforce their rule against all '*stated*' clerical engagements. They have offered no objection to the union of the offices of Session-Clerk, Registrar, or Inspector of the

[1] See Report of 1854.

Poor with that of Schoolmaster. The office most incompatible with the proper discharge of school duties is that last mentioned ; and it is not improbable, that were it usual for teachers in the three counties to hold it, its claims would be found to conflict so seriously with the work of the school as to call for special consideration.

CHAPTER IV.

ADMINISTRATIVE AND OTHER CHANGES SINCE 1854.

Assistant-Substitutes—Temporary Substitutes—Music—Side-Parochial Schools.

Assistant-Substitutes.—The principal changes introduced since the date of the last Report (1854) were rendered necessary by the Parochial and Burgh Schoolmasters Act of 1861. The extent to which this Act modified the parochial system, as settled in 1696, and reformed in 1803, has been already explained (p. 220). One of the most important of its provisions, however, both in itself and in its relation to the Bequest, was that contained in the 19th clause, which enacts that the heritors may superannuate teachers, granting them " a retiring allowance, the amount whereof shall not be less than two-third parts of the amount of the salary pertaining to the office at the date of such resignation thereof, and shall not exceed the gross amount of such salary." The defects of former Acts in respect of superannuation, had been to a great extent supplied by the judicious arrangements of the Bequest Trustees, who had used their powers to facilitate the transference of schools into the hands of assistant-substitutes, on terms which have been already explained.

The Trustees did not cancel their subsisting rules in consequence of the clause above quoted; but where teachers resign office under it, they of course *ipso facto* cease to have any interest in Mr. Dick's settlement; the Trustees being precluded from recognising, directly or indirectly, those who, by demitting the office of " parochial schoolmaster," have removed themselves beyond the reach of the Bequest. As, however, they were of opinion that the new Act did not call for the discontinuance of their previous practice with reference to Substitutes, they requested Presbyteries to continue to examine them as to their qualifications, and resolved to hold a Presbyterial certificate of competency to be an essential condition of participation in the fund.

Again, in order to prevent the continuance of their arrangement for securing retirement from active duty operating so as to relieve heritors of the additional burdens imposed on them by the Statute, the Trustees resolved that in all future cases of retirement to which they should become parties, the heritors should be required, in addition to the salary paid to the retiring teacher, to appropriate to the substitute a salary of not less than £35 where there was one parochial school in the parish, or £25 where there were two or more.

Further, the Parochial Schools Act having raised the minimum assessment for salary to £35 where there was one school, and to £50 where there were two, the Trustees, carrying out the principles already in operation, thereupon resolved that no schools should be in future admitted to participation, as second or side-parochial schools, where the emoluments provided by the heritors for the teacher amounted to less than £35 per annum, including the value of the house and garden.

Temporary Substitutes.—Teachers acting temporarily for a master during the absence of the latter at College are recognised by the Trustees only if they have had a university education, or hold a Government certificate of merit of the first division, second year.

Music.—The only remaining change in the administration of sufficient importance to merit special consideration, is the resolution to give a certain value to the successful teaching of Music in the annual allocation. The nature and grounds of the change will be best learned from the Minute of the Trustees on the subject:—

MINUTE OF DICK BEQUEST TRUSTEES OF 17TH JANUARY 1860.

"*Singing from Notation.*

" The Trustees having received communications from some of the clergy in the three counties, stating their anxiety that encouragement should be given to the teaching of Music in the parish schools, and being themselves impressed with the desirableness of promoting the improvement of psalmody in our parish churches, by the regular teaching of Singing from Notation to the children attending the schools, resolved to require their Visitor, in all his future Reports on the condition of the schools inspected by him, to report specially in each case whether Music is embraced in the school curriculum, as well as what measure of success has attended the teaching in this branch of education. It was further resolved, that in future, in the ascertainment and allocation of the yearly allowances, the teaching of Music shall be taken as an element in fixing in each case the amount to be given in respect of 'Merit in Teaching.' The Clerk was instructed to send an Extract from this Minute to the ministers of the three counties, and to all teachers connected with the Bequest, in order that they may be aware of the regulation now introduced."

Side-Parochial Schools.—One of the benefits which the Bequest has conferred on the three counties has been the encouragement which it has given to the institution of side-parochial schools. In other parts of Scotland the compulsory requirements of the Parliamentary Acts are complied with in respect of the institution of one parochial school, but there are comparatively few districts in which the power residing in the heritors to increase the number of parochial schools has been so liberally interpreted as in the counties of Aberdeen, Banff, and Moray. The number of parishes embraced by the Bequest is 124, the number of parochial schools in these is 154, showing 30 side-parochial schools. The schools added since 1854, and recognised by the Trustees as parochial schools under the Act, are TARVES—*Barthol Chapel;* HUNTLY —*Kinnoir;* BOHARM—*Maggyknockater;* CROMDALE —*Dulnan Bridge;* AUCHINDOIR—*Lumsden;* ABERDOUR—*Auchmedden;* CABRACH—*Invercharrach;* AUCHTERLESS—*Badenscoth.*

CHAPTER V.

THE RELATION OF THE BEQUEST TO THE PRIVY COUNCIL.

SINCE the date of last Report to the Trustees, a considerable number of the parochial schools in the three counties have taken the benefit of Privy Council grants. These grants are claimable by school managers on behalf of teachers, who, having passed the Government examination for a certificate of merit, receive from the heritors a salary of at least £15 in excess of the statutory minimum. In addition to the increase of salary which teachers can in this way obtain, they have the further privilege of being allowed to employ apprentice-monitors (called pupil-teachers) at the expense of the Privy Council.

A certain proportion of the parochial schoolmasters (at present two-fifths[1]) have qualified for these privileges. The Trustees did not feel it incumbent on them to advert to this new source of emolument and supervision, so long as the Minutes

[1] In 1855 one-sixteenth of the schools were in connexion with the Privy Council; in 1860 rather more than one-fifth. The amount at present expended on them must be about £1600 per annum.

under which the Privy Council administered the Parliamentary grant did not tend in any way to contravene or defeat the purposes of the Bequest.

In the Revised Code of 1864, however, it was proposed to reduce all Government grants to schools by the amount of any endowment enjoyed by them. The Trustees, after deliberating on the probable effect of this clause, resolved to oppose its application to the Dick Bequest, on the grounds that the Bequest was not in the proper sense of the words a charitable endowment, and that the application of the new Minute to the parochial schools in the three counties would tend to weaken the peculiar influence of the Bequest in raising the standard of acquirement in teachers and of literary attainment in schools. The clause would have had the effect feared, for this reason, that the teachers, being compelled to forego the one or the other source of income, would naturally prefer the Privy Council augmentation, as being, if not larger in amount, yet obtainable on easier terms than the Dick Bequest, both as regarded personal scholarship and the character of the school work. In this way it was obvious that the Bequest would gradually become practically inoperative as a means of "encouraging active schoolmasters," and of "elevating the literary character of the parochial schoolmasters and schools." The statement drawn up by the Trustees and supported by them in person before the Lord President, is printed as Appendix v. of this Report.

The suspension of the application of the Revised Code to Scotland, in consequence of the appointment of a Royal Commission for the purpose of inquiring into the state of education, allayed the apprehensions of the Trustees.[1]

So much has been said of late years as to the tendency of the Privy Council grants, whether under the Original or the Revised Code, to lower the quality of the education given in the Scotch parochial schools, that it might not be out of place to consider here whether there are real grounds for such apprehensions. But to do so would be superfluous, as the whole subject of the relation of the Privy Council to Scotch schools is at present under consideration by the Commission above referred to. Of two things there can be no doubt,—*First*, that no parochial teacher is entitled to devote his attention to the instruction of his senior pupils in Latin and Mathematics whose junior pupils are unable to pass the examination in reading, writing, and arithmetic prescribed by the Revised Code : and, *secondly*, that whatever system of grants may be devised for the future, the conditions on which they will be obtainable will not counteract the higher parochial education of the three counties with which

[1] In the Code of 1865, the clause complained of is made inapplicable to those rural schools in which the Government grant and the endowment do not make a total sum exceeding the rate of 15s. per scholar, according to the annual average of attendance. That Code, however, has been suspended in Scotland till June 1867.

the Trustees are concerned, so long as the principles on which they administer the Bequest are not rendered nugatory by some such provision as that which they gave their influence, not without effect, to resist.[1]

[1] The influence of the Privy Council on the higher parochial school education, is again adverted to in the chapter on the Higher Instruction of the Parochial Schools.

CHAPTER VI.

VISITATION OF THE SCHOOLS.

OF the 154 parochial schools in the three counties of Aberdeen, Banff, and Moray, 20 are excluded from participation on account of non-compliance with the regulations of the Trustees. The remainder are visited once in two years. Unless special circumstances arise, the report of the Presbytery during the year of non-visitation is accepted as sufficient.

It used to be a frequent subject of complaint that the schools were visited in the summer season, and urgent requests were made that the visitation should be made in early spring, before the beginning of field labour dispersed the highest class. During the last nine years the desires of the teachers have in this particular been generally complied with, because it has happened to be as convenient for the Visitor to inspect the schools in March and April as at any other season. The Trustees, however, have never resiled from their original position that a well-conducted school will show its true quality at whatever period of the year it may be inspected. Even the entire absence of the senior class will not necessarily affect the opinion of an inspector respecting the efficiency of a school if he be competent for his work. The results produced in the highest class are by no means, taken by themselves, a sound measure of the quality of the work of a school. Indeed the temptation which the teacher feels to devote an undue share of his time to his oldest pupils causes him to rely so much on the excellence of a highest class, that he is scarcely aware of the defects of all the others. This is to misapprehend the main object of the parochial school, as of all education, and at the same time to exhibit an entire misunderstanding of method. The perusal of the first portion of this Report will show with sufficient clearness what is meant. It has been written to little purpose if it does not show that the importance of the classes is in proportion to the youth of the pupils, and this in all essential subjects of instruction as well as in the prosecution of the great purpose of education. A sound organization embraces every part of the school equally, and reveals itself even in a mere fragment of the whole. A wise discipline is of more moment, as well as of more efficacy, in the junior classes than in the senior. It is in the opening years of the young child's mind that religious instruction requires the most skilful handling, makes the most lasting impression, and yields the richest reward. It is at the same period that moral acts assume in the mind of the child the character of right or wrong, and the great gulf is fixed between bad and good. It is at the same period that the gentler sentiments best respond to careful direction, and that mutual consideration can be most easily made to take the place of natural selfishness. It is at the same period, that the habit of intelligent apprehension of any subject to which the mind may apply itself is best formed. And finally, it is at the same period that the *character* and *style* of every mental acquirement, whether it be reading, writing, or any other, is permanently given. "Let the teacher take care of his junior classes, and the senior classes will take care of themselves," is probably not an extreme statement. It constantly happens, when discussing with a teacher some great defect in a senior class, that the inspector has to point to the six or seven-year old pupils as the portion of the school to which the remedy must be applied.

Holding the above views as to the periods, nature, and methods of school-work, consistency requires that I should maintain that a competent inspector can judge a school as fairly during the thinned attendance of summer as during the full attendance of winter. Given the same agricultural conditions, it is certainly possible to fix the relative capacity of farmers by the harvest which they lead home; but that man would be an indifferent judge who could not find materials for as sound a judgment in the seed-time.

Further, believing, as I do, that the chief faults of Scotch parochial schools have been, and still are, defective organization, haphazard discipline, comparative neglect of the junior classes, undue postponement of the essential studies,—writing and arithmetic,—and a tendency to relaxation of effort at the season at which agricultural operations begin, I am not certain that summer visitation does not, on the whole, best fulfil the purposes of the Dick Bequest.

What has been said on the period of visitation, when taken in connexion with the first part of this Report, sufficiently indicates the objects which I keep in view when visiting. It is sometimes necessary to guard against the attempts of some teachers to mislead the judgment of a Visitor, by giving prominence to one or two strong points, and by using all sorts of devices, including prompting and leading questions, to throw an illusory glare of efficiency over a badly taught class.

The excuses with which some teachers overload every subject as the inspector approaches it in turn, are of course received only as an indirect confession of defects felt to be censurable and known to be inexcusable.

It is highly creditable to the character of the masters of the three counties that the cases are rare in which either of the above faults is met with. And it has also to be recorded, to their honour, that, although my visits are unannounced, I have never, to the best of my recollection, found a master absent from his post, except for sufficient reasons.

At the same time, it is to be confessed, that having

found, in the first years of inspection, that counsel regarding improved methods had little effect on minds unprepared by special training to take an ideal and artistic, which is at the same time a *professional*, view of their task, it became necessary to demand certain specific *results* in respect of quality and quantity of acquirement. The practical direction which my demands took will appear in the chapter on the "Progress of the Schools." My reason for adopting this course simply was that it was one which was intelligible to all, and that by insuring results of a certain *kind* in the highest classes the teacher was necessarily forced to the prior and early practice in the initiatory classes of certain sound methods and apt expedients. But, while taking my first rough measurement of a school by the broad *results* in respect of acquisition and intellectual capacity, I give weight to these, only to the extent to which they are seen to be the *bonâ fide* fruit of careful organization, of rational and graduated methods, and of good discipline.

It has always been the practice for the Dick Bequest Visitor to enter the schools unannounced, and to proceed at once with the examination, beginning generally with the class which happens to be on the floor when he enters. The Report made to the Trustees is, accordingly, simply a historical record, more or less detailed, of all that takes place in the school while the Visitor is there, and of his judgment on every class which passes under examination.

Having now spoken of the visitation in general, I proceed to record, for the benefit of future, if not of present participants in the Bequest, the actual state of knowledge and the habits of teaching which are generally met with in the schools, pointing out, where necessary, the defects prevalent and the remedies required.

CHAPTER VII.

NOTES OF VISITATION.

(1.) Reading. Examination on the Reading-Lessons. Course of Lessons.

THE average annual enrolment in each of the parochial schools is 113. All learn to read, with the exception of a few big lads who attend only during the winter season for lessons in arithmetic. The lesson of the day, presumed to have been prepared over-night, is read once or twice down the class. The master then usually asks the pupils to spell and define the more difficult words, and proceeds to examine on the substance of the lesson. His examination for the most part simply consists in throwing the categorical propositions of the lesson, which has been read, into an interrogative form. He puts the questions to the pupils in succession, beginning at the top. This interrogatory exercise, of course, varies in its efficiency in proportion to the intellectual power and earnestness of the master. It assuredly adds little to the child's knowledge of the lesson. Its value consists in its power of rousing in the pupil an effort of intellect to follow the master, and of memory to recall the words which have been read.

The benefit to be derived from this kind of examination manifestly depends solely on the amount of intellect exhibited by the teacher, and reproduced in the pupils through sympathy with him, and on the earnestness with which he takes up the lesson as something really worthy of being retained in the mind.

Now it is always desirable, in determining the procedure to be followed with a view to give effect to the right method of teaching any subject, to devise expedients which leave as little as possible to hang by the capacity of the master. In schools, as elsewhere, we can only reckon on an average amount of ability, and a moderate share of earnestness; and while we may freely exempt the thoughtful and ardent schoolmaster from all directions imposed *ab extra*, we must discover rules of working which will give the fullest practical effect to average qualities. In every profession the mass of men are imitative, not originative, and unfortunately this disposition is strongest in the direction of imitating themselves. Our duty, accordingly, is to give teachers a good start in professional life, so that a good habit may be early formed. By this means we may possibly lend to the ordinary mind some of the power of the higher.[1]

Keeping in view these considerations, and the purpose and method of teaching Reading, as these have been explained in the first part of the Report, I would suggest the following course of procedure :—

---

[1] Hence the great utility of Normal Schools, and the necessity there is for the professional training of teachers.

1. Let the teacher, when he gives out the lesson for the following day, either read it to the pupils, or, where time fails for this, shortly sketch its purport, pointing out the more difficult words.

2. When the lesson is read, let him not go slavishly down the class from top to bottom, but, letting the children clearly understand that they are presumed to know both the language and the subject-matter, select those who are to read. The reading should be individual, but if the style be bad, the master should require the pupils to enunciate in concert with him, so that they may gradually acquire his style. To *tell* a child to "speak out," or to "mind the stops," is an utterly useless expenditure of words. The temptation to adopt the simultaneous method of reading should be avoided, but *three at a time* may be occasionally required to read, observing together the same pauses and emphasis. This will not only save time, but be of great virtue as a corrective of slovenly reading.

3. There are five qualities in Reading, each of which should be made the subject of separate and successive study and training :—(1.) Correct pronunciation of the words. (2.) Firmness, articulateness, and distinctness in the enunciation of words. Teachers do not seem to be aware to how great an extent progress in reading depends on a habit of firm articulation. (3.) Deliberateness in the enunciation of the several clauses making up each sentence : these three qualities secure intelligibility. (4.) Emphasis. (5.) Expression. The first three qualities form the principal

aim of the elementary teacher. Emphasis can come within the sphere of his work only when correctness, distinctness, and deliberateness have been attained. But inasmuch as it is the fruit of an intellectual perception of the interdependence of clauses, it should be, as soon as practicable, required of every pupil. Its existence is the best possible indication, test, and measure of the intelligence which the child has been taught to bring to bear on his reading, and of the suitableness of the books which are put into his hands. Expression, again, belongs to the æsthetics of Reading, and has reference to the moral and sentimental appreciation of what is read, and should not be attempted until the emotional nature is old enough, not merely to *feel*, but consciously to reproduce what another person feels. Fine, or rather superfine, reading or recitation by children is, *in itself*, essentially a delusion and a snare, though it may have its uses by holding up, purely imitative though the whole intonation and exhibition be, a standard of style, and thereby elevating the art of reading as an art in the eyes of the school.

4. While the pupil is reading let no corrections be made. When he has ceased, those who have detected errors may hold out their hands. This compels the attention of the whole class to every sentence. Usually each boy attends only to his own.

5. If the boy who reads gives evidence of want of preparation, enter in a book a bad mark against him, taking care that it is want of preparation and not

inaccuracy which is so punished. The more or less of accuracy will be rewarded or punished by the boy's place in the class. To regulate a boy's position on the school scale merely by the number of his mistakes, is to confound the intellectual with the moral.

6. If a schoolmaster wishes to teach his pupils to read well, let him first learn to read himself.

The teacher will find the formal setting apart of certain occasional afternoons for the special exhibition of Reading-style by himself and his pupils, a means of impressing the school with the importance of the subject. The same device may be successfully resorted to in every branch of study.

Examination on the Lesson.—The reading of the lesson being finished, the next object is to extract from it as much discipline as possible. This will depend on the variety and solidity of the reading-book, and the character of the lesson of the day will of course determine the extent to which the class is to be examined. I have already dwelt, in the first part of this Report, on the peculiarly educative power of the reading-lessons in forming as well as informing the mind, when the school uses and purposes of teaching the art of Reading are rightly and largely understood. And I would fain iterate and reiterate the grounds of the opinions already expressed there, that the education of the school means, and must mean, the Reading of the school, more than all other subjects united. But to do so would be to add nothing to the comprehension either of the teacher who has fully grasped what has been already said, or of him who is unable or unwilling to understand it. The extraction of the educative uses of Reading from the lesson of the day is a work so much more dependent than the mere art of Reading in its narrower sense on the character of the teacher, that technical rules are almost useless. One man will reach the best results in one way, another in another. It is a matter of idiosyncrasy. One tendency, however, every young teacher requires to be guarded against,—the tendency to expound and preach rather than to teach. Even to explain is not to teach. To *explain* is to unfold a subject as a subject; to *teach* or *instruct* is to explain the subject in relation to the mental capacity and already existing knowledge of the pupils, at the same time setting in motion and guiding their intellectual activity, so that they may meet the explanation half-way. The good teacher is, in matters intellectual, the moving, guiding, and correcting power, but little more. An exaggerated instance of the tendency to do *for* the pupils what they ought to do for themselves, I find in my reports for 1856, and as it puts in a strong light a not uncommon misconception of the art of teaching, I quote it :—

. . . "The master then proceeded to examine on the subject-matter of the lesson. Beginning calmly, and with considerable gravity, he gradually waxed warm, until he lost himself entirely in his subject, utterly forgetting the existence of his pupils. It was, in fact, a dramatic exhibition of the lesson thrown into an interrogative form, the short and scattered replies of the members of the class only serving to sustain the excitement of the 'examiner.' Spite of the energy and superfluous gesticulation which was exhibited, it was quite evident that the teacher was beating the air, and that it never for a moment occurred to him to think of the actual mental condition of his pupils. The consequence was, that when the examination was taken out of his hands, utter barrenness was found. The master, in fact, monopolized all the energy, and laboured under the not uncommon illusion that his own activity and interest were shared by his pupils." . . .

It will save space and time if I state the mode of procedure which I have recommended, when it was certain that the recommendation would not fall upon an outer crust of indurated habit.

1. The habit of converting categorical into interrogative clauses is not an examination of any efficacy. The lesson should be viewed *as a whole*, having a beginning and middle and end, and the children should be asked to give an account of it in their own words. One or two of the more fluent attempting this, the rest will be too happy to lie in wait for omissions and errors, with a view to supply and correct them. In this way the lesson, whether it be a narrative, a preceptive extract, or an information lesson, will be reproduced by the combined efforts of the class. The cultivating nature of this exercise, apart from its effect in securing the preparation of the lesson, is at once manifest. Such exercises in oral composition should be found at *every* stage of progress, and are as much in their place in the infant and initiatory as in the juvenile and advanced

classes. This being done, with the help of the master where a point is missed or a difficulty not overcome, the first step in the examination is taken.

2. The second stage is the familiar and colloquial illustration and extension of the subject of the lesson by the master, in more or less detail, according to the time at his disposal. He will now call on the pupils for voluntary contributions to the subject in the form of facts or thoughtful suggestions. It is at this stage that the practical application of the lesson will be most suitably made, and the whole brought into connexion with the daily life and out-door experience of the pupils.

3. The third stage there can seldom be time to complete, but it ought always to be partially accomplished. It has to do mainly with the language of the lesson. The amount of language which a man understands is, roughly speaking, the measure of his intellectual capacity. In extending the boy's knowledge of language, therefore, we increase his intellectual grasp, and, in a sense, his knowledge of things; things of intellectual and moral, as well as of external and visible reality. The linguistic discipline, therefore, which reading-lessons give is of the utmost consequence. Idiomatic correctness, grammatical accuracy, and great variety in structure and style are of great value, if not indispensable.

The most common mode of examining on the lesson read by the pupils is referred to in the following extract from my annual Report:—

... " The fault I had to find with Mr. ——'s otherwise thorough mode of examining was that he expected too much from the class. He went to the details of a difficult lesson at once, without first making sure that each individual sentence was understood. This is a common blunder. After the *general* substance of the lesson has been reproduced and illustrated as a whole, the next step ought to be the going over the lesson with the book open, and filling in simple, and if possible, Saxon, expressions, for the more difficult words and phrases. The *sentences* once thoroughly understood, the connexion of these, constituting the detailed argument of the lesson, should only then be taken up by the master."

Another style of procedure is reported on in the following terms :—

... " The above report gives only due credit to Mr. ——'s great and self-sacrificing labours, and may possibly leave an impression on the mind of the reader that this school is almost too good to live ; but a closer inspection reveals a weakness which insures its vitality if not longevity. This is, in truth, a school of memory and facts. The children are instructed with a painful expenditure of labour in facts, Biblical, historical, geographical, grammatical, and arithmetical, but their intelligence is feeble. When examined from sentence to sentence on the meaning of the words read and the purport of each clause, they displayed an ignorance and a want of capacity to comprehend what had been said to them, which one could scarcely believe to be compatible with such unusual excellence in other respects. After a display of seeming knowledge, which astonishes the listener, a clause of the lesson is taken up, *e.g.*, ' The white ant is an extraordinary species of insect,' and the children are asked the meaning of ' extraordinary.' After every facility and encouragement has been given, the smartest boy ventures on the definition ' insect.' In the same way 'species' is defined to mean ' extraordinary,' and so forth ; nor was it possible to establish any intelligent colloquial relations between them and myself. Further examination on the same principle in other things broke the back of the school."

The linguistic treatment of each sentence of the

lesson by the master, which constitutes the third stage of examination, when time permits, may be illustrated thus, the pupils being understood to have their books *open*, otherwise the exercise degenerates into one of memory.

[I presume that the class under examination is the *highest* class of a good parochial school in one of the three counties.]

The pupil reads :—

"*Every student who enters on a scientific pursuit, especially if at a somewhat advanced period of life, will find not only that he has much to learn, but much also to unlearn. Familiar objects and events are far from presenting themselves to our senses in that aspect, and with those connexions, under which science requires them to be viewed, and which constitute their rational explanation.*"

Q. What kind of student is referred to here?
A. The student who enters on a scientific pursuit.
Q. What is said of such a student?
A. That he has much to learn.
Q. Is anything else said of him?
A. That he has much to unlearn.
Q. The author says that every student of a science has much to learn and unlearn; but he says that this is more particularly true of a certain class of students : what class?
A. Those who begin at an advanced period of life.
Q. What is meant by the word " student?"
A. One who studies.
Q. And what do you mean by studying any subject?
A. Reading about it, and thinking about it.
Q. The student referred to is, you have told me, the student " who enters on a scientific pursuit"—pursuit here means subject : what is meant by a "*scientific* pursuit or subject?"

A. A subject carefully arranged, so as to show its facts, causes, and reasons.[1]

Q. This explanation is difficult for you to understand; you will best explain it by an example.

A. Astronomy, Geology, etc., are "scientific subjects" or sciences: that is to say, the real facts about the stars, not merely what seem to be the facts at first sight, arranged so as to show their connexion and causes, is the science of the stars, or Astronomy (and so of Geology).[1]

Q. Can any of you now, looking carefully at the sentence, shut the book, and give me the substance of it in your own words?

A. A person beginning to study a science will find that he has much to learn as well as to unlearn, and this all the more if he is grown up before he begins.

Q. Very good. Now I shall read the sentence as it stands once more over. You can now easily tell me, in the words of the grammar-book, What is the *subject* of this sentence?

A. " Every student" down to "life."

Q. Yes, that is the thing spoken about. Now what is said about it; in the words of the grammar, what is the *predicate?*

A. " Will find" to the end.

Q. What is the principal word or *verb* of this predicate?

A. " Will find."

Q. But *find* is a transitive verb, and therefore part of what follows must be its *object:* what part?

A. The whole of what follows; there are two objects, *learning* and *unlearning*, and they are connected by the conjoining or conjunctive word *but.*

Teacher. We shall now take the second sentence.

(*The teacher here reads it slowly while the pupils follow with the eye.*)

Q. What is said here about "familiar objects and events."

A. That they are far from presenting themselves, etc.

Q. What things are "far from presenting themselves?" etc.

A. " Familiar objects and events."

---

[1] Of course an answer of this sort is worked out by the help of the master, and must be the result of many leading questions.

Q. In the science of Astronomy, for example, what would the "familiar objects and events" be ?

A. The heavenly bodies and their motions.

Q. Which are the *objects*, and which the *events ?*

A. The bodies are the *objects*, and their motions are the *events*.

Q. Now the author says that these objects and events are "far from presenting themselves in a certain aspect and connexion :" what do you mean by "aspect ?"

A. Appearance.

Q. What by " connexion ?"

A. Their union with each other, or other things, or their relation to these things.¹

Q. What kind of appearance and connexions do they fail to present themselves to our senses in ?

A. The appearance and connexions under which science requires them to be viewed.

Q. Does the author say anything else about that "appearance" and "connexion ?"

A. Yes. He says that they " constitute their rational explanation."

Q. What " constitute the rational explanation" of *what ?*

A. A certain aspect and certain connexions of objects and events constitute the rational explanation of these objects and events.¹

Q. Can we accurately say that an aspect or appearance and certain connexions constitute an explanation of anything ?

A. No. What is meant is that the presentation of them to the mind in a certain light, and with certain connexions, " constitutes their rational explanation."

Q. What is meant by " constitute their rational explanation ?"

A. That the kind of presentation referred to is such an explanation as satisfies the reason of a man.

Q. Now, can any of you, looking carefully at this sentence, shut your book and give me the substance of it in your own words ?

A. The author says, that "Things to which we are accustomed, are not always seen in such a way as science requires them to be looked at, and that the way of looking which science requires, gives us an explanation of these things which satisfies our minds."

¹ See foot-note on previous page.

Teacher.—Now, take your slates and go to your seats. Your composition lesson to-day will be putting these two sentences in your own words. In doing this you may make as many sentences of them as you please.

The above is analysis of sentences in relation to thought, and requires no special instruction in difficult terminology. It is, in truth, merely the explicit evolution of a process which *must* go on in the mind of every person who reads the sentences with understanding. Need I point to the great value of such an evolution as a discipline of intellect and an exercise of concentration of the will on an object outside itself. It is an exercise which disciplines every faculty of the understanding. This is the kind of analysis which has been spoken of in the First Part of this Report, as alone properly entering into the work of the parochial school, until the boy has reached the age of twelve. Thereafter formal or technical analysis may be introduced as a logical exercise of a still more minute kind, if time permit. Ordinary parsing even, in any systematic form, will be best omitted till the boy has reached eleven or twelve years of age, if only the parts of speech be gradually extracted from his Reading-lessons, with a view to the further elucidation of the meaning of sentences, and to enabling teacher and pupil to make verbal references without circumlocution.

Whatever course be taken in examining on a lesson, this at least may be fairly insisted on in every case, viz., that the teacher shall himself know what he is aiming at in his examination. The eye hastily cast over the open page, rather than the thought of the master, almost universally seems to determine what is to come next. Such cases as the following are not uncommon :—

Extract from Report on ——— School.

" The teacher of this school is a good scholar, and, so far as I can see, conscientious in the discharge of duty ; but he does not seem to realize in his own mind the purpose or plan of the lessons which he gives, or to think that this is necessary. Nor has he any mental standard by which to judge the progress which each class may make."

Occasionally the teacher will find himself compelled to be satisfied with an examination on the general scope of a lesson in the form of oral composition, or with a written reproduction of its general purport (step 1, p. 257). The time at his disposal must determine such things. It will frequently happen, too, that he will depart from the analysis of sentences in relation to thought, and substitute for it the analysis of *words*, and the fruitful exercise of word-building, with the help of prefixes and affixes.[1]

If there be one habit of teachers more absurd than another, it is the asking for definitions of the words of a lesson with the book shut. The words

---

[1] " Roots," in the form of Latin and Greek, are a waste of time. But a knowledge of the most common prefixes, and exercises in constructing words with the help of them, and on the basis of the root in its *English form*, are of great utility as a discipline.

are thus treated as isolated vocables, and a signification given by the pupil or suggested by the master, perhaps quite away from the sense in which the word is employed in the lesson. No definition of a word is a definition at all unless it can be put in the place of the word defined and leave the meaning of the proposition unaltered, at the same time that it is simplified. From this it manifestly follows that significations should be asked with the book open and as clause by clause is read. When all the more difficult words are in this way explained, the pupils should be required to re-read the sentence, putting the simpler definitions in place of the difficult words. This is not paraphrasing (an art much liable to abuse) but *substituting:* it might, indeed, be called *translating*. One sentence so reconstructed is of more value as a discipline of the intelligence than the recitation of a whole page of isolated terms, with their lexicon definitions. To the exercise of *substitution* or *translation* I attach very great importance.

Valuable as the skilful examination on a reading-lesson may be, the teacher must beware of tarnishing the beauty of a lesson which is addressed to the imagination or feelings of the pupil by following the same course with it as with the other pieces in the reading-book. Not every lesson affords fit material for stammering reproduction, much less for the vulgarizing process of sentence-analysis. Lessons which appeal to the affections, the sentiments of devotion, or the beautiful, should, after they have been read as usual by the class, have their purport simply and unaffectedly sketched by the master, and be then appropriately and expressively read by him to his listening pupils. In this way only can the lesson they are meant to teach be really taught.

Course of Lessons.—In selecting the course of lessons through which he is to carry his pupils, the teacher should have constant regard to the fact that the pupils of parochial schools receive *all* their cultivation within the walls of the schoolroom, and are excluded by their circumstances from those numerous influences of an intellectual, moral, and æsthetic kind which belong to the classes above them in the social scale. His objects in teaching reading are instruction of the mind, discipline of the intellectual powers, cultivation of the imagination, and moral and religious training. In carrying his pupils through a course thus largely conceived, he should not be discouraged by observing that the subject-matter of the more difficult lessons, whether semi-scientific or moral, seems to be quickly forgotten by the pupils. In truth, what is forgotten in the process of learning is often as efficacious an educative agent as what is remembered. A perception of this fact must have prompted Bishop Berkeley's pertinent query, " Whether those parts of learning which are forgotten may not have improved and enriched the soil, like those vegetables which are raised not for themselves, but are ploughed in for a dressing of the land ?"

Nor is the teacher to be discouraged by occasionally finding it difficult to make his pupils fully comprehend the lesson read. Habitually to require pupils to work at the unintelligible is permanently to stunt the mind by obstructing the free action of intelligence. But *never* to demand of them a conscious effort to master difficulties of thought and language is to weaken the intellectual energy. The power of grasping any sequence of thought that has been the subject of a reading-lesson depends of course on the maturity of the learner and his perception of the general relations of the subject to things already thoroughly known by him, and which form the natural props of new knowledge. But we are not to suppose that knowledge which may occasionally transcend the stage of mental development which the pupil has reached, is therefore useless in respect of the mental cultivation which the fresh thoughts give. These thoughts, while adding little to the bulk, may contribute largely to the organic growth of mind. Still more true is this when we have regard to the discipline derivable from the analysis of the language in which the fresh knowledge is conveyed.

A word or two of personal reference to the teacher, bearing on all the work of the school as well as on instruction in reading :—(1.) Let him take up such a position on the school floor with respect to his class as shall insure that each pupil will feel himself addressed by every question and explanation, and that every boy in the class will hear every answer given and every sentence read as distinctly as the teacher himself. This position should not be changed during a lesson. For the concentration of the eyes of the class on the master's face aids the concentration of mind on the subject in hand. (2.) Let him discard the book, both when listening to the reading of the class and when reproducing the general purport of the lesson. (3.) Let him, in all he says, be deliberate, precise, curt, avoiding all talk, and remembering that he is merely the guide and example of *others* who are working. (4.) Let him keep in mind that the more conversational is his tone the more surely does it reach the minds with which he is conversing, and that all loudness is inconsistent with the quiet and calm process of thinking. (5.) Let him attempt little at a time, and do that little *thoroughly*, and this on moral as well as intellectual grounds.[1]

(2.) *Writing* (*Dictation Exercises*).

Of the 113 annually enrolled (on the average) in each of the parochial schools of the three counties, 91 are engaged in learning to write. Writing on paper with pen and ink is usually begun when

[1] I would here guard against its being supposed that by dwelling as I do on common defects, I mean to convey the impression that the schools participating in the Dick Bequest are to any very large extent characterized by these defects. The condition of the schools as to efficiency will be recorded in its proper place.

the pupil is about the age of eight. Copy-books with head-lines are used. As soon as the child is able to form the letters, however, he has been of late years usually exercised in transcribing on his slate, words, lines, and sentences from his reading-lesson, and this exercise is continued throughout the whole school course, in addition to the daily exercise in the copy-book. This slate-writing becomes, in the second highest class, writing from dictation; and in the highest class, the latter exercise is combined with composition exercises. The copy-books used are much more unobjectionable than they used to be in respect of the quality of the paper, while the cheapness of steel pens has put a good instrument within the reach of the poorest. More attention than used to be common is now paid to keeping the pupils to a uniform series of copy-books, thereby securing a certain amount of system and graduation in the successive exercises. Where the teacher is without assistance, the whole school capable of using the pen generally writes at the same hour daily.

On the whole, the Writing of the three counties is very satisfactory in the senior classes. The thing to be regretted with reference to the state of this branch of instruction, is the late age at which children exhibit any proficiency in it. This, however, is not the fault of the teachers so much as of the parents, and of the bad system of charging fees according to the number of subjects taught,—a custom which retards the instruction of the junior classes both in this subject and in arithmetic. The parents seem to imagine that by requiring that only reading and spelling shall be taught to their children for the first two years of their school life, they secure a greater amount of attention to these subjects, both on the part of pupils and teacher, than would be given were writing and arithmetic added; while the separation of the fee for writing from that for reading gives an apparent justification to this delusion, and brings into play the additional argument of economy. The rectification of this is easy, and is gradually being forced on the country by the operation of the Revised Code, which, in this respect, if in no other, will be universally admitted to be correcting a great educational mistake.

That the whole school should be engaged in the writing lesson at one and the same time seems to indicate defective organization, and a badly constructed time-table. But if we bear in mind that the writing lesson is one requiring, quite as much as any other, effective supervision and direction, it will be admitted that, where there are no assistants, this can be secured only by setting the master free for the purpose. Some masters seem to imagine, that with a head-line and pen and ink, instruction in writing will take care of itself, and hence the lessons are frequently almost totally valueless. The slovenly pages, the misspellings, repeated in every successive line, the omission on the part of the pupil to refer his eye back to his model, all reveal to the visitor the view which the teacher takes of this part of his duties. Writing requires to be actively *taught* by the master, especially in the earlier stages and till a good habit is formed, quite as much as any other subject. He should not only vigilantly superintend the writing lesson, but affix a mark to every copy written by the child, and allow places to be taken for this as for other lessons.

These remarks apply to the present method of teaching writing. The more practical method, recommended in the first part of this Report, and to which I would here refer the teacher, requires copy-books specially constructed with a view to its application. The substance of the remarks there made, however, applies to any system, and it is this : Begin children with slate and pencil from the very first day of their entering the school, teaching them to copy printed letters from a wall-sheet or the black-board, until they can read the Primer, and then introduce them to script letters. In this way much time at present utterly wasted in idleness, or in acquiring a distaste for the confinement of school, will be profitably employed ; and when the child, at the age of eight, has pen, ink, and paper given to him, he will be found to be already competent to transcribe the sentences of his lesson-book.

In the chapter on Method I have summed up the object of teaching Writing. If that object be kept in view, dictation exercises will follow transcription and enter very early into the daily round of school work. In connexion with this, let me beg teachers to husband their own strength, and read the words they dictate *only once* to the pupils. Teachers are apt to forget that every lesson, however humble, has a higher than its *apparent* purpose to serve, if rightly taught. If the words are read out only once, the pupils not only get a lesson in writing from dictation, but also in attention and in concentration of mind. If any boy fails to follow, he must leave a blank on his slate at the forgotten word, which blank will of course count an error.

It would be to carry out this Report into superfluous detail to enter upon the many little devices (little, but not petty or unimportant) which suggest themselves to various minds for expeditiously correcting the mistakes of the dictation exercise, and otherwise giving full effect to it. One thing, however, must be specially urged on teachers, and that is, the importance of requiring the pupils, after the mistakes have been pointed out, to go to their seats and write out *several times* correctly the words which they have misspelled, afterwards showing the corrections to the boy or boys who have done the exercise without errors, should the master be too much occupied for the work of revision.

(3.) *Arithmetic.*

Of the 113 annually enrolled (on the average), in each of the parochial schools of the three counties, 71 learn Arithmetic.

Mental calculation generally accompanies the first stage of arithmetical teaching in the three counties. This stage is learning to write the figures from dictation; it is followed by lessons in addition, worked out on the black-board by the master, and afterwards imitated by the pupils on their slates. The pupils, however, begin this branch late, partly for the reasons given in the last chapter; but the result generally is, that, when I visit a school, I find about 13 per cent. of those present ready to work questions in Vulgar Fractions, and in Simple and Double Proportion. Such a result would be quite satisfactory, where the average age is twelve, were the working of questions involving some thought readily done. This, I regret to say, is not the case. In accordance with my conviction that the arithmetic of the people, and of the future student too, should be economic, I consider the power of manipulating questions, which are numerically stated, to be a very poor accomplishment, whether viewed arithmetically, or in its relation to intellectual discipline. So taught, Arithmetic is a very inferior educative agent; taught in a more practical sense, it is one of the most potent.

On this subject I might quote many illustrative passages from my annual Reports, but it will be more to the purpose to give the opinion of Professor Kelland, who accompanied me during a portion of the tour of 1865, and whose experience of the Dick Bequest schools is now very considerable :—

"EDINBURGH, 20 CLARENDON CRESCENT,
July 10, 1865.

"MY DEAR LAURIE,—In the decennial Report to the Trustees of the Dick Bequest, on which you are now engaged, I think it would be well, as was done in the previous Report, to direct attention to the comparative neglect of Arithmetic as a branch of education proper. Arithmetic, as a mere technical art, is indeed more or less imperfectly taught in the schools which have come under my notice, but I have very rarely seen it used as a discipline. In truth, the masters themselves are for the most part unable rapidly and with certainty to think out a process of arithmetic which is not purely mechanical. The tendency of modern education is to sacrifice depth to breadth, and thus the humbler science of arithmetic suffers. In my examinations I have proposed, with little success, both to masters and to scholars, such questions as the following :—

"If by selling at 16s. 6d. a yard you lose 10 per cent. on the outlay, what do you gain or lose per cent. when you sell at 20s. a yard?

"In 1000 ozs. troy how many ozs. avoirdupois?

"Two *equal* wine-glasses are both *filled* with wine and water: in the one the proportion of wine to water is 1 to 4; in the other 1 to 5. When both are poured together into a tumbler what is the proportion of wine to water in the mixture ?

" Surely to think out such problems is more conducive to *education* than to blunder over the elementary rules of Algebra or the Greek alphabet.—Believe me, yours very truly, PHILIP KELLAND."

All that it is necessary to say on the questions of the purpose and method of this branch of study has been already said in the first part of this Report; and I shall only further advert to one or two prevailing defects easy of cure.

(1.) The teaching of Arithmetic should begin earlier than it does, and begin with the ball-frame. In its initiatory still more than its highest form, school arithmetic should be concrete.

(2.) Much greater prominence should be given at every stage to mental arithmetic.

(3.) To teach the simple rules without a previous training in the principles of Notation, and concurrent instruction in the principles of the rules which the pupils are taught to apply, is to make uninteresting, if not stupefying, an exercise which ought to be preeminently attractive and invigorating. It is, moreover, wilfully to forego a large portion of the discipline of the reasoning powers which Arithmetic is supposed to give. A boy, it is true, must work by rules, but he can be safely exercised in and enlightened by principles where these have to do with subjects quite outside himself.

(4.) It follows from the preceding paragraphs that the master should never yield to the temptation of indulging the indolence of his pupils by reading to them, or allowing them to read, figures instead of the numbers which they denote.

(5.) In Arithmetic, accuracy is in a special sense imperative. The pupil must be taught to see, as indeed he cannot help seeing, that the whole process is utterly futile, except in so far as it is accurate. A function of Arithmetic in the school is to teach accuracy, as a function of Language is to teach precision.

(4.) *Music.*

Singing lessons are of comparatively recent introduction into the schools of the three counties. The sol-fa system, affording, as it does, facilities for producing rapid and showy results, is chiefly in favour; but the best singing and the most thorough training are found in those schools which prefer the ordinary notation.

This important and cultivating art is not yet so general in the schools as the Trustees desire that it should be. It is found in only about 20 per cent. of the schools. But I think it may be safely said that it almost always forms a part of the school curriculum, when the master himself is able to sing.

Of one school I report as follows :—

... " Music from notation exceedingly well taught. Six boys, whose age averaged eleven and a half, were prepared to write down the notes of a tune, entirely new to them, when sung once over by the master. I selected a tune, and the result was quite up to the profession. Sacred and secular pieces were very well sung, the children taking parts."

Of another school it is reported :—

" Music from notation carefully and very successfully taught. The children sang at sight a tune (quite new to them) written on the board in the ordinary notation."

Even, however, where Music is pretty successfully taught, its relation to the general routine of the school, and its powerful moral and religious influence in the formation of character, are not yet properly understood. If the pupils can exhibit a song or two, the master too often thinks his work in this department is done. This is a great error. The function of Music is to lighten the labour, cheer the spirits, intensify the sympathy, and instruct the hearts of the children, and, more than this, to harmonize the whole work of the school. Music ought, therefore, like the spirit of religion itself, to permeate the labour of the day. If it did so, it would not fail to sweeten the temper and promote the vivacity of both teacher and taught.

(5.) *Geography.*

Of the 113 scholars annually enrolled (on the average) in each of the parochial schools of the three counties, 52 are returned as receiving instruction in Geography. This is too small a proportion. It is an error to suppose that Geography is a "higher subject." It is, when properly understood, the most "elementary" of all subjects, though not ranking among the indispensable studies.

The general outlines of the Map of the World, and the special *topography* of the British Isles, and of Palestine, are, for the most part, carefully taught in the schools benefiting by the Bequest. There are usually two geography classes, and these receive lessons three times a week. The manufacture, the commercial characteristic, or the historical incidents for which towns are noted, are generally given.

The defects in the teaching are—(1.) The manner in which the children are introduced to the subject. (2.) The presentation of a chart of the world, before the eyes and minds of the children have been familiarized with a sphere. (3.) The almost total omission of physico-industrial geography. (4.) The limited amount of attention given to map-drawing.

To dwell on these points in such a way as to develop fully their importance, would be to repeat what has been already said in another part of this Report in its proper connexion. But the last two defects suggest the further remark, that when Physical Geography is taught, it is almost always taught as a special and advanced department of study. Now, this is entirely to mistake its proper uses in the elementary school. The Physical Geography of the school, as distinct from the science of Physical Geography, is such an account of a country, its position, configuration, soil, and climate, as explains its industries and its people. The very first steps in geographical instruction, therefore, should associate the county or country which is the subject of the lesson with these facts, as being the things mainly worth knowing. Around geographical teaching, so conceived, will naturally gather all that "general information" which the school ought to give, but which might be irrelevant in connexion with any other lesson, and might tend to encourage too discursive a style of teaching.

Of one school the report is to this effect :—

. . . "In geography the highest class made an excellent appearance on Scotland. The way in which physical and industrial and political geography are woven into each other by Mr. ⸻ is creditable both to his intelligence and to his sense of duty in the teaching of this subject."

Of only a few others could so favourable a report be given.

To the apology so frequently made that there is no time for map-drawing, the reply is sufficient that the best schools find time. But if it be desired to avoid the unfavourable criticism on the school organization which is implied in such a reply, the teacher may safely be told to substitute slate map-drawing for one of his oral lessons. The slightest reflection will convince any man that a single attempt (succeeding in the attempt is a matter of secondary moment) to outline a wall-map of Scotland on the slate will do more to fix in the pupil's mind the shape of the country and the relative localities of the principal rivers and towns than four or five oral lessons.

Map-drawing furnishes a fresh illustration of the truth more than once adverted to in the course of this Report, namely, that the best method of teaching any subject is not only the most philosophic, but also the most practical; not only the most sound, but also the most sure and rapid; not only extracting out of the subject to which it is applied the highest discipline which it affords, but contributing, over and above this, to the general discipline of the mind in a manner not always at first view obvious. For in this humble exercise we have all the characteristics which I have enumerated, and the *further* benefit of a discipline of the eye in accuracy of perception, of the hand in neatness and cleanness of execution, and also, to some extent, a training of the sense of the fit, the harmonious, and the lower forms of the beautiful. Teaching the right subject in a right *manner*, according to right methods, and with right aims, is in truth a great art, fruitful in more important results than even those men, whose life-craft it is, imagine.

(6.) *History.*

A succession of names, confused genealogies, dates, causeless and eventless battles,[1] with here and there a dozen lines about a heroic man or deed—such is school History. And even this is given only in a fragmentary form; for the *continuous* record of even

[1] To the *child* "causeless and eventless."

such things is, owing to the shortness of attendance, perused by not more than 20 per cent. of those who read the school manual. It is with the deepest regret that I have to record that the occupation of the senior pupils with this comparatively barren subject has very largely increased in the North within the last four or five years.

To find reading of the scope and character of a school history given to the highest class in a parochial school is to me a great vexation. All the progress made during the past ten years (for there has been visible progress in many things) is more than counterbalanced by the abandonment of the more difficult and thoughtful extracts of an advanced collection for such miserable food; miserable whether we regard its substance, or the language in which it is generally conveyed. A Visitor may, in such circumstances, find much to applaud in the discipline, the religious knowledge, and the whole junior work of the school, but he feels that he has not even the materials afforded him of testing either the knowledge or the intellectual capacity of the senior classes.

(7.) *Grammar and Composition.*

About one half of the pupils attending the parochial schools in the three counties are returned as receiving instruction in English Grammar. There are no special returns under the head of English Composition, but the proportion regularly instructed in this branch cannot fall short of 23 per cent. The grammatical instruction does not *really* reach, in an adequate sense, a larger proportion of the pupils than this.

The pupils learn to distinguish the parts of speech, with the number and gender of nouns, in the second highest class, except in those schools in which pupils remain beyond the age of eleven; in such cases the children of the third highest class are initiated in these elements. In the highest class the declensions of nouns, pronouns, and verbs are learned, and parsing acquired. Parsing means the discrimination and naming of the concords and governments that subsist between the different words of a sentence. The results are, considering the nature of the subject, very fair in the *average* school. In a large number of the schools the highest class show a most thorough acquaintance with the syntax of even involved sentences, such as those of Milton's *Paradise Lost*.

The principal defect found in the teaching of Grammar, according to the above system, is want of accuracy and precision. This defect manifestly vitiates the whole teaching, and renders the subject worse than useless.

In one of my annual reports I find the following remark, which illustrates the all-importance of precision :—

. . . " The importance of grammar for boys and girls lies in this, that it is a valuable exercise of mind in the making of verbal distinctions, and, therefore, cultivates the power of distinguishing in general ; and above all, of distinguishing between things which are objects of reflection (notional) and not merely of external observation."

If the distinctions made cross each other, or are vague and indefinite, parsing is an illusion. Grammatical teaching can have only two possible objects in a parochial school—the discipline of the intellect, the more thorough understanding of reading lessons, or the art of composition. The first is not only not promoted, it is unquestionably retarded, by looseness of definition or the slurring over of difficulties; the second and third are not to be attained by mere parsing, unless it take the form of analysis, and be supported by actual practice in the art of constructing sentences and paragraphs.

It has been said above that the results of grammar teaching are very fair even in the average school. But I would qualify this observation by saying that merely "very fair" results in a subject of this kind are of little practical value, disciplinary or other. Hence the opinion stated in a former part of this Report, that systematic grammatical teaching should be postponed till after the pupil has attained the age of eleven, except so much of it as is necessary to throw light on the speaking and writing of sentences. For this purpose syntactical rules, declensions, etc., are quite unnecessary. The parts of speech are perhaps required, in order to abbreviate explanations and references, but beyond these, the essential knowledge is a knowledge of the elements of a sentence, and of the relationship of principal and subordinate clauses. All of analysis that it is necessary to teach at this stage may be composed in four or five propositions.

The chief requirement is constant practice in oral and written sentence-making.

When pupils remain at school *beyond* the age of eleven, a portion of the time cannot be better spent than in parsing, based on sentence-analysis. But in connexion with this, and as a further indication of the prior claims of Elementary Composition (or Practical Grammar), I can confidently assert that I never yet found thorough and thoughtful parsing which was not based either on some knowledge of Latin, or on a training in the analysis of sentences.

In teaching sentence-analysis, masters are apt to make the great error (the error which pervades almost every department of instruction) of attempting too much, and thereby securing showy quantity instead of thoroughly good quality. The point to keep in view is this, that the sole object of all grammatical analysis as such, and apart from its practical object—composition, is to enable the pupil to perceive the connexion and interdependence of the words and clauses of a sentence, and through this (but unconsciously), of thought. The importance of grammar in this respect, when it is properly taught, is pointed out in the following extract from the annual Reports:—

From Report on —— *School.*

. . . " An examination on the syntax of a piece of poetry which the Visitor selected revealed the intimate connexion which subsists between grammatical teaching (in the sense of elementary analysis) and the comprehension of everything said or written which goes beyond a mere repetition of ordinary peasant talk. If boys have not been trained to the detection of the syntactical relation of the words and clauses of sentences, it is evident that—except where there is a naturally strong intellect, or that cultivation in language and thought which the children of the educated classes unconsciously absorb from day to day—they will utterly fail to find their way through either prose or poetry of which the construction is in the least degree involved. This is nearly equivalent to saying that they will fail to understand the works of our best authors."

To avoid the facile descent to rote-work, which belongs to the subject of grammar as much as to any, although the very conditions of its existence would seem to render rote impossible, pupils should always be required, when parsing, to give in full the definitions and rules which they are presumed to be applying. The master should never assume that they know the "why" of the statements which they so glibly utter. English sentences should be parsed and construed precisely like Latin, in so far as practicable.

Composition.—The schoolmasters, in the very great majority of cases, have of late years acquired the habit of training their highest classes to a kind of *précis*-writing on the slate. This exercise has been much encouraged by me, because it is of great disciplinary and practical value in itself, and at the same time furnishes a standard by which the master may safely measure many of the results of his labours. Grammar, spelling, writing, and general intelligence, are all tested by the power of composing an independent account of the lesson of the day, or of a story read aloud by the master. Moreover, by keeping steadily in view the practical result—Composition, the teacher will be guided as to what he should or should not do in the years of teaching which must precede the attainment of it.

Although the subject of Composition now receives a great deal of attention, some teachers curiously, I had almost said ingeniously, fail, even with the best intentions, to produce any facility in the art worthy of the labour they bestow on it. This comes of the omission to *organize* the course of instruction. As soon as the pupils can write fairly from dictation the teacher at once plunges into narrative composition. He will find the progress made by his pupils much more intelligent, as well as more rapid and assured, if he spend two preliminary months in exercising them in the construction of single sentences, writing on the black-board the words which are to enter into these sentences. By this kind of exercise alone can the boy learn to know what is and what is not a sentence. When he knows this and can apply his knowledge, but not till then, he may be required to write an account of his lesson or of some tale read to him. Meanwhile the habit of *oral composition*, already spoken of in connexion with examination on the lesson of the day, may be formed.

What remains to be said on Grammar and Composition concerns the general object and method of these subjects in their relation to the supreme purpose of the school rather than to the expedients and rules for teaching, and these are treated of in the first part of this Report.

(8.) *Organization.*

The high education of the Northern schoolmasters stands them in good stead in all that concerns the actual work of instruction and of influence on the character of those committed to their charge. This higher education, it is true, cannot supersede the study of Method (except when it is found conjoined with an elevated conception of the purpose of school work and an instinctive sympathetic appreciation of teaching processes), but it is certainly a better qualification for the efficient discharge of even the humblest duties in a parochial school than an empirical knowledge of methods obtained at a Normal College. But when we come to questions affecting school organization, many portions of discipline, and the important small matters of the schoolroom, the advantages of professional training are at once visible. Of Organization especially is this true.

When I first began my visitation, very few teachers in the North had given any thought to this subject. Even classification seemed to be roughly arranged, and the masters did not appear to be sensible of the extent to which grouping and graduation tend to retard or expedite the progress of a school. Still less was all that department of organization, which is represented by the word " time-table," understood. So conspicuous were the shortcomings of the schools in these matters, that many years ago the Trustees issued a circular letter directing attention to them, and enclosing the blank form of a time-table, a copy of which they now require to be sent up along with the annual statistical return. The following is a copy of the letter then issued :—

"EDINBURGH, 18*th May* 1857.

" DEAR SIR,—In the Reports which from time to time have been laid before the Trustees of the Dick Bequest, attention has been directed to the want of adequate organization in many of the schools. There are several teachers, it is true, who display considerable skill in this important department of school-management ; but it may be safely said that the majority do not give that prominence to the subject which it certainly merits, when its bearing on the whole work of the schoolroom is well considered.

" The Trustees have, consequently, instructed me to communicate with you on this subject, and to enclose for your adoption, the skeleton form of a Time-Table, in the belief that the careful filling up of such a Table at the commencement of the summer and winter seasons, and the regulation of your daily work by it, will do much to remove the defect adverted to above, by promoting a more skilful arrangement of classes, and a more methodical distribution of school time than is at present general.

" The Trustees will henceforth require that copies of these Time-Tables be transmitted to them along with the Annual Schedule. They would also recommend that they be suspended in a conspicuous part of the schoolroom.

" By the means which the Trustees now take of drawing your attention to the subject, you will perceive that they understand by organization such a classification of the pupils, according to the development of intelligence, or extent of acquirement, as will confine each to that stage of study, and secure for him *that kind of teaching*, for which he is best fitted, and from which, consequently, he will derive most benefit. You will perceive also, that a well-organized school provides for the occupation of every class, and at all times during the school-hours. In the words of an eminent educationist, ' Every child should always have something to do, and a motive for doing it.' But while each class pursues, as far as may be practicable, an independent course throughout the day, it should be apparent that it forms part of a whole in which unity of purpose and spirit is conspicuous. A too great tension of the pupil's faculties is, no doubt, to be most carefully avoided ; but this can always be done by providing intervals of idleness (which in the case of junior classes should be frequent), whether these are to be spent in the open air, or in the schoolroom with such amusement as pencil and slate can afford." . . .

A large proportion of the teachers did not know how to use the table sent down to them; but being desirous to comply with any request made by the Trustees, they filled it up with an account of the way in which they themselves spent the school hours. Some of those who so misunderstood the object of the Trustees complained, I believe (and from their point of view perhaps justly complained), that the new form was inquisitorial!

The uses of a time-table have been already explained in the first part of this Report, and also the bearing of organization on the attainment of all the objects of the school. - The most practical supplement to what has been there said will be a specimen of a time-table for a school of sixty pupils. The insertion of such a model is by no means superfluous, for, notwithstanding the progress which has been made in many directions, the parochial schools of the North (and the remark is true of all Scotch elementary schools known to me which are not taught by trained teachers) are, so far as I have seen or can learn, very far behind the majority of schools south of the Tweed in respect of organization. I would again urge on masters the importance of this subject. Those who deliberately contemn the *machinery* of their work exhibit by so doing their entire misconception of the means which are available for the attainment of school ends, and it is even doubtful if they understand what those ends are.

T

Daily Time-Table for a School

FORENOON.

HOURS.	CLASS I.	CLASS II.	CLASS III.	Class IV.	CLASS V.	CLASS VI.
10 to 10.25	Not assembled.	Not assembled.	Preparing.	Preparing.	Religious lesson.	Religious lesson.
10.25 to 10.40	Oral religious lesson.	Oral religious lesson.	Writing from dictation under a monitor a verse of the New Testament.	Writing from dictation under a monitor a verse of the New Testament.	Preparing reading lesson.	Preparing reading lesson.
10.40 to 11	Preparing.	Preparing.	Religious lesson.	Religious lesson.	Preparing reading lesson.	Preparing reading lesson.
11 to 11.20	Copying letters and words on slate.	Copying letters and words on slate.	Reading lesson under the master.	Copying out on slate the difficult words of the day's lesson.	Writing.	Writing.
11.20 to 11.40	Reading lesson under master.	Reading lesson under monitor.	Slate exercise on the lesson.	Arithmetic.	Arithmetic.	Arithmetic.
11.40 to 12	Making figures on slate from black board	Making figures on slate from black board.	Arithmetic.	Reading lesson under master.	Arithmetic.	Arithmetic.
12 to 12.15	Reading lesson under monitor.	Reading lesson under master.	Dismiss.	Dismiss.	Dismiss.	Dismiss.
12.15 to 12.40	Dismiss till 2 p.m.	Dismiss till 2 p.m.	Writing, a monitor overlooking.	Writing, a monitor overlooking.	Writing, a monitor overlooking.	Reading lesson under master.
12.45 to 1			Dictation under a monitor.	Dictation under a monitor.	Reading lesson under master.	Slate exercise on reading lesson.

N.B.—The above Table is so constructed as to call for the assistance of a monitor for little more than two hours daily, though, in addition to this, he will be required to see that the transcribing on the slates is carefully and accurately done, and that the errors in the dictation exercises are properly corrected. This amount of aid one of the senior boys will always be ready to give in return for a free education. The work of arranging for each lesson should always be thrown on one of the boys of the class. This saves the master much trouble, and helps to train the boys to independent order. One of the *with an average attendance of* 60.

AFTERNOON.

Hours.	Class I.	Class II.	Class III.	Class IV.	Class V.	Class VI.
2 to 2.20	Preparing.	Preparing.	Lesson in arithmetic by master.	Reading lesson under monitor.	Preparing reading lesson.	Preparing reading lesson.
2.20 to 2.40	Lesson from master.[1]	Copying on slate from black board.	Preparing reading lesson.	Arithmetic.	Dictation under monitor, alternated with geography.	Composition or slate exercise on lesson.
2.40 to 3	Copying on slate from black board.	Reading lesson under master.	Copying a few lines from reading lesson on the slate.	Copying a few lines from reading lesson on the slate.	Arithmetic.	Arithmetic.
3 to 3.15	. . . MUSIC. *Then dismiss Classes I. and II.*					
3.15 to 3.40		....	Arithmetic.	Lesson in arithmetic under master.	Slate exercise on reading lesson.	Arithmetic.
3.40 to 4		....	Reading lesson under monitor.	Copying on slate.	Reading lesson under master.	Map-drawing on slate.
	Dismiss Classes III., IV., V.					
4 to 4.20		....	....	....		Special exercise on the grammar and language of the reading lesson, alternated with a special lesson in the principles of arithmetic or geography.

[1] Ten minutes being given twice a week to object-lessons·

advantages of a table constructed on the above principle is, that it can be worked only where there is great order, quietness, and precision in movement. There are other ways of arranging the work of the school-day, but none, so far as I can see, which secures three reading lessons daily to Classes I. and II., and two reading lessons to Classes III., IV., and V., the Fifth Class being *twice* under the *master's* direct tuition. Latin and Mathematics should be taught from 9 A.M. till 10.

The teacher will of course occasionally depart from the strict order of the time-table, for the purpose of giving prominence to some special department of instruction. The direct moral instruction, for example, is presumed to be given in connexion with the reading and the religious lessons, but the occasional suspension of the work that may be due at a particular hour, for the purpose of explaining some moral duty, of enforcing some point of discipline, or exhibiting some religious truth in its practical bearing, will be frequently found necessary or desirable. Again, a whole afternoon may be devoted occasionally to singing, or to specimens of good reading given by the master himself and his best pupils.

(9.) *Discipline and Minor Morals.*

Discipline, in so far as it means the enforcement of order and of obedience to passing commands, is sufficiently well attained in the schools of the North, and that without the exercise of severity either in language or punishment, save in a few cases. The superiority and dignity of character which belong to men of considerable cultivation suffice to enable the northern masters to obtain unconsciously as much respect for their authority as secures the order and quiet which are essential to the conducting of the school. It is very doubtful, however, whether the masters ever deliberately contemplate discipline and its objects in their relation to the leading purpose of education.

I do not know that there is any school from which corporal chastisement is theoretically excluded; but in the very great majority of schools it is regarded as a last resort. The infliction of bodily pain as a corrective of every petty misdemeanour is to be found only in a few schools.

Of one large school, in which I found very good teaching, I report:—

"Mr. —— stands, with one or two others, at the head of the Bequest, and it is much to his credit to be able to say that the very high results visible in every department are attained without any seeming pressure on the children."

Again, of another school I report:—

"Spite of the very limited accommodation this is a pleasing, busy, and orderly school. The master is kindly towards his pupils, and there is a freedom and a naturalness about the children which it is always gratifying to see when the master can prevent these characteristics degenerating into license."

Similar testimony might be borne to effective discipline, accompanied with gentleness, in very many cases. Of one successful teacher, on the contrary, I report:—

"He owes everything to energy, and is destitute of that gentleness and sympathy which, when combined with firmness, tell more powerfully on a school than intellect, energy, and methods combined."[1]

---

[1] The two kinds of school discipline are well illustrated by Dr. Morell in his Report for 1857: "In the Stockport and Draylesden schools *equally* the order is *rigid;* the discipline maintained with the utmost

Where a teacher, without exercising severity, has educated his pupils to general obedience and to honest and independent work, he has done much.[1] There are, however, objects of discipline higher than these, which can be attained only where there is a deliberate purpose to attain them, and a well-considered method of working out that purpose. These objects are the cultivation of moral habits, by means of the lessons of the day, and the vigilant regulation (without espionage) of the mutual intercourse of the pupils. Nor will apt opportunities be wanting of informing the mind with Religious principles, and subjecting the will to motives which transcend mere justice, honesty, and courtesy. The purposes of discipline and the indirect moral teaching which it gives have been dwelt upon elsewhere : my

exactitude ; the spirit pervading the whole of the classes, one in which subordination, carefulness, and systematic instruction are steadily *enforced*, not harshly indeed, but with stringent regularity : and the result of all this is seen in the *uniform progress* of the children through all the classes, and in the mechanical perfection of the details. In the school I am now referring to a different system is pursued ; the order, at least in appearance, is not so strict ; the mechanical details are not so perfect ; the gradations from class to class not so uniform. But in place of this there is a peculiarly friendly relation established between the teacher and the children, which, while it does not interfere with the necessity of *his will* being the law of the school, puts less restraint on the pupils, and renders their mental development more free and natural. Hence, while on the one hand you have perhaps less *measurable* progress, you secure more personal influence, more action on the feelings and dispositions of the mass of the scholars, and probably more direct moral effect."

[1] Mr. Middleton, in his Report for 1865, says with truth : " The *morale* of a school is very high indeed when the children are quiet, and do their written work honestly, and their oral work without prompting, and where the teacher can be safely trusted to read the set dictation to one class while the inspector is dictating arithmetic to another."

wish here is to point out the fact that in its higher meaning, Discipline does not seem to be a distinct and specific object of thought or method to the great majority of parochial teachers.

The defective view generally taken of the larger objects of discipline shows itself in all that has to do with the petty moralities of the school. Politeness and cleanliness are not insisted on, and the moral influence of such arrangements in the school as please the eye is generally ignored by the master. The sense of the beautiful, even in those lower manifestations which we call order, propriety, fitness, and decency, is closely allied with moral perceptions. Hence the moral suggestiveness of good external arrangements, and their influence in promoting the higher objects of the school: they extend to the poorer classes the refinements of civilisation, and make them sharers to some small extent in the higher quality of mind from which those refinements spring. Well-lighted, well-ventilated, well-cleaned, well-arranged schoolrooms, are not only the best external aids to the mere doing of the day's work: they are also moral agencies.

Nor is it beneath the dignity of the subject to class among these agencies the teacher's own clothing, and personal habits. These tell on the minor moralities of the school quite as powerfully as the habits of will and the manners which he is hourly exhibiting tell on the growth of character in his pupils.

It is not necessary again to refer to the relations

of courtesy between the sexes, as these have been spoken of at sufficient length in the first part of this Report.[1]

(10.) *Direct Moral Instruction.*

Direct moral instruction is conveyed in the schools of the North by the censure of faults and offences as they arise, and by the enforcement of the moral lessons which occur in the reading-books and in the Bible.

This is not enough: it seems to me that a master should draw out for himself a scheme of school-moralities, to be taught in their proper order and completeness. The inculcation of truthfulness, honesty, integrity, justice, love, in the ever-varying forms which they assume, should be deliberately set down by every teacher as part of his round of work, and should be designedly presented again and again to the pupils in the various forms of parable, biography, and precept. It is probable that boys who go through a full parochial school curriculum obtain from their Catechism, Bible, and reading-books, in an irregular and haphazard way, such a course of instruction in morality as I have indicated. But this would certainly be more effectively given if, when any moral question incidentally arose in the course of other work, it was recognised by the

[1] See Mr. Matthew Arnold's Reports to the Privy Council for 1860 and 1861.

master, and felt by the pupil to stand out from the other topics preceding and following it, as a matter of super-eminent importance. This can happen only where all such incidental teachings form part of a pre-arranged scheme of moral instruction. The pupil should, of course, be kept in ignorance of any such formal scheme; but the master, by working in accordance with a pre-conceived purpose, would be led to give more weight and prominence to casual lessons, and thereby to lay on the minds of his pupils a deeper impression of the vital importance of the truths he might from time to time expound or enforce. Such carefully devised and elaborated plans of moral teaching are perhaps less necessary among the teachers of the three north-eastern counties than elsewhere, because they are all men of superior education; men, moreover, who, in the majority of cases, have added a theological to an Arts university curriculum. Accordingly, the matured and grave character of the master, his settled conclusions, and consequently his high and decided (though possibly curt) manner of handling all moral questions, to a large extent attain the ends of teaching quite as surely as these could be attained through the methodical and deliberate inculcation of a complete circle of moral duties by a man less highly qualified. This fact, however, does not weaken my position with regard to the importance of organizing and methodizing moral instruction in parochial schools.

Further, it is the teacher's business, as has been

shown in the first part of this Report, to give those pupils who stay sufficiently long with him, detailed instruction in the bearing of the moral law on those habits of daily life which are in constant variance with it. I refer to the bearing of morality on health and the means of preserving it, on economy, foresight, manly independence, filial as well as paternal responsibilities, and so forth. These things are not attended to in our schools, and consequently are not understood by the lower strata of the population outside the school.

(11.) *Direct Religious Instruction.*

Direct Religious teaching is given on the basis of the earlier books of the Old Testament, the New Testament, and the Shorter Catechism, in all the schools visited. It is, however, a mistake to suppose, as some seem to do, that in the introduction of certain portions of religious teaching, no regard is had in Scotland to the age and advancement of the pupils. Children under eight years of age receive only occasional oral religious instruction originated by the master, or suggested by the reading-books[1] used in the elementary classes. About the age of eight or nine years they begin to read the New Testament, and to be examined on the chapter of the day.

[1] This practice shows the importance of giving religious lessons in the earlier books of a reading series.

About the same age, speaking generally, they begin to learn by heart the Shorter Catechism, continuing to repeat and revise it during their whole future attendance at school, sometimes adding the Scripture "proofs" of the answers. In some cases the "Mother's Catechism" precedes the Shorter. After the child has spent about a year, or it may be more, in reading the New Testament, he is introduced to the Old Testament, and the rest of his school time is spent in perusing and reperusing the earlier books. The two highest English classes are generally united in the reading of the Old Testament, and receive instruction together. This united class is called the "Bible" class, for by "the Bible" both schoolmasters and pupils colloquially mean the Old Testament only. The principal religious lesson of the day is given immediately after the opening of morning school, the day's work being begun with prayer, and sometimes also with praise. These exercises and the religious lesson together occupy from thirty to forty-five minutes.

The result of all this is that the upper classes are well informed in the earlier half of the Old Testament history, and are familiar with the Shorter Catechism. So far as Old Testament historical and also general dogmatic religious knowledge are concerned, the state of the northern schools is quite satisfactory.

But while saying thus much in the way of well-merited laudation, I must add some words of censure. And first, with respect to the *historical* knowledge :—

I found when I first undertook the work of Visitor, that, in very many of the schools, the highest classes, while armed at all points with early Old Testament history, were ignorant of the more important facts and truths of the Gospels. Accordingly, for a time, I assiduously set myself to assume that the Old Testament narrative was familiar, and to examine exclusively in the life, parables, and acts of our Saviour. It might be supposed that, as the reading of the New Testament had preceded that of the Old, the pupils would be sufficiently familiar with the story of the Gospels. This, however, was not the case. On the contrary, the ignorance found in very many schools was inexcusable. It was grievous to think that the boys and girls before me were passing out of the school into the world with only a dim and fragmentary knowledge of the life and teaching of the Saviour, and even that knowledge, such as it was, intimately associated with the laborious spelling-out of lessons some two years before the termination of their school course: nor was it any consolation to find that the same children were impregnable in an examination on the Creation, the Fall, and the Exodus. This defect is to a large extent removed; but it is still necessary to urge on many of the masters attention to the fact that the period of school attendance is limited, and that, consequently, in the inculcation of Bible facts and truths they are bound in duty to make a *selection*. Their power in this matter of religious teaching is very great, and lays on them the most solemn responsibility. No man indeed, fired with the zeal of a true teacher, can think, without a certain awe, of his opportunities of giving a permanent direction to the religious current of the minds under his charge. But if the master do not familiarize the child's mind with the solemn narrative of the life of Christ from birth to death, if he do not store his memory with those divine sayings which will be his best guide and consolation through life, and with the devotional utterances of such of the psalms as are best adapted to youthful comprehension; and further, if he do not make all this the basis of the Christian teaching, he foregoes his opportunities and misdirects his influence.

Again, exception has to be taken to the lateness of the age at which it is usual to begin religious teaching. The oral instruction which precedes the reading of the New Testament is, in the majority of schools, so far as I can discover, of the most desultory and capricious kind. Now it is the teacher's duty to *organize and methodize his instructions* in religion, and to provide milk for the babes as well as stronger meat for the maturer minds of the school. So far from dealing perfunctorily with the religious instruction of the infant classes, the master should direct his chief efforts towards them, labouring to simplify truths and to adapt them to their childlike conceptions. The elevating, purifying, and harmonizing ideas of Christian truth, should be early infused into a child's mind, that they may grow there with his growth and strengthen with his strength, and thereby become, unawares, a constituent part of himself. They should possess him, not he them. It is only by thus pre-occupying the infant mind at the most impressible period of its life, that religion can be woven into the character, and that a religious people can be reared. Hence the infinite importance of a more thorough religious training of the infant classes—a training so thorough as perhaps to be possible only through the agency of separate infant and initiatory departments, under the management of qualified Female teachers.

What has been now said, if read in conjunction with what has been written in the first part of this Report on the subject of Methods, makes it unnecessary to refer at greater length to the religious teaching of the schools.

The substance and method of the religious teaching are open to the objections which have been stated. But these objections I should almost have been disposed to refrain from stating, had I been able to report favourably on the *manner* of the religious teaching. The younger the pupil the greater is the influence of the *manner* (as opposed to the matter) of instruction. Pre-eminently is this true in the department of religion. A manner in discord with the gentleness, the love, the holiness, the purity, and the loftiness of the sacred theme, degrades and perverts the teaching. The sentiments of love, awe, devotion, purity, are the bases on which must repose the superstructure of divine truth, and these will hardly manifest their life, except as a reflection of what is seen by the child in another. It is therefore of the greatest moment that every word and act bearing directly or indirectly on religious topics should be uttered and done with an appropriate outward manner, if the religious instruction is to be enforced and supported, instead of being debased and subverted, by the associations along with which it is first presented to the mind of the young.

What is true of the manner of the master is equally applicable to the external circumstances in which religious teaching is given. The subject should be surrounded with an atmosphere of calmness, coolness, and order. In the words of my predecessor in office, "the sacredness of the [religious] lesson requires every attainable protection."

Finally, I have already, in the chapter on Method, stated the use which should be made of the Bible in religious instruction. It is happily no longer used for purposes of spelling and grammar. But until it shall have ceased to receive prominence as a *reading-lesson* book, Scripture instruction will never be placed on a perfectly satisfactory footing.

(12.) *The Higher Instruction of the Parochial Schools.*

English Composition—Latin- Greek —Mathematics.

English Composition is now introduced into all the schools of the three counties, and taught with considerable success. In many cases the results are admirable. It would be superfluous to add to the observations already made on this subject under the head of Grammar (p. 281) and in the first part of this Report. Up to a certain point it is an elementary subject; beyond this it belongs to the higher intellectual instruction.

The centesimal proportion of pupils learning Latin in the northern counties is 6·7; Greek, 1·5. The results in these departments are, on the whole, good. Greater attention to thoroughness and precision in translating from Latin and Greek into English, and the introduction of verse-making, would, it seems to me, be an improvement, whether we look to the attainment of sound scholarship or the mental discipline afforded by the classical languages. The rendering of English into Latin, in the sense in which schoolboys perform this exercise, demands certainly discrimination in applying the rules of syntax, and is a valuable training in exactness of habit, but, beyond this, it is an exercise of memory more than of intellect. The converse process, on the other hand, is an exercise almost solely of intellect. Latin verse-writing has special claims of its own to cultivation, and might be safely permitted to share the ground at present occupied by Latin prose.

The number of Greek pupils has not largely increased during the past ten years, but the extent to which the language is studied is considerably greater. The boys of the senior Greek classes exhibit, for the most part, considerable familiarity with the language of the Anabasis and with Arnold's First Greek Prose Composition : they frequently also profess portions of the Iliad and the New Testament.

By Mathematics is understood Mensuration—which is taught during the winter months to farm lads, who generally may be found clustered in a remote corner of the schoolroom—the first three Books of Euclid, and Algebra to Quadratic Equations inclusive. The latter branches are seldom attempted except by those boys who are destined for the University.

Lest, however, any general reader should imagine that this somewhat high-sounding phrase, " destined for the University," implies the possession by those so destined of shoes and stockings, it may be as well to say at once that it does not do so. To be *on* the parish poor-roll and *in* Virgil are not always incompatible. The parish schools afford a sound elementary classical education to all without distinction, who give any indication of superior talent. In the north-east of Scotland, if nowhere else, the pathway to learning and eminence is not only theoretically, but *practically*, open to the poorest. A free education (for the parochial schoolmasters of Scotland never boggle about fees in the case either of the clever or *the poor*), embracing Latin, Greek, and Mathematics, is at the door of every boy endowed by nature with a capacity for a higher sphere of activity than that in which he has had the accident of being born. This peculiarity of the Scotch system is one to be jealously guarded.

Many specimens might be quoted of schools in which the higher branches are well taught and which are at once elementary and middle schools of the old Scotch parochial type. In one of many similar reports I find the following remarks on one of these schools, which may be fairly accepted as representing many others:—

... " One-fourth of the pupils present worked questions in simple proportion, double proportion, and fractions, readily and accurately.

" Two boys were engaged with algebra, and showed a very fair knowledge of equations.

" Six boys in Cæsar made an excellent appearance throughout.

" One boy in Livy and the Anabasis of Xenophon was very promising.

" Two girls in French translated well."

It is commonly averred that the proportion of Latin pupils in the parish schools of Scotland generally is smaller than it used to be, and that this is attributable to the inability of the new race of schoolmasters to give the required instruction. I have taken some trouble to inquire into the accuracy of these statements, and on comparing the Return which I take up annually for the Education Committee of the Church of Scotland, with older documents, I find that in the three north-eastern counties Latin is much more extensively taught than it was thirty-five years ago, and Greek more extensively.

The centesimal proportion of pupils learning Latin in the three north-eastern counties is, as before stated, 6·7, and learning Greek 1·5 ;[1] in the rest of Scotland the proportion is, learning Latin about 4, and learning Greek, about one-half per cent. It does not appear that the number learning Greek in the parish schools was at any time greater throughout Scotland than it is now, but those learning Latin seem to have numbered about 6 per cent. of all the scholars. There is here therefore a falling off, as regards the country at large; but great as is the falling off in respect of quantity, the deterioration of the quality of the Latin professed in landward parishes (the north-eastern counties excepted) is doubtless much greater. The falling off in respect of scholars is quite adequately accounted for by the facilities which railways afford —(1.) For obtaining for the clever sons of peasants, small farmers, and petty tradesmen, remunerative occupation as attractive to the common mind as the Ministry; (2.) For obtaining a higher education in

[1] On page 348 the table shows an increase of classical scholars in the north.

some of the great centres of population than the parochial school ever at any time provided for boys of the middle and upper classes. It seems to me that higher qualifications in the teachers would not have materially arrested the operation of these two causes, and that in the course of another decade, a considerable reduction in the numbers learning Latin will have to be reported, even in the districts for which the Dick Bequest is intended, where the masters are unquestionably more highly qualified for teaching the higher branches than any other class of Scotch schoolmasters, past or present.

With regard to the qualification of the new race of schoolmasters for giving the higher instruction, and the influence of the Privy Council on it, it will be universally admitted, that while the *general* qualifications of the teacher, whether we regard the knowledge he professes or the training he receives, have been very much raised under the influence of the Government Minutes, his special qualification as a teacher of Latin and Greek has been lowered. This result is the necessary consequence of the Normal School programme of study, which is arranged by Government with a view to the educational wants of England, and then, without inquiry, applied to Scotland. Nor is it probable that any plan of training teachers can ever be devised, even under more favourable circumstances as regards the central administration, which will be suited in all respects to the requirements of Scotch parishes, so long as our Universities are ignored as schools for teachers, and left outside the machinery employed for producing them.

This brings me naturally to speak more explicitly than I have yet done of the class of teachers who occupy the parochial schools in the north-eastern counties which benefit by the Bequest.

CHAPTER VIII.

THE CLASS OF PAROCHIAL TEACHERS IN ABERDEEN, BANFF, AND MORAY.

THE teachers of the north-eastern counties are almost without exception graduates of the University of Aberdeen, and four-fifths of them are licentiates in theology. Only a very small proportion are excluded from participation in the Dick Bequest in consequence of failure to pass the examination of the Trustees. These facts guarantee not only the solid acquirements of the teachers, but, which is of more importance, an elevation and solidity of moral and intellectual character, which are of inestimable value in attaining the true ends of the school. Those schoolmasters who have received their preparation for their work in our Normal Colleges certainly exhibit, in the very first year of their professional life, a capacity for organization, a knowledge of good methods, and a skill in teaching, which University men attain only after many years of conscientious labour. Nor, indeed, save in a few exceptional cases, do the latter ever come to a full appreciation of the ways and means and the important little things of the schoolroom. This is a defect which can be cured only by the careful study of teaching as an art resting on philosophic principles, and upon the critical observation of the organization and methods of model schools. But, on the other hand, the University men not only bring higher accomplishments and more disciplined powers to the work of the school; they also bring that force of character which tends to reproduce itself in those committed to their care. Accordingly, although in certain respects the Normal teacher cannot fail to excel his less skilful competitor from the University, he falls very far short of him in training the young to thoughtfulness and intensity of character. Now it is precisely this result which has in the past been, and still is, the peculiar and distinguishing feature of the Scotch parochial school, and this frequently to the detriment of technical facility in reading, writing, and arithmetic, and almost always to the comparative neglect of the junior classes. These technical accomplishments it is the teacher's duty to give, nor can any pretext of cultivating the intellect exempt him from the thorough discharge of that duty, and from laying strong and broad in the junior classes the substructure on which higher profession must rest, if it be sound. But while it is comparatively an easy matter for the University-trained teacher to adapt his powers to the discharge of this duty, or to the attainment of any desired result in the school, whether of method or acquirement, the higher discipline which almost unconsciously flows from him is quite beyond the reach of the more shallow product of the Government Training College. The curriculum laid down for our Normal Schools embraces subjects so multifarious, and calling so largely on the mere cramming power of the student, that they divert him from the close pursuit of any one subject involving a thorough intellectual discipline. The consequence is that the students leave the Colleges with minds very inadequately trained, in the larger sense of the word,—full of facts and figures, but wanting that firm hold of either language or mathematics which will insure the further prosecution of these subjects, and which tends to give the student that solidity of intellect which thorough acquirement in any one direction scarcely ever fails to confer. Coming to the Training College after having exercised premature authority as pupil-teachers, and already by anticipation revealing some of the less attractive features of their profession, the Normal students too often leave it, we fear, confirmed in their self-esteem ; and this, partly because their intellectual horizon is diligently confined by a Government programme which does not admit of a liberal discipline. Now, it stands to reason that a lad who has to fight his way to the University gives a guarantee in that very fact that he possesses *moral* qualifications for the work of a teacher, which must be altogether wanting in the young man who, from the age of thirteen, has been the *protégé* of the Government, whose every step has been made easy, and for whom perfect security has at every stage been carefully insured, as if by a paternal hand. The atmosphere, moreover, into which the former has successfully fought his way is much healthier than that which can be breathed in a Seminary purely professional in its aims. In a University, the whole circle of knowledge is being continually suggested to the most obtuse ; a consciousness of ignorance and of partial views is in this way pressed on the student ; and the training thus unconsciously given, even when little visible work is done, is of a higher kind than can be gained from the most faithful acquisition of facts in a regulation college. Again, the influence of great names in the several departments of thought, and friendly intercourse with young men of different classes in society and having diverse predilections and pursuits, have, in a University, free room to act in the formation of character. There are, besides, the purely intellectual advantages which flow from the deeper study of one or two important subjects, and from the higher University ideal continually held before the student. These various influences cannot fail to result in a more liberal cultivation, and in that deeper reverence and finer *morale* which (except in singularly coarse natures) accompany cultivation, and which are notoriously wanting in the mass of students who leave our Normal Colleges—qualities not to be lightly esteemed in those who are to leave their mark on the youth of the country.

That high intellectual qualifications unfit men for the humblest elementary work of the school is contrary to fact. The neglect of junior classes by schoolmasters is to be ascribed to an unsympathetic nature, mistaken methods, or a lax conscience, not to excess of intellectual endowment. Of twenty-one teachers who at present hold marks for special distinction in scholarship, only two have failed in the north-eastern counties to attain average efficiency as schoolmasters, while fourteen outstrip the mass of their fellow-teachers. Indeed, it may be safely predicted that the highest scholarship and the most effective school-keeping will be found to go together.

It is commonly urged as an objection inherent in the arrangements which secure for the North such high-class schoolmasters, that a very small proportion regard the school in any other light than as a stepping-stone to the pulpit. That nine-tenths of the graduates appointed to parochial schools regard the work of teaching as a merely temporary avocation, and certain to lead to preferment in the Church, is true, and has been so far recognised by the Dick Trustees that they have modified their regulations so as to admit of the winter absence of teachers at the Theological Hall where they go in order to complete their studies for the ministry. After some fluctuation of opinion, my conviction is that the system is, in the present and past circumstances of parochial education, a good one; and for this reason, that even the high emoluments attached to the schools in the three counties would not, but for the collateral advantage of a prospect of Church preferment, secure teachers so well educated as those who now offer themselves for every vacancy. Doubtless, were there an organized system of schools of different grades throughout Scotland, which might furnish a career of progress to elementary schoolmasters (and without this career the occupation will never probably take rank in the eye of the vulgar as a profession),[1] the inducement to become parochial schoolmasters would be provided in a more legitimate way than at present: but until such inducement is provided, those interested in education must gladly accept the aid which the Church indirectly lends to the school. It is to be feared, however, that the practice of using the school as an avenue to the pulpit would end in gross abuses were there no inspection of the parochial schools, outside, and apart from, the various interests involved.[2]

[1] A properly organized system of middle or grammar schools in Scotland would directly elevate the parochial schools by holding out inducements to enter the teaching profession.

[2] In Appendix V. will be found a list of the teachers of the three counties, extending over the last ten years, which contains the names of those who have died during that period, and shows the occupations to which those betook themselves who demitted office, in so far as these can be ascertained.

CHAPTER IX.

PRESENT STATE OF THE SCHOOLS—CLASSIFICATION—
CHIEF DEFECTS IN RESPECT OF RESULTS—PROGRESS
MADE DURING THE LAST TEN YEARS.

UNDER the various heads of school-work I have animadverted on defects in method still prevalent in the North (and probably to a greater extent elsewhere). These defects are not to be regarded by the Trustees as universal. With the best schools no fault can be found, and of the great majority I can report in favourable terms. It is true that the methods of teaching followed are not always, nor perhaps generally, such as contribute most to the development of the intelligence, nor the discipline always such as promotes most surely the formation of good moral habits : but, in the majority of cases, the results, both technical, intellectual, and moral, are such as to merit commendation. This cannot, however, be said of the Religious instruction. Inadequate methods, where there is industry and resolution, may produce satisfactory results in all matters that have to do with the imparting of a certain amount of knowledge, or the producing of a certain quantity of intellectual power ; but when our object is to produce a certain *state of mind*, method is in the school all in all. Looking merely to the amount and accuracy of the scriptural and catechetical knowledge of the *highest* classes in the schools, I should say that no subject was better taught than religion. But while in previous parts of this Report full value has been assigned to this the historical portion of the religious work of the school, and a solid argument has been furnished in favour of the somewhat premature acquisition of abstract dogmatic religious propositions, the infinite importance of method and manner in religious training has been dwelt upon with more than usual emphasis.

When, to the defective method of religious instruction are added the want of method in teaching geography, inattention to the arithmetic (especially the mental arithmetic) of junior classes, and the neglect of deliberateness, emphasis, and expression in reading (which in other respects is good), the *principal* defects at present to be found in the parochial schools of the three counties have been exhausted.

Terms of praise or blame are, however, so vague, and have such varying values attached to them, that general commendation or general censure conveys little information; and I shall therefore classify the schools of the Bequest under the heads of *Inferior, Fair, Good, Very Good,* and *Excellent,* first quoting from the annual Reports to the Trustees examples of schools belonging to each of these classes. I take almost the first which come under my eye in opening a volume of the manuscript Reports.

I. *Extracts from Reports on "Inferior" Schools.*

(1.) " The decline of numbers here is not satisfactorily explained by the number of other schools in the parish. The master is a man of narrow, shallow nature, without breadth or depth, or imagination or sympathy ; cutting, keen, quick, and hard ; short-tempered, and more likely to confirm than to remove stupidity in his pupils. On the occasion of my first visit, I remarked these defects of character, but recommended admission to participation, although the results were precisely similar to those ascertained to-day, because I saw that the teacher was (as he is) really working, and I hoped that he would soon succeed in securing better results, both moral and intellectual. I have been disappointed. The school is stereotyped, and I doubt its ever being much better than it is while in Mr. ———'s hands.

" The highest class (8) read from a History of England very fairly but with exceeding monotony. No grammar or composition professed.

" Writing from dictation professed only to the extent of monosyllables.

" Knowledge of words very fair."

(2.) " The third class (8) was on the floor when I entered, and read, with the exception of three, fairly from the third of the Irish Series. When examined they made little or no response. I doubt their being regularly examined, although the master assured me they were.

" Two, composing the second class, read badly, but they had newly come.

" The highest class (5) read very monotonously, but with sufficient fluency, from a History of England. They exhibited, when examined by me, great ignorance of the signification of words. Parsing very bad. Composition not practised, and writing from dictation poor.

" The reading of the fourth class from Constable's second book was fair. Spelling scarcely fair ; the class is not thoroughly taught one lesson before proceeding to the next.

"In arithmetic five professed proportion, and worked inaccurately and stupidly.

"The Bible class (19) were examined in the master's singularly sleepy way, on the first five chapters of St. Luke, but only a few followed him.

"Writing fair.

"I have been very patient with Mr. ———, encouraging him from year to year, and taking the most lenient view of his school-work, but it is impossible, in justice to the other teachers of the counties, and to the children of ———, to connive longer at the continuance of such an incubus on the parish as Mr. ———. He is young, but lifeless; destitute of the will to do. I consider his to be a quite hopeless case. Had not great pains been taken with him, and every chance given him in vain, it might seem harsh to recommend, as I now do, that he be cut off from the Bequest altogether, until a future visit shall reveal progress. [He is an assistant-substitute.]

II. *Extracts from Reports on " Fair" Schools.*

(1.) " This school is taught by a man of very humble acquirements and capacity, but distinguished by a strong sense of duty, and a power of applying himself assiduously to his work.

"The highest class (4) read from *Robinson Crusoe* fluently. Knowledge of words moderate. Parsing not worth mentioning ; but in winter this subject is carried much further. Writing from dictation very fair.

"The second class (5) read from the fifth Progressive Reader fluently, but monotonously.

"The master examines with care. The pupils have the expression of children honestly taught. Though slow, they are fairly intelligent and perfectly well disposed towards their work. Writing from dictation very fair.

"The Bible class made a good appearance on the first seven chapters of Judges.

"Writing fair.

"In arithmetic two in proportion worked well.

"I directed Mr. ———'s attention to more distinct enunciation in reading, and to the earlier introduction of slates and writing."

The following is a Report on a School which was found to have declined from "Good" to "Fair," if not to "Inferior."

(2.) " My last two visits to this school made me doubt Mr. ———'s claims to a continuance on the merit scale; but the excuse in 186— was so good . . . that I reported the circumstance, and recommended only a slight reduction of Mr. ———'s merit marks. As there was no excuse offered to-day it seemed desirable to sift the school thoroughly, and every class was accordingly minutely examined. I kept the master by me, and brought out the results *through* himself. The process only very slightly annoyed his great good-nature.

" The highest class (7) read a piece of poetry (Macaulay's *Armada*) very well. Intelligence good. The master examined in parsing very skilfully, by bringing out answers *suggested* by himself —*apparently* responded to by the whole class, but in reality only by one boy and partially by a second. I stopped this, and made him examine each boy individually, that he himself might distinctly see that only one boy knew anything about grammar. He examines so well, and becomes so interested in his subject and unconscious of his audience, that probably he is not aware that he puts answers into the mouths of his pupils.

" Composition scarcely fair.

" The second class (7) read monotonously, but very fairly, considering the difficulty of the book. I pointed out to the teacher that the pupils of this class were not at all fitted for the book which they were reading—the fourth of the Irish Series. The master examined, as usual, extremely well (apparently) on the meaning of the words and sentences, sustaining the attention of the children and moving on in a smooth flow of well-connected questions and clear explanations, but wilfully or unconsciously blind to the fact that not a single child could answer a question. He willingly accepted such answers as he himself suggested from the class *as a whole*,—an old vice of his, to which his attention has several times been called.

" Writing from dictation professed by only two of this class, and badly done.

" The same process was gone through with the third class (16), attended by the same results, with this difference, that the reading was bad, the book being very much too difficult,—the fifth of the Irish Series. This class did not practise copying on their slates from their books.

" In geography an elaborate examination on the world was gone through, but only three really answered the questions, the rest of the class ignorantly chiming in.

" Ten professed proportion, but only four were correct, and all were slow.

" The religious knowledge of the school is very good, and the writing very good.

" These two last points, and the good moral tone of the school and excellent character of the master, relieve somewhat the gloomy picture drawn above.

" I spoke at length to the master on the defects of his school, and I fear (though my remarks were well received) that it will be necessary, while striking off his merit marks, at the same time to inform him that still further reductions await him if grammar, composition, writing from dictation, and arithmetic, are not more fully taught, and if greater care is not exercised in putting books into the children's hands for which they are really fitted."

III. *Extract from a Report on a " Good" School.*

" I found here three Latin classes and one Greek class. I examined the Greek and the second highest Latin class, and found both subjects well taught. The teacher has an unclean and rough aspect, and on first entering, an unfavourable impression is consequently made on the Visitor, but a careful examination reveals very satisfactory results.

" The highest class (10) read, from the fifth of the Scottish Series, fluently and accurately. They gave evidence that they read with understanding, and displayed great attention under examination. Six members of this class could parse well, and had begun analysis. The same wrote well from dictation. Etymology is taught.

" I was glad to find that slate-writing was begun at a very early stage, and I had specimens shown me of the morning's work. Next visit I expect to see the good effects of this, and to find composition as well done by the highest class as dictation now is, and more advanced dictation in the second class.

"The writing of the whole school is clean and pretty good.

"In arithmetic five professed proportion, but though they worked readily and with accuracy, as regards processes, they did not exercise that thoughtfulness necessary to secure an accurate answer.

"The second geography class had a very satisfactory knowledge of general geography.

"The first and second classes united made a good appearance when examined on the Gospel of St. Luke.

"The reading of the second class was, like the first, fluent and accurate, and characterized by considerable intelligence.

"On the whole, this school is a very satisfactory one, though not brilliant in its results, or effective to the eye in its organization, discipline, and general arrangements. I think the teacher deserves 100 for merit."

IV. *Extracts from Reports on "Very Good" Schools.*

(1.) "Mr. —— has always been distinguished for the simplicity and good-humour, combined with intelligence and thoughtfulness, which pervade his school.

"The highest class (8) read from the first Book of Milton exceedingly well, not only with accuracy but with as much expression and seeming perception of the meaning, as if they had been grown men. Knowledge of grammar most thorough. Composition very good.

"The second class (19) read from the fourth of the Irish Series very distinctly. Intelligence carefully developed in connexion with the subject-matter of the lesson and signification of words brought out in a common-sense way. Parsing intelligent as far as it went.

"The same remarks apply to the third class.

"Writing from dictation good.

"Writing very good.

"In arithmetic twenty professed proportion and worked very well.

"In Latin two boys translated and parsed well from Virgil. The same boys were reading Xenophon's Anabasis.

" The organization and discipline are very good. The spirit of willing work pervades the whole school, and *every* child gives and receives attention.

" Mr. —— continues fully to deserve his high position on the merit scale, and even a further increase of marks."

(2.) " The highest class (8) read distinctly and fluently from a history of England. Grammar exceedingly good. Knowledge of words excellent. Composition good.

" The second class (12) read from the fourth of the Irish Series very fairly. Copying from the book on the slate practised by this class. The master is a careful, and with the junior classes, a kindly and not unsuccessful examiner. There can be no doubt that no labour is so gratefully responded to, and none so fruitful in its results, as that expended in conversationally exercising the intelligence of young children.

" The third and fourth classes made a better appearance than the second, reading well from the third of the Irish Series, and having a good knowledge of words and of the lesson read.

" In arithmetic seven worked proportion thoughtfully, and in the the main, accurately.

" The Bible-class answered well when examined on the leading points of the Jewish history.

" Writing exceedingly good.

" One boy was examined by me in Livy, and was thoroughly grounded.

" The same boy translated a few sentences of the Anabasis with facility, and made an excellent appearance in turning a piece of simple English into Greek."

V. *Extracts from Reports on " Excellent" Schools.*

(1.) "A visit to this school was not properly due, nor do I pretend on this occasion to have inspected it, but as I had to pass the door, and understood that Latin and mathematics were now introduced, I called for the purpose of learning the state of these branches.

"Nothing could be more satisfactory. Of eight boys reading Cæsar (six of them peasants' sons, and under twelve years of age), it would be impossible to say which displayed most intelligence, zeal, and thoroughness of knowledge. I could not imagine a better class. The mathematics was quite elementary.

"The writing is, as formerly reported, excellent.

"On previous occasions I have had the pleasure of recording the great success which attends Mr. ———'s efforts to teach English reading, grammar, and geography, and Bible history. The Presbytery continues to speak, in terms almost extravagant, of the high state of these branches, and the terms which they employ are consistent with facts. A better Scotch parochial school, if we look at the state of every branch of instruction, and at the moral influence of the master, I could not wish to see. Mr. ——— certainly takes a place next to his neighbour of ———, and second highest on the Bequest. I think Mr. ——— merits a letter of congratulation on the results which he has achieved."

(2.) "This excellent school continues, under the quiet and thoughtful management of Mr. ———, not only to maintain its character but even to make progress.

"The highest class (3) read from Milton's *Paradise Lost* rather rapidly, but with manifest understanding. Knowledge of grammar, of words, and of analysis, excellent.

"Composition exceedingly good.

"The second class (18) read extremely well from the fourth of Constable's Series. An attentive, well-ordered class, exhibiting strongly the peculiar feature of Mr. ———'s school, namely, the equality of the top and bottom of the class. The attention and order pervading the whole school, as well as this class, were admirable.

"The writing from dictation of the second class was excellent.

"The arithmetic was very good. Three boys worked equations accurately.

"Writing exceedingly good.

"The third class (20) were examined on a portion of Bible history, and displayed great familiarity with it. The third class (18) read extremely well from the third of Constable's Series.

" All the junior classes copy on their slates from their books.

" There are several Latin classes. The highest boy read a portion of an Ode of Horace admirably, and was very thoroughly grounded."

(3.) " When I entered I found the fifth highest class had just finished writing a long passage on their slates, and working sums in addition and subtraction. Both exercises were remarkably well done for so young a class.

" The third and fourth classes wrote admirably from dictation.

" The highest class (17) read a difficult lesson from the Advanced Reader of the Scottish Series exceedingly well. I asked very many questions on words, roots, and the allusions of the lesson, also on analysis and parsing, and in not one case did the class fail to give an accurate answer. All too were eager, attentive, and desirous to excel.

" The composition of the highest class was excellent. Some members of the second and third classes having listened to the passage I read as a composition exercise for the highest class voluntarily attempted it, and with success.

" In the department of geography, map-drawing receives great attention, and some good specimens were shown.

" The third class read extremely well from the fifth of the Scottish Series. They were skilfully and most thoroughly examined by the teacher, and displayed great intelligence and interest in their work.

" In arithmetic fourteen worked simple and compound proportion quickly and accurately.

" The highest Latin class read from Livy well. I do not think the Latin, however, the strong point of the school.

" Mr. —— deserves a higher place on the scale of merit and a letter of very cordial commendation. His school has always been good, but never has reached so high a pitch of excellence as now."

(4.) " The order,—not oppressive in its character,—which pervades this school, the affectionate terms on which teacher and pupils live, and the excellence of the teacher's character, impress me more strongly in this school than in almost any other.

" The Bible class (40) was examined on the 1st Book of Samuel, and made an excellent appearance, following the story with interest, the master requiring to make no effort to secure the respectful and serious attention of every boy in the class.

" The highest class (5) read from the Advanced Reading Book of Constable's Series as well as any Visitor could wish, whether we regard the intelligence and distinctness or the emphasis and expression. Analysis of sentences and knowledge of words very good. Parsing excellent ; composition excellent. And this remark applies also to the composition of the second class (17), which wrote admirably the same exercise as that prescribed by me for the first.

" The second class read on barter and money, from the sixth of Constable's Series, very intelligently. Analysis very fair. Parsing exceedingly good.

" Some forty or fifty worked proportion and fractions exceedingly well.

" The fourth class made an excellent appearance.

" Music good.

" There are four Latin classes. I heard the highest, which acquitted itself very well.

" It is now eight or nine years since I first inspected Mr. ——— here, and every successive visit has revealed fresh excellences in his character and his school. On the whole, I am disposed, taking moral as well as intellectual merits into consideration, to regard ——— school as almost at the head of all the schools in the three counties."

It is not necessary to apologize for quoting from the special annual reports on each school at such length, because without a sufficient variety of specimens of the internal working of the schools, the following classification would be valueless :—

Classification of Schools according to Merit.

Inferior.	Fair.	Good.	Very Good.	Excellent.	TOTAL.
8	33	34	40	15	130

Progress of a marked kind has been made during the last ten years in those departments of school-work to which I have chiefly devoted my attention when inspecting, viz. :—*Reading* (which, however, is still very defective in respect of style), *Writing from Dictation, English Composition, Mode of Examining on Lessons, Map-drawing, Organization,* and *Greek.* In the last named branch, however, the progress has been due to the higher requirements of the Universities. In a small proportion of the schools, the Government inspectors have been advising and stimulating very much in the same direction as myself; but in the great majority the improvement, in so far as it is due to external agency, is due to the operation of the Dick Bequest.[1] When I began the work of visitation nine years ago, not five per cent. of the schools systematically taught Writing from Dictation, not two per cent. attempted Composition as a separate subject of study; Map-drawing was very rare, and Reading was not regarded as an *art.*

I have already adverted to the work which still remains to be done (p. 317).

The direct effect of the Bequest in improving schools which have fallen into the hands of teachers who are inefficient in consequence of negligence or of ignorance of their profession, has been dwelt upon in previous Reports. It is unnecessary, therefore, to

---

[1] The present results were already attained four years ago, when fewer than one-fourth of the schools had formed a Government connexion.

do more here than quote, by way of illustration, the last case of the kind which came officially under my notice :—

Extract from Report of a Visit in 1863 *to* ⸺ *School.*

"The small attendance was caused by the prevalence of an epidemic.

"Mr. ⸺ is visited for the first time.

"The highest class, which had dwindled to two in consequence of the prevailing epidemic, read distinctly and intelligently from the History of England, and had a fair knowledge of words. Parsed and composed pretty well.

The second class (6) read from the fifth of Constable's Series, on the whole, well. Knowledge of words poor. The teacher thinks that the parents object to their children being asked the meaning of words! Intelligence of this and the other classes quite undeveloped. Writing from dictation fair.

"The third class read from Wilson's Elementary Reader fairly.

"The Bible class was examined on the Exodus, and exhibited a satisfactory acquaintance with the facts.

"Writing pretty good.

"Arithmetic, except in the case of one boy who worked well, backward.

"Latin a farce.

"Organization and discipline bad.

"No music.

"Mr. ⸺ is an intelligent, amiable, good-looking youth, disposed to consider himself ill-used, and to become depressed and hopeless. His manner in the school is listless, and he seems resigned to failure. I had much talk with him in the hope of rousing him to greater mental and bodily activity. In his listlessness and want of resolution and hopefulness lies the source of the school's feebleness. He is quite well disposed, however, and if the Trustees will admit him on a preparatory scale of three-fourths at present, I am confident that I shall be able to report in much more favourable terms when I next visit him."

Extract from Report of Visit to same School in 1865.

" The highest class (7) read prose and poetry fluently, intelligibly, and distinctly.

" Grammar thoughtful, and in its results very satisfactory.

" Composition very good.

" The second class (7) read from the fifth of Constable's Series with fluency, and with distinctness of enunciation.

" Writing from dictation good.

" The geography is well and practically taught. Every boy in the highest class exhibited a very creditable specimen of map-drawing.

" In arithmetic eight worked proportion steadily, and five with accuracy.

" Writing good.

" Fourteen, composing the New Testament class, made a very pleasing appearance when examined.

" In Latin three boys made a very fair appearance in Jacob's Latin Lessons.

" Music very fair.

" When I visited Mr. —— for the first time two years ago, I found things in so deplorable a state, in many essential respects, that I had little hope of his ever becoming a good teacher. I am happy to say that he has profited by the advice then given him, and, as the above report testifies, now presents a school largely increased in numbers, and quite above the average in respect of efficiency.

" I think Mr. —— should be complimented on the improved condition of his school, and allowed — for merit in teaching."

Many similar cases might be cited. Twenty had been marked for quotation, but no purpose could be served by multiplying such extracts.

CHAPTER X.

THE BEARING OF FEES AND DATE OF ENTRY ON ATTENDANCE AND ORGANIZATION—GRATIS SCHOLARS.

IN Scotland the importance of insisting on a fee for schooling, where it is at all possible to obtain one, is almost universally recognised. It has been felt that fee-paying, like mercy (to use an illustration of my predecessor's), is twice blessed, blessing both him that gives and him that takes. It is a mistake to suppose, however, that all the scholars attending the parochial schools pay fees. Although use and wont might entitle masters to disregard the words of the Act of 1803, which requires them to give a certain amount of gratuitous instruction when the heritors and minister think it necessary, yet they exercise the greatest possible leniency in the exaction of fees when the circumstances of the parents make payment a heavy burden. Returns from 124 of the schools show upwards of 750 gratis scholars on the school books, exclusive of those paid for by the Milne Bequest, who number upwards of two thousand. The above 750 are confined to sixty-nine schools not admitted to the benefit of the Milne Fund, giving an average of more than ten per cent. for each school. The returns from the schools on the Milne Bequest show thirty five per cent. of gratis scholars, although the grant of the Trustees (£20 per annum) is intended to cover the fees of only twenty-five scholars, or about twenty-four per cent. of the total number enrolled.[1]

In a considerable number of parishes in Scotland an attempt is being made to introduce monthly or quarterly instead of weekly payments. Weekly payments notoriously facilitate irregularity of attendance. If a child is unable to go to school on a Monday, he is kept at home for the rest of the week, because the parents think that they will not get full measure for their twopence or threepence, as the case may be. Payments taken up in advance, and for a longer term, help to cure this evil. Quarterly payments, though almost universal in the north-east,[2] may be regarded as imposing too great a burden on the resources of the parents, as well as on their foresight. Monthly payments seem better suited to the circumstances of most districts of the country.

An objection to the practice of weekly payments, of equal importance with that just adverted to, is its interference with the organization of a school. This objection is of equal force where quarterly payments prevail, because the length of the term compels teachers to admit pupils whenever they please to present themselves for enrolment. Pupils dropping in at pleasure, and taking their places in classes whose

[1] The above numbers do not include those scholars whose fees are in arrear.   [2] Vide p. 342, foot-note.

progress they must retard, are a great obstruction to the work of a teacher, and discourage his efforts to secure efficient organization. Monthly payments will, however, not provide a remedy for this evil unless the teacher fixes a monthly date *on which day alone* new pupils can be enrolled.

Fees and attendance are here associated in the same chapter, because the mode of exacting school pence tells powerfully on the regularity of the pupils, and because, in the absence of direct or indirect compulsory education laws, it is a duty to make use of every available device for palliating the chief obstacle in the way of the education of the poorer classes. Even in the favoured counties to which this Report refers, upwards of fifty per cent. of the pupils are returned as not attending 140 days annually. If, however, we are to avoid the error common to almost all educational statistics, we must deduct at least ten per cent. from the above number on account of those children who, having entered during the currency of a session, have not had time to complete 140 days before the expiry of the year to which the return applies. This leaves upwards of forty per cent. who attend for fewer than 140 days. Although various devices might be resorted to whereby shortness and irregularity of attendance would be considerably reduced, and their evil consequences to some extent obviated, there can be little doubt that it is only by the extension of the compulsory laws, now in partial operation, that the evil can be effectually remedied. There would be less opposition to such an extension were it more distinctly dissociated in the minds of the public from the idea of State restriction of the liberty of the subject. We are too apt to forget that the only restriction proposed is a restriction on vicious parents, and that, by the enforcement of such a restriction, we protect the rights of children. In the words of M. Jules Simon, "Recevoir l'instruction élémentaire est *le droit de chacun, et tous ont intérêt à ce que chacun la reçoive.*" This short sentence, and the following quotation, sum up the whole *moral* side of the argument:—

> "This sacred right the lisping babe proclaims
> To be inherent in him, by Heaven's will,
> For the protection of his innocence ;
> And the rude boy—who, having overpast
> The sinless age, by conscience is enrolled,
> Yet mutinously knits his angry brow,
> And lifts his wilful hand, on mischief bent,
> Or turns the godlike faculty of speech
> To impious use—by process indirect
> Declares his due, while he makes known his need.
> This sacred right is fruitlessly announced,
> This universal plea in vain addressed
> To eyes and ears of parents, who themselves
> Did, in the time of their necessity,
> Urge it in vain ; and, therefore, like a prayer,
> That from the humblest floor ascends to Heaven,
> It mounts to reach the State's parental ear." [1]

When however, we pass from the moral to the social and political difficulties which beset the question of obligatory instruction as a national measure, we encounter many important questions not easy of

[1] Wordsworth's *Excursion*, book IX.

solution. The extension, however, of the existing Factory laws to other industries than those to which they are at present applicable, can present no insuperable difficulty.

The average fee for children learning Reading only, is twopence a week in the three north-eastern counties. Those children who are considered to be sufficiently advanced to learn Writing, Arithmetic, Grammar, and Geography, pay 4d. or 5d. a week. Latin, Greek, Mathematics, and French are also paid for separately.[1] I have already, in another place, adverted to the fact that Scotch parochial schoolmasters have been in the habit of devoting themselves chiefly to the higher classes to the neglect of the lower. They are now disposed to correct this great error; but they can never effectually do so until the present mode of regulating the fees by the subjects taught is discarded. A smaller charge should, of course, be made for children under eight years of age than for those above that age; but the charge, whatever it may be, should be understood to pay for the *whole* school curriculum. The teaching of Reading, Writing, and Arithmetic should begin on the same day; and a small slate should be put into every child's hand, along with his Primer, on the day on which he enters school. By such an arrangement, too, the power of objecting to this or that particular subject being taught to their children would be taken out of the hands of ignorant parents.

[1] *Vide* p. 342.

CHAPTER XI.

SCHOOL ACCOMMODATION—FURNITURE—APPARATUS—
SCHOOL LIBRARIES—TEXT-BOOKS USED.

THE schoolrooms are well built, and in most respects adequate, with the exception of six, four of which are *side*-parochial schools.

There is not in Scotland such careful attention to offices for the pupils, and such a strict regard to cleanliness, decency, and propriety as may be found south of the Tweed.

The School Furniture is sufficient, but in the majority of cases awkwardly and unskilfully made. The subject of school furniture has not yet been so much studied in Scotland as it ought to be, and we have a great deal to learn on this subject from the United States.

The apparatus consists in all cases of maps and a black-board, and occasionally globes are also to be found. No parochial school, in my opinion, is adequately supplied with apparatus which has not— (1.) A large black-board affixed to the wall. (2.) A smaller movable black-board specially intended for the junior classes. (3.) A black-board ruled for music. (4.) A pair of globes. (5.) A set of maps, including a large physical map of the world. (6.) A numerical ball-frame. (7.) A supply of objects for object-lessons, etc. (8.) Coloured pictures illustrative of Scripture narratives. (9.) Simple materials for exercises in Colour and Form.

School-libraries are, when they are met with, and this is much too seldom, composed of works which the children do not care to read. It is obvious that as reading from the library is supposed to be a voluntary act, the books in it must be attractive if the library is to be of any use. A liberal supply of fairy tales, fables, ballads, voyages imaginative and real, illustrated books of natural history, and such religious books as contain in themselves an interest *apart from the fact that they treat of religion*, ought to form the staple of the library. Moreover, sets of books suited to the different stages of progress in the school should be provided. I was grieved, but not much surprised, to be guided one day by a Banffshire boy of twelve years of age, son of a small farmer, who had never heard of Jack the Giant Killer, the Babes in the Wood, or Robinson Crusoe! A mind growing up with imagination so starved must consolidate into something strangely different from the richly fed minds of the children of the middle and upper classes. When there exists a school-library really suited to the needs and desires of the young, permission to take the books may be used as a reward for lessons thoroughly acquired. The school will be a brighter place for little children when, the lesson once thoroughly acquired, a story-book or picture-book will be put into their hands to amuse, and, through amusement, to instruct. Why should not the teacher himself occasionally take a book from the library-shelf and read a story to his school? It would relieve the monotony of his work, and help to maintain friendly and pleasant relations between himself and his pupils.

The School-books used by the masters vary to a considerable extent. Those issued by the Association of Scottish Schoolmasters, parochial teachers have a personal interest, I believe, in using; if not a personal, at least a corporate interest. It is contrary to my practice to interfere with the books used, except when I find that inferior results can be distinctly traceable to badly graduated lesson-books. From a return recently taken up, I am able to record here (and it is a subject of some historical value) the books at present used in the parochial schools of Aberdeen, Banff, and Moray:—

Reading-Books.—Scottish School-Book Association Series, Constable's Series, M'Culloch's Series, Nelson's Series, and in a very few schools, the Irish Series, and Chambers's Narrative Series.

Arithmetic.—The treatises of Gray, Melrose, Scottish School-Book Association, Ingram, Thomson, Colenso, Barnard Smith, H. Smith, and Currie.

Geography.—The treatises of the Scottish School-Book Association, Reid, Anderson, and Clyde.

338   REPORT ON EDUCATION.

English Grammar.—The text-books of Morell, Lennie, and Scottish School-Book Association.

Algebra.—The text-books of Colenso, Chambers, and Cassell; Wood and Todhunter where there are advanced classes.

Euclid.—The editions issued by Chambers and Cassell.

Latin.—Edinburgh Academy Rudiments, Melvin's Grammar, Ferguson's Grammatical Exercises, Arnold's Prose Composition, Melvin's Versions, and the usual Classics.

Greek.—Geddes's Grammar, Xenophon, Homer, and the New Testament.

In the studies usually comprehended under the expression "English branches," the manuals that may be used are probably of comparatively little consequence, with the exception of the Reading-books and the text-book of Arithmetic. To state here all that might be said on this most important subject, however, would be to recur to the questions of Method already handled in previous chapters, and substantially to repeat in a different form what has been there said. One thing only I would here urge on the attention of schoolmasters—that the reading-books of parochial schools constitute substantially *the whole literature* of their pupils. Let them, therefore, estimate books from this point of view. Both grammar and geography will probably be best taught when the principal portion of the teaching is oral, and the text-book the black-board. The same is true of arithmetic in the *initiatory* stages.

CHAPTER XII.

GENERAL STATISTICS OF EDUCATION IN THE COUNTIES
OF ABERDEEN, BANFF, AND MORAY.

THE population of those portions of the three counties of Aberdeen, Banff, and Moray, embraced by the Bequest (see p. 344), is, by the census of 1861, 272,361.

The number of parishes in the three counties is 124, and in these there are 154 statutory parochial schools and 554 non-parochial schools, besides 12 parochial female schools.

Parochial schools taught	by masters,	.	154
Parochial do.	by mistresses,	.	12
Non-parochial do.	by masters,	.	215
Non-parochial do.	by mistresses,[1]	.	339
		Total,	720 schools.

There is consequently a school for every 378·27 of the population in the three north-eastern counties of Scotland. A novel feature in the above figures is the number of *Female* parochial schools established under the 5th clause of the Act of 1861.

Parochial Schools.

Emoluments of Schoolmasters. — The parochial schools are supported by statutory assessment, which

[1] The proportion of *Female* schools which are merely sewing-schools is not ascertained.

yields an average of £43, 4s. 11d. of fixed salary to each teacher. In addition to this the teachers are provided with dwelling-houses and gardens (or compensation in lieu of them), the annual value of which may be very moderately stated as £10. The average number of rooms in the dwelling-houses is very nearly six, and they are for the most part substantial and comfortable edifices. The average amount of school-fees *actually received* is £28, 9s. 8d. In addition to these emoluments the majority of the schoolmasters enjoy small salaries as session-clerk and registrar of the parish, which may average for both offices about £9. In Aberdeenshire 70 parochial schools receive £20 per annum from the Milne Bequest, for which they have to teach 25 children gratuitously. The amount paid under the Dick Bequest for year to Whitsunday 1863 averaged £31, 11s. 8d. to each teacher.

The average emoluments of parochial schoolmasters accordingly may be thus summed up :—

	£	s.	d.
Statutory salary,	43	4	11
Value of house and garden,	10	0	0
Fees actually received,	28	9	8
Session-clerk, Registrar, etc.,	9	0	0
Dick Bequest,	31	11	8
Average income,[1]	£122	6	3

Attendance.—The average daily attendance at each

[1] To which has to be added £20 of Milne Bequest to 70 of the Aberdeenshire schools, and Government grants where the schools happen to be in connexion with the Privy Council.

of the parochial schools during the year 1864 (not the average enrolment, which was 118·9*) was 71·4 ; of these, 52·1 were boys, and 19·3 were girls. Of the above 71·4, 44·9 attended 150 days and upwards. The number actually present on the day on which the return was taken up—a very stormy day in January—averaged for each school 68·4.

Age of Pupils, etc. etc.—The average age at which children enter the parochial schools of the three counties is 6·3 ; the average age at which they leave is 13.

Accessibility of Schools.—The *greatest* distance which pupils travel to the parochial schools *averages* 3·1 miles. The average distance of the pupils from school is about 1½ miles. The greatest distance from which any boy comes to school is five and a half miles; but there are only 5 schools which are attended by boys who come more than four miles. In 60 schools are to be found a few children who come more than three miles.

Hours of Meeting.—In summer the schools generally meet at half-past nine and dismiss at four o'clock, there being from half an hour to an hour of interval; in winter they meet about ten and dismiss about a quarter-past three, the period of interval allowed being, during that season, only about twenty or thirty minutes.

Vacations.—The vacations are determined by the

* 131 schools return this.

grain harvest. In the great majority of cases they last six weeks, beginning in the third or fourth week of August.

Fees.—The school-fees run from 2s. a quarter (in a few cases 1s. 6d.) for the youngest children, who are supposed to learn only reading and spelling, to 5s. a quarter for those above eight who are learning arithmetic, geography, writing, and grammar. Where Latin, Greek, and mathematics are taught the fee is frequently 7s. 6d., and in a few cases 10s. They are for the most part paid quarterly, but only in about 16 per cent. of the schools are they paid *in advance*.[1]

Non-Parochial Schools.

I have little to add on the subject of non-parochial schools to the figures already given on p. 339, because the returns are imperfect. Of the 554 non-parochial schools, I find that 531 return their daily attendance as averaging 42·3 ; and 393 return their fees as averaging £15, 17s. 9d.

In 26 of the 124 civil parishes, the only non-parochial schools existing are taught by mistresses. Ten parishes have no schools save the parochial.

[1] Fees are paid as follows in 123 parochial schools *making returns under this head :*—103 quarterly ; 2 half-yearly ; 6 yearly ; 1 weekly and quarterly ; 3 quarterly and half-yearly ; 3 at Whitsuntide and autumn vacation ; 1 three times a year ; 1 quarterly, half-yearly, and yearly ; 1 at end of herring fishing ; 1 no rule.

N.B.—Of these 98 are *not* paid in advance.

Notwithstanding the ample means of education provided for the population of the three north-eastern counties, 681 persons above ten years of age are returned as unable to read, and 3922 as unable to write. From these figures, however, have to be deducted immigrants from the Highlands, and children of ten or eleven years of age, who are at present at school, and will learn to write before leaving it. Had the query been limited to persons above twelve years of age the number returned as unable to write would certainly not have exceeded 1000.

CHAPTER XIII.

PAROCHIAL SCHOOLS IN CONNEXION WITH THE BEQUEST.

OF the 154 parochial schools admissible in the 124 civil parishes, 134 only are connected with the Dick Bequest. The reason of the non-participation of these 20 schools is, that they have not complied with the conditions of the Trustees, as these have been explained in the chapter on the Administration of the Trust.

The population of the three counties, and of those portions to which Mr. Dick's Bequest is applicable, is shown in the following statement :—

Population by census of 1861 of the counties of—

Aberdeen,	221,569
Banff,	59,215
Moray,	42,695
	323,479

Deduct districts not within the range of the Dick Bequest :—

ROYAL BURGHS, viz.—

1. Aberdeen, the six town parishes—

East,	5,182
West,	11,450
North,	6,273
South,	4,291
Greyfriars',	7,143
St. Clement's,	7,623
	41,962

COMPARATIVE STATEMENT. 345

Brought forward,	41,962	323,479
2. Banff (not landward),	3,557	
3. Elgin,	7,543	
4. Forres,	4,112	
		57,174
		266,305

Add portions of parishes in other counties, viz.,

Abernethy,	788	
Banchory-Devenick,	2,303	
Drumoak,	235	
Duthil,	325	
Cromdale,[1]	1,405	
		6,056
		272,361

The following figures show the statistical state of the parochial schools benefiting by the Bequest :—

Attendance.—The average number enrolled at each of the parochial schools, taking the average of the last ten years, is 112·7 (the average for 1862, was 113·1). Of this number 49·8 are returned as having attended 140 days or upwards. The number of school-days averaged 246 annually, taking the average of the ten years. In consequence of the recent but already nearly universal custom of closing schools on Saturday, the number of school-days is now reduced to 235.

[1] The parish of Cromdale contains a population of 566 in Moray and 3376 in Inverness, together 3942. There are two schools in the parish now admissible to the Bequest, which would embrace say one-half the population, or 1971, whereof 1405 in Inverness-shire might with propriety be added to the above.

Subjects taught.—Of the average number enrolled (112·7) there are returned as learning—

English Reading,	111·2
Writing,	88·2
Arithmetic,	65
English Grammar,	48·7
Geography,	52·9
Mathematics,	4·8
Latin,	6·7
Greek,	1·5
French,	·5

In some sea-coast schools Navigation is taught. Singing from notation is now introduced into about 20 per cent. of the schools. Drawing is only occasionally met with.

CHAPTER XIV.

COMPARATIVE STATEMENT, HAVING REFERENCE TO
PREVIOUS REPORTS.

Fees.—THE fees have not materially altered since the date of the last Report, 1854. But whereas only 24 schools received their fees quarterly at that date the great majority now do so.

Attendance.—The regularity of attendance has improved very considerably. The proportion attending for 140 days and upwards was in—

1837.	1852.	1862.
32.6	42.2	57.1

This is a very gratifying feature of the most recent returns.

Subjects taught.—For 123 schools, the number studying Mathematics is 603, as against 700 in 1852. The number learning Latin is at present 860; the number learning Latin in 1852 was 803. The number learning Greek is 196, as against 186 in 1852. The number learning French is 88, as against 48 in 1852.

The following Table exhibits the numbers learning

the various branches at different decennial periods since the Bequest came into operation, the calculation being made for 123 schools :—

	1833.	1842.	1852.	1862.	Increase from 1833 to 1842.	Increase from 1842 to 1852.	Increase from 1852 to 1862.	Total Increase from 1833.
English Reading,	10,108	12,842	13,937	13,815	2·734	1·095	b	3·707
Writing, . .	6288	10,094	11,082	11,221	3·806	·988	·139	4·933
Arithmetic, . .	3022	5542	7583	8,746	2·520	2·041	1·163	5·724
Grammar, . .	1060	3712	5947	5,992	2·052	2·235	·45	4·932
Geography, . .	582	4032	6555	6,373	3·450	2·523	c	5·791
Mathematics, .	279	531	700	603	·252	·169	d	·324
Latin, . . .	488	560	803	860	·72	·243	·57	·372
Greek, . . .	81	61	186	196	a	·125	·10	·115
French, . . .	9	44	48	88	·35	·4	·40	·79

a. Decrease, 20.   *b.* Decrease, 122.   *c.* Decrease, 182.   *d.* Decrease, 97.

The much larger proportion of the pupils enrolled for English who *also* learn writing and arithmetic is even more satisfactory than the increase in the numbers studying Latin, Greek, and French.

School Accommodations.—The dwelling-houses (the average number of rooms being now nearly six, whereas it was reported as being nearly five in 1854), school-houses, school-furniture, and apparatus, have much improved during the last decade (p. 335).

Emoluments.—The incomes of the teachers from all sources[1] have risen from an average of £101, 1s. 7d. to £122, 6s. 3d. The following Table exhibits the increase in the emoluments of the parochial teachers since 1833 :—

AVERAGE.

1833.	1843.	1853.	1863.
£55 12 4	£97 16 6	£101 1 7	£122 6 3

[1] Exclusive of Government grants.

Cost of Schooling.—The education of each child enrolled on the parochial school-books of the three counties costs about 21s. per annum, including fees (but excluding from the calculation the value of schoolroom, Privy Council grants, and the Milne Bequest, which would raise it to about 25s. per scholar in Aberdeenshire).[1]

It would be ungracious as well as unjust to conclude this Report without recording the satisfaction which I have had in my official intercourse with the masters connected with the Bequest. Conscientiousness, thoughtfulness, courtesy, and openness and fairness of mind, I have found to be characteristics of the great majority of the teachers. The work of visitation, accordingly, has been to me a pleasant labour of co-operation rather than a disagreeable critical task.

[1] The Milne Bequest does not extend its benefits beyond the county of Aberdeen.

STATE showing AVERAGE ANNUAL ABSTRACT of RETURNS from Autumn Vacation 1852 to Autumn Vacation 1862, and DISTRIBUTION OF FUNDS OF THE DICK BEQUEST from Whitsunday 1853 to Whitsunday 1863.

Year from Autumn Vacation to Autumn Vacation	Number of Schools Admissible to Bequest	Number of Schools Returned	Average Number of Scholars Enrolled during Year	Average Number of Scholars Attended 140 Days or more	Average Number of Scholars Studying — English	Writing	Arithmetic	English Grammar	Geography	Mathematics	Latin	Greek	French	Average Number of Days School Taught during the Year	Average Salary	Average Amount of School Fees received	Amount of School Fees in Arrears	Number of Gratis Scholars	Number of Scholars on Ellis Bequest	Amount on Buildings and Repairs by Heritors	Year from Whitsunday to Whitsunday	Fund for Distribution	Maximum Allowance	Average Allowance	Minimum Allowance
1852-3	146	111	114	487	1121	897	614	479	59a	5	64	1b	4	2601	£29 14 2	£25 18 8	£163 19 5a	619k	2207u	£714 12 6ee	1853-4	£3748 16 0*	£47 1 2	£29 0 6	£22 2 2
1853-4	146	114	108e	473	1084	845	599	489	52	4b	65	1b	4	2554	29 17 5	24 16 11	176 3 11b	799l	2020v	195 4 5f	1854-5	4014 9 3	51 9 4	31 12 3	24 1 3
1854-5	146	126	105e	438	1071	833	601	477	52	41	61	1b	4	2513	29 16 7	23 13 8	173 10 6c	820m	2251w	487 6 10gg	1855-6	4236 0 6	53 3 10	34 10 6	26 9 7
1855-6	146	119	1117	47	1099	861	627	498	53b	44	65	1b	4	2579	29 17 6	25 10 9	166 15 10d	791n	2011x	601 9 3hh	1856-7	4250 12 4	52 4 3	33 6 10	26 16 6
1856-7	148	116	1109	427	1068	861	618	475	52	53	64	1b	4	2417	29 17 2	25 5 6	168 13 0e	484o	1860y	969 14 4ii	1857-8	4491 2 9	54 14 11	36 13 0	28 11 11
1857-8	149	116	1151	488	1133	894	692	499	557	52	68	13	4	2446	29 16 9	27 0 6	168 5 0f	447p	2013z	691 1 3j	1858-9	4378 16 5	54 18 1	35 6 0	25 7 9
1858-9	149	118	1164	512	1149	929	685	508	538	51	70	18	4	2307	29 12 7	28 0 3	199 6 6g	653q	2000aa	223 17 0kk	1859-60	3951 2 4	44 16 0	30 2 0	20 14 10
1859-60	150	119	1159	546	1148	913	687	50	515	49	7	16	4	2453	29 19 2	28 4 1	202 14 1h	659r	1986bb	905 12 1ll	1860-1	3844 13 11*	42 5 11	28 4 0	18 19 5
1860-1	151	120	1129	575	1112	864	667	478	48	48	65	16	4	2291	29 10 7	26 12 5	240 10 3l	603s	1828cc	1434 16 2mm	1861-2	4247 11 7	46 18 11	30 7 9	21 6 1
1861-2	152	124	1131	571	1123	912	711	481	518	49	7	16	7	235	44 11 6	28 9 8	245 18 5j	752t	1978dd	1396 12 4nn	1862-3	4276 18 4	45 13 10	31 11 8	20 0 1

a. 83 Schools. b. 92 „ c. 96 „ d. 88 „ e. 88 „ f. 96 „ g. 90 „ h. 93 „ i. 104 „ j. 104 „

k. 51 Schools. l. 66 „ m. 70 „ n. 62 „ o. 40 „ p. 40 „ q. 63 „ r. 63 „ s. 63 „ t. 69 „

u. 54 Schools. v. 52 „ w. 57 „ x. 54 „ y. 50 „ z. 54 „ aa. 54 „ bb. 53 „ cc. 50 „ dd. 55 „

ee. 18 Schools. ff. 11 „ gg. 17 „ hh. 18 „ ii. 13 „ jj. 7 „ kk. 9 „ ll. 21 „ mm. 15 „ nn. 24 „

* In each of these years an addition was made to the free revenue of the year of a sum taken from the reserved allowances.

APPENDIX.

APPENDIX.

I.

RULES OF EXAMINATION, ADOPTED 6th February, and REVISED 21st December 1849.

1. Every Schoolmaster, claiming the benefit of the Bequest, must be examined by the Trustees' Examiners at either the *first* or the *second* Examination immediately following his election.

> NOTE.—1. Every Claimant may thus employ at least twelve months after his election in preparation, without forfeiting the Bequest for any period.
> 2. A Schoolmaster failing to undergo examination within the time required, forfeits all claim for the period prior to the time at which he shall actually be examined.

2. No extraordinary distinction shall be bestowed, however eminent may be a Candidate's merits in particular branches, unless he profess the whole subjects of Examination at his first appearance.

> It is desired that every Candidate should undertake the whole branches at his first appearance. From feelings of indulgence, considerable latitude has for some time past been allowed in making only a partial profession. No benefit, however, has been experienced from this course. On the contrary, it has tended to an indefinite protraction of the examination of Candidates through successive years, which is not only inconvenient, but shown by experience to confer no advantage upon Candidates themselves. These considerations have led to the adoption of the following

Regulations for Examinations extending beyond one year.

3. All the branches must be professed by each Candidate within two successive years. If at the Annual Examination in those years he be pronounced *fair* in all the branches, his Examination shall be

held to be completed; but if otherwise, his Examination must be resumed under the conditions mentioned in Rule 6.

4. Every Candidate must, at his first attendance for Examination, profess and be examined upon not less than *five* of the ten subjects of written trial, including English, Arithmetic, and Latin, the profession of these three in the first year being indispensable.

5. Whatever modified allowance the Trustees may in their discretion allocate in respect of partial profession and success in the first of these two years, the amount shall be reserved, and no payment be made until the entire Examination is completed in terms of Rule 3.

6. In the event of a Candidate being found *deficient* in any one of the ten branches at the end of the second Examination, then all his past appearances, with the exception of those marked *good*, shall be held null for *every* purpose; it being open to him again to compete for admission by passing through the Examination anew, but always in the same way, and under the same conditions, in conformity with these Rules, as if he had made no previous appearance in any branch not marked *good*.

In transmitting the foregoing Rules to newly elected Parochial Schoolmasters in the Counties of Aberdeen, Banff, and Moray, the Trustees of Mr. Dick's Bequest beg to invite their serious attention to the objects of the Bequest, the Testator's express direction being that the Fund shall be distributed in such manner as " *shall seem most likely to encourage active Schoolmasters, and gradually to elevate the literary character of the Parochial Schoolmasters and Schools*" in these Counties. In order to accomplish these important objects, the Trustees have adopted such Regulations as appeared best calculated to attain them: and with a view in particular to the elevation of the literary character of the Schoolmasters, they instituted an Examination of newly elected Teachers, upon such branches of literature and science as it is reasonable and proper to expect should be known by Schoolmasters claiming the advantage of this Bequest, in addition to their ordinary emoluments.

But it is manifest, that whatever rules the Trustees may prescribe, the success of these must mainly depend upon the Schoolmasters themselves,—upon their earnest and faithful exertions to attain the literary elevation desired by the Testator, without the possession of which every conscientious Teacher must feel that no portion of the Fund can properly belong to him.

It has been a source of great satisfaction to the Trustees to witness the manner in which Mr. Dick's design has been seconded by various Teachers, whose examination has proved that they have imbibed the spirit and cultivated the attainments which the Bequest requires. One of their most pleasing duties has consisted in conferring both special and permanent distinctions on such candidates.

The appearance of the Teachers just referred to has satisfied the Trustees both of the practicability of Mr. Dick's design, and that the Examination instituted is, in respect of its subjects and extent, within the capacity of all Teachers eligible to the Parochial Schools of the three Counties.

On the other hand, it cannot but be a source of pain to the Trustees to be compelled at any time to take a different view of any Schoolmaster's appearance, and to find that he is not worthy to participate in the Fund. The Testator's directions, however, leave them no other course; and whatever feelings of indulgence and consideration may have prevailed at the outset, while the Examination was new and comparatively untried, the Trustees regard it as their plain duty to require, now that the Examination has been established for fourteen years, and its nature and details are generally known and understood, *that every Teacher examined shall in accordance with the foregoing rules exhibit a fair degree of attainment, as the condition of his receiving any share of the Fund.* The Trustees think it right to call the attention of all newly appointed Schoolmasters to this announcement; and they are well aware that it will afford satisfaction and encouragement to the deserving—a class which, it is hoped, may in future embrace every Teacher appointed within the district. They are earnestly entreated to bear in mind Mr. Dick's purpose, and the necessity of intelligent and honest exertion upon their part to secure its success, and they need hardly be reminded that the consciousness of such exertion will add a double value to any allowance which they may receive.

EXAMINATION PAPERS, 1864.

NOTICE.

To Candidates preparing for Examination in September 1865, the following hints may be of consequence :—

1. In examining on Geography an acquaintance must be presumed with at least the outline of the Geography of the globe at large, and the *Elements of Physical Geography*. But Candidates will be expected to possess a much more minute and exact knowledge of the Geography of Europe, and more particularly of Great Britain and Ireland; together with that also of Ancient Palestine. Questions in Classical Geography will be confined to Ancient Italy, Greece, and Asia Minor. The Examination will not extend beyond what is contained in Clyde's School Geography, and Pillans' First Steps in Classical Geography.

2. The Examination on History and Chronology will relate to (1.) Bible History; (2.) History of Ancient Rome; History of England and Scotland in the 17th and 18th centuries.

3. In the department of English, a general acquaintance will be expected with the history of English Literature, its chief epochs, and their characteristics. On this subject, Spalding's History of English Literature is recommended; and Candidates will be expected to be well versed in the outline of our Literature as there presented. The special study of a definite work is moreover required; and the main object and drift of the Examination will be to test the Candidate's literary information and appreciation in connexion with this work, and especially with reference to a passage selected from it,—his knowledge of the sources, structure, etymology, and syntax of the English language, with the application of the principles of general grammar to the construction and resolution of English phrases and sentences. *The work which has been fixed upon for the ensuing year is Cowper's Task.* A further recommendation to be given under this head is the attentive study of some such treatise on the structure and grammar of the English language, as Morell's Grammar and Analysis of the English Language.

4. In Latin, the field of Examination for September 1865 will be limited to Livy (Book V.), and Horace (Ars Poetica), along

with a Latin version; in Greek, to Acts, chaps. xi.-xx., Xenophon (Anabasis, Book IV.), and the thirteenth Book of the Iliad.

5. In the study of Greek, accuracy and precision should be aimed at from the outset. With this view the Student ought, in the first place, to confine his reading for some time to Attic prose alone; endeavouring, by rigorous practice, to acquire an exact mastery of its common forms of inflexion and conjugation, whether regular or irregular, and a firm hold of the ordinary Greek Grammar. And for the same end, while encouragement will be given to higher acquirements by the occasional introduction into the Examination Paper of a short passage from Homer, the main and by far the most important part of the Examination will always be made to turn upon a thorough knowledge of Attic prose. In the next place, while the Grammar which the Student employs should be accurate and trustworthy, his Lexicon should not only be equally so, but should correspond with the former as closely as possible. It is only necessary to add that in reading the Student should constantly have at hand, and refer to, his list of Irregular and Defective Verbs, with their several parts in use, and their modes of conjugation.

6. For attaining due proficiency in Geometry, little can be suggested beyond a careful study of Euclid and the actual application of the different propositions, as they are successively acquired, to the practical solution of exercises.

7. With respect to Arithmetic, it cannot be too strongly impressed, that a loose facility of mere calculation is not enough; that the theory—the ground and reason of the several rules and processes—should be clearly understood, by the help of some such treatise as De Morgan's or Professor Thomson's Arithmetic, or Tate's Compendium; and, in particular, that Proportion and *Fractional* Arithmetic should be thoroughly mastered.

8. In Physics, there will be demanded the Elements of Statics treated mathematically, together with Hydrostatics and Optics.

It is specially ordered that no Candidate shall bring into the room on the day of Examination any books or MS. whatever. The infringement of this rule by any Candidate will, if discovered, vitiate his whole examination.

EDINBURGH, *October* 1864.

ENGLISH GRAMMAR AND LITERATURE.

JULIUS CÆSAR, III. 2.

If you have tears, prepare to shed them now.
You all do know this mantle : I remember
The first time ever Cæsar put it on :
'Twas on a summer's evening, in his tent ;
That day he overcame the Nervii :—
Look ! in this place ran Cassius' dagger through :
See, what a rent the envious Casca made :
Through this, the well-beloved Brutus stabb'd ;
And, as he pluck'd his cursed steel away,
Mark how the blood of Cæsar follow'd it,
As rushing out of doors, to be resolved
If Brutus so unkindly knocked, or no ;
For Brutus, as you know, was Cæsar's angel :
Judge, O you gods, how dearly Cæsar loved him !
This was the most unkindest cut of all:
For when the noble Cæsar saw him stab,
Ingratitude, more strong than traitors' arms,
Quite vanquish'd him : then burst his mighty heart ;
And, in his mantle muffling up his face,
Even at the base of Pompey's statue,
Which all the while ran blood, great Cæsar fell.
Oh, what a fall was there, my countrymen !
Then I, and you, and all of us fell down,
Whilst bloody treason flourish'd over us.
Oh, now you weep ; and, I perceive, you feel,
The dint of pity : these are gracious drops.
Kind souls, what weep you, when you but behold
Our Cæsar's vesture wounded ? Look you here,
Here is himself, marr'd, as you see, with traitors.

QUESTIONS.

1. State what facts are known concerning the life of Shakspeare.
2. (*a*) To what category of his plays does *Julius Cæsar* belong ; and (*b*) what is the probable date of its composition ?
3. From what probable source were the main elements of the play derived ?
4. (*a*) Describe very briefly the historical circumstances of the death of Julius Cæsar ; and (*b*) point out any particulars in which Shakspeare has departed from these circumstances in his representation.

5. " His life was gentle; and the elements
So mixed in him, that Nature might stand up
And say to all the world, 'There was a man.'"
(a) Who speaks here; and (b) who is spoken of?
6. *There is a tide in the affairs of men.*—(a) Who says this; and (b) in reference to what is it said?
7. *The troubled Tiber chafing with her shores.*—In what part of the play does this line occur?
8. " There was a Brutus once that would have brooked
The eternal devil to keep his state in Rome
As easily as a king."
(a) What Brutus is here spoken of; (b) who speaks; and (c) to whom is the speech addressed?
9. *Even at the base of Pompey's statue.*—What is the various reading in this verse?
10. What is the meaning of the line,—
" Whilst bloody treason flourished over us."
11. *The dint of pity.*—(a) What is an equivalent word to *dint;* and (b) what is the derivation of the word?
12. (a) Parse the several verbs in the passage; and (b) classify them according to Mr. Morell's classification.
13. Point out the Saxon words in the passage.

HISTORY.

1. Enumerate the distinguishing epochs of the Bible history.
2. (a) Mention the chief characters on both sides in the war of Greece with Persia; and (b) the causes out of which the war sprang.
3. What were the special and what the general causes of the Peloponnesian war?
4. What part did the Thebans play in the later history of Greece, and who was their great leader?
5. (a) At what age did Henry VIII. ascend the throne of England; and (b) whom did he then marry?
6. (a) What is the date of the battle of Flodden; and (b) what were the circumstances which led to it?
7. (a) What was the cause of Henry's rupture with Rome? (b) Describe the successive steps of the process of the rupture.

8. Mention the most prominent ecclesiastical measures connected with the Reformation in England.
9. (a) Who was Cromwell in Henry's reign; and (b) what were his relations to Wolsey?
10. What was the Pilgrimage of Grace?
11. What two distinguished men suffered martyrdom in Henry's reign in connexion with the progress of Henry's rupture with Rome?
12. Describe the nature of Wyatt's rebellion, and the circumstances out of which it arose.
13. Who were the chief ecclesiastical agents of Mary of England in her persecutions?
14. State the claims of Mary Queen of Scots to the English throne.
15. Who was Sir Francis Drake?
16. Describe the career of Sir W. Raleigh.
17. What was the Babington conspiracy?
18. Describe the relations of the Earl of Essex with Elizabeth, and the charges against him.
19. What was the Hampton Court Conference?
20. (a) Who were the chief Puritans of Elizabeth's reign; and (b) for what special objects did they contend?
21. What were the chief political causes which led to the growth of Puritanism in the reigns of James and Charles I.?
22. What was the Gunpowder Plot?
23. Explain Tonnage and Poundage?
24. *Explain the chief religious grounds of dissatisfaction in the commencement of Charles' reign.
25. Mention the leaders on the Parliamentary and Royal side.
26. State the origin of the "Covenant" in Scotland, and its relation to the civil war.
27. Briefly note the chief events in the career of Cromwell, particularly the chief battles in which he was engaged, and their dates.
28. At what battle did Lord Falkland fall?
29. Describe the career of Montrose, and his connexion with the civil war.

GEOGRAPHY.

1. Explain the following terms of Mathematical Geography:—
   (a) equator; (b) meridian circle; (c) ecliptic; (d) equinox.
2. Explain the following terms of Physical Geography:—(a) glacier; (b) cyclone; (c) mirage; (d) prairie; (e) delta.
3. Why are there two tides daily?
4. Why do isothermal lines not coincide with parallels of latitude?
5. Mention the chief seats of the cultivation (a) of the sugar-cane, (b) of the coffee-plant.
6. Give the names, and describe generally the course, of the leading rivers that spring from the Alps.
7. State (a) the boundaries of Holstein; (b) the chief towns of Holstein and of Schleswig.
8. Mention the counties that border on Northamptonshire, Armagh, and Perthshire respectively.
9. Describe the course of the Trent, the Shannon, and the Tweed, naming the chief towns on their banks.
10. Name the universities and great public schools of England.
11. Where are the following towns situated:—Queenstown, Harwich, Stockport, Alloa, Kidderminster, Dundalk, Dorchester, Beverley, Walsall?
12. Name the chief seats of the manufacture of silks, pottery, and hardware in Britain.
13. (a) What is meant by " Galilee of the Gentiles "? (b) by which of the tribes was it formerly occupied? (c) what were the principal towns in it at the time of our Saviour?
14. Where were Jericho, Joppa, Sychar, Gadara, Carmel, Ascalon, Peræa?

CLASSICAL GEOGRAPHY.

15. Name the chief mountains and rivers of the Peloponnesus.
16. Name the chief colonies of Magna Græcia.
17. State the position of Tarsus, Capua, Hymettus, Sicyon, Thyatira, Lilybæum, Ariminum, Chæronea, Soracte.

LATIN.
To be translated into Latin Prose.

No one, it is plain, experiences the death of relatives without having met with many misfortunes before; so encompassed is human nature with a variety of troubles on all sides. Why, therefore, should one, who has bravely endured heavier or at any rate as heavy trials, lose courage and give himself up to grief, when he ought most of all to become callous and to harden himself against fresh distress? We mentioned a little before, that to act thus was moreover unjust. For nature has given us the use of life, as if of money, without any prescribed term. If, at her pleasure, she demands back her own lent on condition of being restored, why is she arraigned? or why do you not thank nature for delaying to demand back what she might have claimed sooner, rather than assail her with unjust complaint for making the demand at length? For it is beyond doubt that we are allowed not a place for our dwelling, but a lodging for our sojourn; and when we remove from it, we ought to depart with eagerness as from an inn full of troubles and discomforts, and to fly with the utmost joy to the future life as to our native land.

LIVY IV. 30.
To be translated accurately.

Veientes in agrum Romanum excursiones fecerunt. Fama fuit, quosdam ex Fidenatium juventute participes ejus populationis fuisse : cognitioque ejus rei L. Sergio et Q. Servilio et Mam. Æmilio permissa. Quidam Ostiam relegati, quod, cur per eos dies a Fidenis afuissent, parum constabat. Colonorum additus numerus, agerque his bello interemptorum assignatus. Siccitate eo anno plurimum laboratum est : nec cœlestes modo defuerunt aquæ, sed terra quoque, ingenito humore egens, vix ad perennes suffecit amnes. Defectus alibi aquarum circa torridos fontes rivosque stragem siti pecorum morientium dedit; scabie alia absumta. Vulgatique contactu in homines morbi ; et primo in agrestes ingruerant servitiaque ; urbs deinde impletur. Nec corpora modo affecta tabo, sed animos quoque multiplex religio et pleraque externa invasit, novos ritus sacrificandi vaticinando inferentibus in domos, quibus quæstui sunt capti superstitione animi : donec publicus jam pudor ad primores civitatis pervenit, cernentes in omnibus vicis sacellisque peregrina atque insolita piacula pacis deum exposcendæ. Datum inde negotium ædilibus ut animadverterent, ne qui nisi Romani dii, neu quo alio more, quam patrio, colerentur.

QUESTIONS.

1. From what sources did Livy derive the materials for the earlier history of Rome?
2. Where were Veii, Fidenæ, and Ostia?
3. *Colonorum, primores civitatis, ædilibus*—Explain these terms.
4. *Datum inde negotium*—By whom?
5. Give the derivation of *populationis, relegati, cur, perennes, stragem, ingruerant, religio, piacula.*

6. Parse the words *ingenito, interemptorum, egens, suffecit, siti, vaticinando, cernentes, exposcendæ*, conjugating the verbs.
7. Why are *Ostiam, humore, vaticinando, inferentibus, quæstui, deum,* in their respective cases?
8. What are the more usual forms for *contactu* and *tabo?*
9. How do you explain *alibi?*
10. Express the clause *novos ritus, &c.* in such other form or forms as occur to you.

HORACE III. 16.

To be translated accurately into English Prose.

  Aurum per medios ire satellites,
  Et perrumpere amat saxa potentius
  Ictu fulmineo. Concidit auguris
   Argivi domus, ob lucrum
5 Demersa exitio. Diffidit urbium
  Portas vir Macedo, et subruit æmulos
  Reges muneribus. Munera navium
   Sævos illaqueant duces.
  Crescentem sequitur cura pecuniam,
10 Majorumque fames. Jure perhorrui
  Late conspicuum tollere verticem,
   Mæcenas, equitum decus.
  Quanto quisque sibi plura negaverit,
  Ab dis plura feret. Nil cupientium
15 Nudus castra peto, et transfuga divitum
   Partes linquere gestio,
  Contemptæ dominus splendidior rei,
  Quam si quidquid arat impiger Appulus
   Occultare meis dicerer horreis,
20 Magnas inter opes inops.
  Puræ rivus aquæ, silvaque jugerum
  Paucorum, et segetis certa fides meæ
  Fulgentem imperio fertilis Africæ
   Fallit sorte beatior.

QUESTIONS.

1. State when Horace flourished, and describe briefly his character.
2. Mention his leading literary contemporaries.
3. *Mæcenas, equitum decus,*—(a) Who was Mæcenas? (b) What were the *Equites* in the time of Horace?
4. Explain the allusions in *auguris Argivi domus, vir Macedo, munera navium,* and *puræ rivus aquæ*.

5. Parse *satellites, potentius, concidit, demersa, diffidit, perhorrui, fallit*, conjugating the verbs.
6. Point out any phrases or constructions formed after a Greek model.
7. Explain the meaning of the following expressions:—*Majorumque fames, nudus, contemptæ dominus splendidior rei, magnas inter opes inops.*
8. To what philosophical school did the idea expressed in lines 13 and 14 belong?
9. Give any parallel sentiments, or expressions, of Horace that occur to you as illustrative of these verses.

GREEK.

XENOPHON'S ANABASIS, III. 1.

To be translated accurately.

Ἐπεὶ δὲ ἀπορία ἦν, ἐλυπεῖτο μὲν σὺν τοῖς ἄλλοις καὶ οὐκ ἐδύνατο καθεύδειν· μικρὸν δ' ὕπνου λαχὼν εἶδεν ὄναρ. ἔδοξεν αὐτῷ βροντῆς γενομένης σκηπτὸς πεσεῖν εἰς τὴν πατρῴαν οἰκίαν, καὶ ἐκ τούτου λάμπεσθαι πᾶσαν. περίφοβος δ' εὐθὺς ἀνηγέρθη, καὶ τὸ ὄναρ πῇ μὲν ἔκρινεν ἀγαθόν, ὅτι ἐν πόνοις ὢν καὶ κινδύνοις φῶς μέγα ἐκ Διὸς ἰδεῖν ἔδοξε· πῇ δὲ καὶ ἐφοβεῖτο, ὅτι ἀπὸ Διὸς μὲν βασιλέως τὸ ὄναρ ἐδόκει αὐτῷ εἶναι, κύκλῳ δὲ ἐδόκει λάμπεσθαι τὸ πῦρ, μὴ οὐ δύναιτο ἐκ τῆς χώρας ἐξελθεῖν τῆς βασιλέως, ἀλλ' εἴργοιτο πάντοθεν ὑπό τινων ἀποριῶν. ὁποῖόν τι μέντοι ἐστὶ τὸ τοιοῦτον ὄναρ ἰδεῖν ἔξεστι σκοπεῖν ἐκ τῶν συμβάντων μετὰ τὸ ὄναρ. γίγνεται γὰρ τάδε. εὐθὺς ἐπειδὴ ἀνηγέρθη πρῶτον μὲν ἔννοια αὐτῷ ἐμπίπτει, τί κατάκειμαι; ἡ δὲ νὺξ προβαίνει· ἅμα δὲ τῇ ἡμέρᾳ εἰκὸς τοὺς πολεμίους ἥξειν. εἰ δὲ γενησόμεθα ἐπὶ βασιλεῖ, τί ἐμποδὼν μὴ οὐχὶ πάντα μὲν τὰ χαλεπώτατα ἐπιδόντας, πάντα δὲ τὰ δεινότατα παθόντας ὑβριζομένους ἀποθανεῖν; ὅπως δ' ἀμυνούμεθα οὐδεὶς παρασκευάζεται οὐδὲ ἐπιμελεῖται, ἀλλὰ κατακείμεθα ὥσπερ ἐξὸν ἡσυχίαν ἄγειν. ἐγὼ οὖν τὸν ἐκ ποίας πόλεως στρατηγὸν προςδοκῶ ταῦτα πράξειν; ποίαν δ' ἡλικίαν ἐμαυτῷ ἐλθεῖν ἀναμένω; οὐ γὰρ ἔγωγ' ἔτι πρεσβύτερος ἔσομαι, ἐὰν τήμερον προδῶ ἐμαυτὸν τοῖς πολεμίοις.

QUESTIONS.

1. What is the subject of this work of Xenophon? and what are the chief elements of its value?

2. Describe briefly the contents of the Third Book.
3. Parse λαχών, πεσεῖν, ἀνηγέρθη, εἰκός, συμβάντων, ἐμποδών, ἀμυνούμεθα, ἐπιδόντας, προδῶ, conjugating the verbs.
4. Give the derivation or affinity of βροντῆς, σκηπτός, ἀποριῶν, ἐμποδών, ἡσυχίαν, ἡλικίαν.
5. ἐκ τούτου λάμπεσθαι πᾶσαν.—Why is πᾶσαν in the accusative?
6. ὥςπερ ἐξόν—τί ἐμποδὼν μὴ οὐχί.—Explain the syntax, and give the Latin equivalents, of these expressions.
7. ὁποῖόν τι ἐστι κ.τ.λ.—What is the nominative to ἐστί?
8. ἐγὼ οὖν τὸν ἐκ ποίας πόλεως κ.τ.λ.—Resolve this question into a less elliptical form.
9. ὄναρ.—What other forms of the word are in use? What is its opposite?

HOMER'S ILIAD, XII. 230-250.

To be translated accurately into English Prose.

Τὸν δ' ἄρ' ὑπόδρα ἰδὼν προσέφη κορυθαίολος Ἕκτωρ
Πουλυδάμα, σὺ μὲν οὐκέτ' ἐμοὶ φίλα ταῦτ' ἀγορεύεις·
οἶσθα καὶ ἄλλον μῦθον ἀμείνονα τοῦδε νοῆσαι
εἰ δ' ἐτεὸν δὴ τοῦτον ἀπὸ σπουδῆς ἀγορεύεις,
ἐξ ἄρα δή τοι ἔπειτα θεοὶ φρένας ὤλεσαν αὐτοί,
ὃς κέλεαι Ζηνὸς μὲν ἐριγδούποιο λαθέσθαι
βουλέων, ἅς τέ μοι αὐτὸς ὑπέσχετο καὶ κατένευσεν·
τύνη δ' οἰωνοῖσι τανυπτερύγεσσι κελεύεις
πείθεσθαι, τῶν οὔ τι μετατρέπομ' οὐδ' ἀλεγίζω,
εἴτ' ἐπὶ δεξί' ἴωσι πρὸς ἠῶ τ' ἠέλιόν τε,
εἴτ' ἐπ' ἀριστερὰ τοίγε ποτὶ ζόφον ἠερόεντα.
ἡμεῖς δὲ μεγάλοιο Διὸς πειθώμεθα βουλῇ,
ὃς πᾶσι θνητοῖσι καὶ ἀθανάτοισιν ἀνάσσει.
εἷς οἰωνὸς ἄριστος, ἀμύνεσθαι περὶ πάτρης.
τίπτε σὺ δείδοικας πόλεμον καὶ δηϊοτῆτα;
εἴπερ γάρ τ' ἄλλοι γε περικτεινώμεθα πάντες
νηυσὶν ἐπ' Ἀργείων, σοὶ δ' οὐ δέος ἔστ' ἀπολέσθαι·
οὐ γάρ τοι κραδίη μενεδήϊος οὐδὲ μαχήμων·
εἰ δὲ σὺ δηϊοτῆτος ἀφέξεαι, ἠέ τιν' ἄλλον
παρφάμενος ἐπέεσσιν ἀποτρέψεις πολέμοιο,
αὐτίκ' ἐμῷ ὑπὸ δουρὶ τυπεὶς ἀπὸ θυμὸν ὀλέσσεις.

NEW TESTAMENT.—ACTS II. 22-28 ; x. 34-43.

To be translated accurately.

Ἄνδρες Ἰσραηλῖται, ἀκούσατε τοὺς λόγους τούτους· Ἰησοῦν τὸν Ναζωραῖον, ἄνδρα ἀπὸ τοῦ Θεοῦ ἀποδεδειγμένον εἰς ὑμᾶς δυνάμεσι καὶ τέρασι καὶ σημείοις οἷς ἐποίησε δι' αὐτοῦ ὁ Θεὸς ἐν μ'σῳ ὑμῶν, καθὼς καὶ αὐτοὶ οἴδατε, τοῦτον τῇ ὡρισμένῃ βουλῇ καὶ προγνώσει τοῦ Θεοῦ ἔκδοτον λαβόντες, διὰ χειρῶν ἀνόμων προσπήξαντες ἀνείλετε. Ὃν ὁ Θεὸς ἀνέστησε, λύσας τὰς ὠδῖνας τοῦ θανάτου, καθότι οὐκ ἦν δυνατὸν κρατεῖσθαι αὐτὸν ὑπ' αὐτοῦ· Δαβὶδ γὰρ λέγει εἰς αὐτόν· Προωρώμην τὸν Κύριον ἐνώπιόν μου διὰ παντός, ὅτι ἐκ δεξιῶν μού ἐστιν, ἵνα μὴ σαλευθῶ. Διὰ τοῦτο εὐφράνθη ἡ καρδία μου, καὶ ἠγαλλιάσατο ἡ γλῶσσά μου· ἔτι δὲ καὶ ἡ σάρξ μου κατασκηνώσει ἐπ' ἐλπίδι, ὅτι οὐκ ἐγκαταλείψεις τὴν ψυχήν μου εἰς ᾅδου, οὐδὲ δώσεις τὸν ὅσιόν σου ἰδεῖν διαφθοράν. Ἐγνώρισάς μοι ὁδοὺς ζωῆς· πληρώσεις με εὐφροσύνης μετὰ τοῦ προσώπου σου.

Ἀνοίξας δὲ Πέτρος τὸ στόμα, εἶπεν· Ἐπ' ἀληθείας καταλαμβάνομαι ὅτι οὐκ ἔστι προσωπολήπτης ὁ Θεός· Ἀλλ' ἐν παντὶ ἔθνει ὁ φοβούμενος αὐτόν, καὶ ἐργαζόμενος δικαιοσύνην δεκτὸς αὐτῷ ἐστι. Τὸν λόγον ὃν ἀπέστειλε τοῖς υἱοῖς Ἰσραήλ, εὐαγγελιζόμενος εἰρήνην διὰ Ἰησοῦ Χριστοῦ· οὗτός ἐστι πάντων Κύριος. Ὑμεῖς οἴδατε τὸ γενόμενον ῥῆμα καθ' ὅλης τῆς Ἰουδαίας, ἀρξάμενον ἀπὸ τῆς Γαλιλαίας, μετὰ τὸ βάπτισμα ὃ ἐκήρυξεν Ἰωάννης· Ἰησοῦν τὸν ἀπὸ Ναζαρέτ, ὡς ἔχρισεν αὐτὸν ὁ Θεὸς Πνεύματι ἁγίῳ καὶ δυνάμει, ὃς διῆλθεν εὐεργετῶν καὶ ἰώμενος πάντας τοὺς καταδυναστευομένους ὑπὸ τοῦ διαβόλου, ὅτι ὁ Θεὸς ἦν μετ' αὐτοῦ. Καὶ ἡμεῖς [ἐσμεν] μάρτυρες πάντων, ὧν ἐποίησεν ἔν τε τῇ χώρᾳ τῶν Ἰουδαίων καὶ ἐν Ἱερουσαλήμ· ὃν ἀνεῖλον κρεμάσαντες ἐπὶ ξύλου. Τοῦτον ὁ Θεὸς ἤγειρε τῇ τρίτῃ ἡμέρᾳ καὶ ἔδωκεν αὐτὸν ἐμφανῆ γενέσθαι· Οὐ παντὶ τῷ λαῷ, ἀλλὰ μάρτυσι τοῖς προκεχειροτονημένοις ὑπὸ τοῦ Θεοῦ, ἡμῖν, οἵτινες συνεφάγομεν καὶ συνεπίομεν αὐτῷ μετὰ τὸ ἀναστῆναι αὐτὸν ἐκ νεκρῶν. Καὶ παρήγγειλεν ἡμῖν κηρύξαι τῷ λαῷ, καὶ διαμαρτύρασθαι, ὅτι αὐτός ἐστιν ὁ ὡρισμένος ὑπὸ τοῦ Θεοῦ κριτὴς ζώντων καὶ νεκρῶν. Τούτῳ πάντες οἱ προφῆται μαρτυροῦσιν, ἄφεσιν ἁμαρτιῶν λαβεῖν διὰ τοῦ ὀνόματος αὐτοῦ πάντα τὸν πιστεύοντα εἰς αὐτόν.

QUESTIONS.

1. On what grounds do you determine the authorship of the Acts of the Apostles?

2. At what part of the Acts of the Apostles, and in connexion with what event in the life of St. Paul, does the author begin to speak in his own name?
3. Give a brief summary of the events recorded in the first ten chapters.
4. Define the precise meaning of the several expressions used in one of the above passages to denote the miraculous power of Jesus Christ.
5. Parse the following words:—ἀποδεδειγμένον, ὡρισμένῃ, πωοσπήξαντες, ἀνείλετε, προωρώμην, σαλευθῶ, εὐφράνθη, ἐγκαταλείψεις, ἀνοίξας, ἰώμενος, κρεμάσαντες, κηρῦξαι, διαμαρτύρασθαι, ἁμαρτιῶν.
6. Give the derivation of the following words:—ὠδῖνας, διαφθοράν, εὐφροσύνης, πωοσωπολήπτης, εὐαγγελιζόμενος, διαβόλου, προκεχειροτονημένοις, ἄφεσιν, ἁμαρτιῶν.
7. Explain the following phrases occurring in the course of the first five chapters:—
τὸ καθόλου μὴ φθέγγεσθαι.
οἱ νεώτεροι συνέστειλαν αὐτὸν,
ὑπὸ τὸν ὄρθρον.
οἱ δὲ ἀκούσαντες διεπρίοντο.
8. (a) What space of time is covered by the narrative of the first ten chapters; and (b) what is the special significance of the event recorded in the tenth chapter, in relation to the spread of the Gospel?

ARITHMETIC.

1. Find, by Practice, the cost of 19 cwts. 3 qrs. 20 lbs. at £27, 13s. 7d. per cwt.
2. Add together the fractions $3\frac{2}{5}$, $4\frac{3}{13}$, $7\frac{1}{23}$, and $\dfrac{1\frac{1}{2}}{6\frac{1}{2}}$
3. Reduce 4s. 2½d. to the decimal of 5s. 11d., and divide the result by ·0014.
4. If the proportion of deaths be annually 1 in 45 in towns and 1 in 56 in the country, what is the percentage of mortality, when the town population bears to that of the country the proportion of 3 to 7?
5. Extract the square root of $1\frac{13}{30}$, and the cube root of 4 feet 1088 inches cubic measure.

368   REPORT ON EDUCATION.   [APP. I.

6. Two clocks are together at 12; when the first again comes to 12 it has lost a minute, and when the second comes to 12 it has gained a minute. How long must elapse before they are a quarter of an hour asunder?

7. Between 1801 and 1811 the population of Edinburgh increased by $24\tfrac{3}{4}$ per cent., and in the latter year it was 102,987; what was it in the former?

What would it have become in 1821 had the yearly rate of increase from 1811 been 2 per cent.?

8. At an examination, the respective marks attainable are as follows:—For classics, 1500; for English, 1200; for mathematics, 1400; for modern languages, 1000; for geography, 750. The relative proficiency of two candidates in these five departments is indicated by the following numbers:— A's, 3, 4, 2, 5, 1; B's, 4, 3, 5, 0, 2; which should stand first in the examination?

2. If I buy 15 dozen of wine, 6 bottles containing a gallon, for £35, 10s., at what rate must I sell it per quart so as to gain £15 per cent.?

10. Of what is $\tfrac{1}{5}$ the logarithm? Find approximately the logarithm of 6.

ALGEBRA.

1. Multiply $x^2-7xy-8y^2$ by $8y^2-x^2-7xy$, and $1+2x+3x^2+$ &c.$+nx^{n-1}$ by $1-2x+x^2$.

2. Divide $x^3+y^3+z^3-3xyz$ by $x+y+z$; and admitting that $4b^2c^2-(b^2+c^2-a^2)^2$ is divisible by $a+b+c$; resolve it into simple factors.

3. Extract the square root of—
$$(a-b)^4-2(a^2+b^2)(a-b)^2+2(a^4+b^4),$$
and the cube root of—
$$27x^6-27x^5y-45x^4y^2+35x^3y^3+30x^2y^4-12xy^5-8y^6.$$

4. Add together the fractions—

(1.) $\dfrac{x}{a-1}+\dfrac{x}{\tfrac{1}{a}-1}.$

(2.) $\dfrac{1}{6x+6}-\dfrac{1}{2x-2}+\dfrac{4}{3x-6}.$

(3.) $\dfrac{ab}{(b-c)(c-a)}+\dfrac{bc}{(a-c)(b-a)}+\dfrac{ca}{(a-b)(b-c)}.$

5. Prove that—
$$x^2+y^2+z^2 > xy+xz+yz;$$
and that the hypotenuse of a right-angled triangle, together with the perpendicular on it from the right angle, are greater than the two sides of the triangle.

6. Solve the following equations:—

(1.) $\dfrac{2x-1}{3} - \dfrac{3x-2}{4} = \dfrac{5x-4}{6} - \dfrac{7x+6}{12}.$

(2.) $\sqrt{(5a+x)} + \sqrt{(5a-x)} = \sqrt{(10a+2b)}.$

(3.) $x^2+y^2 = 7+xy,\ x^3+y^3 = 6xy-1.$

7. Sum the arithmetical series—
$$1+3+5+\text{etc. to } n \text{ terms};$$
and the geometric series—
$$1+3+\text{etc. to } 20 \text{ terms}.$$

A sum of money rather more than doubles itself in 15 years at 5 per cent. compound interest. Suppose the interest to be such that the sum is exactly doubled in 15 years; it is required to determine how much a penny would amount to from the date of the death of Wallace, 1305, to 1860.

GEOMETRY.

1. Define a square; and a parallelogram. Prove that a square is a parallelogram. In what respect is Euclid's definition of a square faulty? What *consequence* can be deduced from it, if it be admitted?

2. If the square described upon one side of a triangle be equal to the sum of the squares described upon the other two sides of it, the angle contained by these two sides is a right angle.

3. If a straight line be divided into two equal and also into two unequal parts; the squares of the two unequal parts are together double of the square of half the line, and of the square of the line between the points of section.

If the point which, in this proposition, divides the line into two unequal parts, be taken in the line produced, what change ought, from the nature of the case, to be made in the enunciation?

4. The angle at the centre of a circle is double the angle at the circumference.

Assuming that there is no limitation as to the magnitude of an angle, deduce from this proposition, in immediate corollaries, the propositions that "the angles in the same segment of a circle are equal," and that "the opposite angles of a quadrilateral described in a circle are together equal to two right angles."

5. To inscribe an equilateral and equiangular pentagon in a given circle.

6. If two triangles have one angle of the one equal to one angle of the other, and the sides about the equal angles proportionals, the triangles shall be equiangular.

7. Similar polygons may be divided into the same number of similar triangles, having the same ratio to one another which the polygons have; and that ratio is the duplicate ratio of homologous sides.

TRIGONOMETRY, ETC.

1. Prove the relations which exist between radius and (1) sine and cosine, (2) tangent and cotangent, (3) secant and cosecant.

2. The three sides of a triangle are 148, 195, and 329; find its area.

3. The three sides of a triangle are 2, $\sqrt{6}$, and $1+\sqrt{3}$; find the least angle.

4. Prove that $R \sin. (A + B) = \sin. A \cos. B + \cos. A \sin. B$. Find the numerical value of $\sin. 75°$.

5. Determine the volume and convex surface of a cone, the area of whose base is 16 feet, and whose slant height is 3 feet.

PHYSICS.

1. If a straight lever support weights in equilibrium, they are to one another inversely as the lengths of the arms which support them.

2. Two forces, represented by 1 and $\sqrt{2}$, act at an angle of $45°$; find the magnitude and direction of their resultant.

3. Water weighs 1000 oz. avoirdupois per cubic foot; find the pressure on a square yard 100 feet below the surface of the water.

A man just floats in water, what is his specific gravity? If he weighs 14 stone, what is his cubic measure?

4. Explain the action of the siphon. How does this action account for intermitting springs?

5. Enunciate the laws of reflexion and refraction of light. Account for total internal reflexion, and mention some of its applications. Find the positions of the successive images of objects placed between two mirrors inclined to one another by the angle of 30°.

6. State the physical explanations of sound and light. Give the relative values of the notes in the diatonic scale. Are the values of the different colours in the solar spectrum similarly related?

APPENDIX II.

RESULTS OF EXAMINATIONS OF SCHOOLMASTERS AND SUBSTITUTES.

TABLE No. I.—SCHOOLMASTERS.

The classification of Teachers, with respect to their examinations, during the ten years from 1854 to 1863 inclusive, has been made under four divisions, as shown from the Table, viz. :—

I. Teachers who have appeared for examination for the *first* time, ... 61
II. Teachers who did not pass the examination in whole at their first appearance, but were examined a second time, . 49
III. Teachers who failed to pass their first examination, and appeared for a second examination, . . . 6
IV. Teachers who have never been examined at all, although two or more examinations have taken place since their appointment, ... 12

These classes are further subdivided, thus, Class I., containing 61 :—

Teachers who have passed the whole of the examination at their first appearance, and received a special extra allowance as a mark of the Trustees' approbation for distinguished proficiency,	6
Teachers who have passed the whole of the examination at their first appearance, and received the usual allowance for scholarship, but without special commendation,	6
Teachers who have passed only part of the examination at their first appearance, but completed their trials at next appearance,	37
Teachers who have failed on a second appearance, but passed at a second examination,	3
Teachers who have died or resigned before time for second appearance,	2
Teachers who have made a first appearance, but have not appeared to complete examination,	3
Teachers who have failed at second appearance, and have not appeared for a second examination,	3
Teacher who has made a first appearance, but has not returned to complete examination, being in ill health,	1
	61

Class II., containing 49 :—

Teachers who, having passed only part of the examination at their first appearance, have returned and completed their trials at a second appearance,	41
Teachers who have failed on second appearance, but passed at a second examination,	3
[Two of these appeared twice at second examination, and one passed at first appearance.]	
Teachers who have failed on second appearance, and have not returned for a second examination,	5
	49

Class III., containing 6 :—

Passed second examination at first appearance,	1
Do. at second appearance,	4
Failed to pass at second appearance,	1
	6

Class IV., containing 12 :—

Teachers who did not appear for examination at all, in consequence of ill health, and who are now dead, ... 4
Teachers who have not appeared for examination, and have resigned, ... 5
Do., and are still teaching, ... 3

12

TABLE No. II.—ASSISTANT-SUBSTITUTES.

This Table also consists of four divisions; and the same classification has been made as in No. I. It only requires to be noticed that, in the case of Assistants, very few came up for a second examination. The Trustees generally, in the case of an Assistant who fails to pass the examination at his second appearance, request him to resign, without allowing him to come forward for a second examination, unless they have good expectations that he will devote his leisure time to study, and qualify himself for passing in a creditable manner.

Class I., containing 39 :—

Teachers who have passed the whole examination at their first appearance, and received a special extra allowance for distinguished excellence, ... 2
Teachers who have passed the whole examination at their first appearance, but without special commendation, receiving, however, the usual addition to their allowances for scholarship, ... 2
Teachers who have completed their trials at a second appearance, ... 21
Teachers who have been allowed a second examination, and passed [one appeared as schoolmaster], . . . 3
Teachers who died or resigned before time for second appearance, ... 2
Teachers who resigned at request of Trustees after their first appearance, ... 3
Teacher who failed to make a second appearance, but afterwards resigned, ... 1
Teachers who failed on second appearance, and afterwards resigned, ... 3
Teacher who failed on second appearance, and did not appear

Carry forward, 37

	Brought forward,	37
for second examination (being appointed a schoolmaster he could not be called on to resign), ...		1
Teacher who appeared for second examination as schoolmaster, and failed, ...		1
		39

Class II., containing 23 :—

Teachers who passed part of the examination at their first appearance, and completed their trials at a second appearance,	20
Teachers who failed to complete their examination at a second appearance, and resigned afterwards, . . .	3
	23

Class III., containing 4 :—

Passed second examination at first appearance,	1
Do. at second appearance,	1
Failed to pass second examination, and resigned,	2
	4

Class IV., containing 2 :—

Teachers who did not come up for examination at all, in consesequence of bad health ; one resigned and one died, . .	2

Teachers who have failed to pass examination 1854-1863 :—

Of the 61 schoolmasters who have come up for examination for the first time, those who have failed to pass, as on page 372, are,	6
Of the 39 assistant-substitutes, do., as on page 373, . .	9
Schoolmasters who have not come up for examination at all, as on page 373, ...	12
Assistant-substitutes, do., as on page 374, . . .	2

After the examinations of 1863, the teachers on active duty, whom the Trustees have been unable to admit on account of failure to attend the examinations, were :—

(1.) Those who have not yet been examined at all, though two or more examinations have passed since their election, .	7
(2.) Those who have failed to attend a second or subsequent examination, ...	13
	20

No. I.—TABLE OF RESULTS OF EXAMINATIONS, 1854-63.—SCHOOLMASTERS.

YEAR	Number examined first time.	Passed. Highest class, and special exemption allowance for deficiency.	Passed. Distinguished, with allowance for scholarship.	Incomplete.	Completed examination at next appearance.	Failed to appear, or to complete examination at second appearance.	YEAR	Number examined.	Passed.	Failed on second appearance. Deficient.	Passed at a second examination.	Did not appear for a second examination.	First appearance.	Second appearance.	Judgment on examination.	Number who have never been examined at all, although two or more examinations have taken place since their appointment.
1854	3	1	..	2	2	....	1854	4	3	1	..	1	..	1	Passed	{ 1 who resigned before next examination. 1 who resigned in 1861.
1855	6	..	..	6	2	{ 1 resigned and went abroad before examination of 1856. 3 failed to complete examination in 1856, but 2 passed afterwards, and 1 did not reappear.	1855 1856	3 5	3 2	.. 3	2 ..	.. ..	.. ..	.. ..	....	1 who still teaches.
1856	6	..	1	4	2	{ 1 failed in 1857, but passed in 1858. 1 did not appear to complete examination.	1857	3	2	1	1	..	2	..	{ Past in part, and completed next year.	{ 1 who died in 1860. 1 who resigned in 1860. 1 who resigned in 1861.
1857	6	..	1	5	4	{ 1 did not appear to complete examination.	1858	4	4	..	..	..	1	2	All passed.	{ 1 who died in 1862. 1 who died in 1860. 1 who died in 1861.
1858 1859	4 7	.. ..	.. ..	4 6	4 5	....	1859 1860	4 6	4 6	.. ..	.. ..	2 ..	.. ..	.. ..	....	{ 1 who still teaches. 1 school declared vacant under Act 24 and 25 Vict. cap. 107.
1860	8	..	..	8	5	{ 2 failed to complete in 1861, and did not reappear. 1 did not appear to complete examination.	1861	7 (4 appeared as assistant-substitutes last year.)	5	..	..	1	..	..	....	....
1861	5	1	..	4	3	{ 1 died before examination of 1862.	1862	6	6	2	3	2	2	2	{ 1 passed in part, and completed in 1864. 1 failed in 1864.	1 still teaches.
1862 1863	8 6	2 1	3 ..	6 4	6 3	{ 1 did not appear in 1864, being in ill health.	1863	..	..	..	..	..	..	..	....	....
	61	6	6	49	37	12		49	41	8	3	5	..	..		12

No. II.—Table of Results of Examinations, 1854-1863.—Assistant-Substitutes.

	First Examination—First Appearance.					First Examination—Second Appearance.				Second Examination.			
Year.	Number examined first time.	Passed. Highest class, with special extra allowance for distinguished proficiency.	Passed. Distinguished, with allowance for scholarship.	Incomplete.	Completed examination at next appearance.	Failed to appear, or to complete examination at second appearance.	Year.	Number examined.	Passed.	Still deficient.	First appearance.	Second appearance.	Judgment.	Number who have never been examined, although two or more examinations have taken place since their appointment.
1854	4		2	2	1	{ 1 allowed to appear next year for a second examination. 1 failed next year, and resigned. }	1854	2	2		1	1	{ Both failed and resigned. }	{ 1 who resigned before next examination, being in ill health.
1855	2	1		1		{ 1 resigned before next examination. }	1855	1	1		1	1	{ Completed examination next year. }	1 who died in 1857.
1856	3*			3	2	{ 1 did not re-appear, but resigned afterwards. }	1856	1		{ 1 resigned afterwards. }				
1857	4			4	2	{ 1 reappeared as a schoolmaster afterwards for second examination, but failed to pass. }	1857	2	2			1	Passed.	
1858	5	1		4	1	{ 2 failed next year, and resigned. 1 died before next examination. }	1858	2	2	{ 2 resigned afterwards. }				
1859	5			5	4	{ 1 resigned before next examination. }	1859	3	1					
1860	4			4	4		1860	4	4					
1861	10			10	3 (As assistants.) 3 (As schoolmasters.)	{ 2 did not appear in 1862, but passed afterwards, 1 as an assistant, and 1 as a schoolmaster. 1 failed next year as a schoolmaster, and did not reappear. 1 school declared vacant under new Act, and a different schoolmaster appointed. }	1861	4	3					
1862	1			1	1		1862	1	1					
1863	1			1		{ 1 resigned before next examination. }	1863				1		Passed.	
	39	2	2	35	21	14		23	20	3	2	2		2

* Four Candidates appeared this year, but the examination of one was cancelled, and allowed to be commenced de novo.

APPENDIX III.

REPORT BY THE PRESBYTERY OF —— REGARDING SCHOOLS IN THE PARISH OF ——.—1864.

The Trustees of Mr. Dick's Bequest have prepared this Formula, and now transmit it, agreeably to the wish and suggestion of several clergymen in the three counties. It has not proceeded from any wish to interfere with the plan of the copious and valuable Reports with which the Trustees have been favoured by some Presbyteries. But if the Presbyteries generally shall think it advisable to act upon the suggestion, to issue this Schedule, it is believed that it will tend to simplify and facilitate the discharge of this important branch of their functions, while the uniformity thus introduced into the nature and detail of reports influential in determining the apportionment of the Bequest, will obviously afford material assistance to the Trustees.

It is unnecessary to specify minutely the nature of the observations with which the Trustees hope to be favoured. They have no doubt that these will comprehend what may be worthy of notice respecting particular branches, and, in general, the considerations of the method pursued—success evinced by the accuracy and extent of acquirement in the scholars—peculiar excellence of any kind—improvement in any department since a previous examination—knowledge of the Holy Scriptures and of Christian doctrine and duty, and any other important information.

PRIVATE SCHOOLS.

Total number of day schools in the parish, *besides the parochial schools*, ... 2
Total number of scholars attending these, . .

PAROCHIAL SCHOOL.

Examined upon the —— day of February 1864.

Number of scholars attending, ... 58
Number present at examination, . . . 47

Number learning Religious Knowledge, . 52
Ditto, English, . . . 58
Ditto, English Grammar, . . 29

OBSERVATIONS.—The pupils very well taught from the alphabet class onward to highest.
The spelling very good, and remarkably good in all the more advanced classes. The scholars generally gave a good account of the lessons, which in all cases were selected by the visitors. The English reading is so distinct as to create the expectation that the lesson will be found to have been well entered into and appreciated, when a minute examination is made. Lessons in verse were well read, and pieces of poetry tastefully and correctly recited by many of the pupils. The Catechism had been thoroughly attended to, and the answers were accurately, readily, and intelligently given. Paraphrases well recited.

The Holy Scriptures were read well; by the junior class, New Testament history successfully attended to. The examination by the visitors was on the Acts, particularly on Paul's history, journeys, and preaching. The senior Bible class did equally well on the Old Testament. The department of English grammar is very well taught; and the scholars have entered heartily into this branch of education, and have profited accordingly.

Number learning Analysis of Sentences, . 10

OBSERVATIONS.—The pupils in this branch are in two divisions, and are carefully instructed; the junior division well grounded, and the senior able to analyse with very considerable acuteness. They are instructed from Morell's Grammar.

Number able to compose a simple Narrative satisfactorily, 7

OBSERVATIONS.—These scholars did the prescribed exercise not only satisfactorily but remarkably well. The subject was chosen by the visitors, and was one on which they had never written before, but with which it was known they should have been well informed; and the result on examining their narratives very much gratified the examiners.

Number learning Writing, . . 40

OBSERVATIONS.—Careful attention must have been bestowed on this branch of school-work. The copies were all clean,--the progress manifest; and the writing of many of the more advanced pupils was very good indeed.

Number learning Arithmetic,   .   .   .   40

OBSERVATIONS.—The youngest class had got through simple addition, and did very fairly. The middle class were on through compound addition, and also did very fairly. The highest class were on to compound proportion and fractions. They worked out various questions put by the visitors very readily, and could give a good account of the mode adopted for getting the answer.

Number learning Geography, Political and Physical, 22

OBSERVATIONS.—Junior class: The examination here by the visitors was on the British Isles, Europe, and part of Asia. They had been taught from the Young Child's Geography, with the aid of good maps; and they made a very good appearance.

Senior class: The examination here was on all the Continents generally, and on Europe and the British Isles specially. Clyde's smaller class-book had been used, and used with success. This department of geography very well taught.

Number learning Mathematics,   .   .   None.
Number learning Latin, ...   3
    Ditto,   Greek,   .   .   None.
    Ditto,   French,   .   .   None.

OBSERVATIONS.—The three Latin pupils were reading Cæsar's Commentaries. The parts read were chosen by the visitors from what they had gone over with the teacher. They did remarkably well, considering their years and opportunities. They analysed and parsed the sentences with readiness and accuracy.

Number taught to sing from notation, .   .   None.
Number learning the elements of outline drawing,   None.

GENERAL REMARKS.—The parish school of —— is in a very efficient state, and maintains a high character. The order is very good; and the scholars are lively and hearty at their school-work. The visitors hold that it has not suffered in efficiency during Mr. ——'s absence at college. His substitute-assistant is a good scholar and a very painstaking teacher, and has carried on the work with diligence, intelligence, and success. *One-half* of the pupils have entered for the *first time* during Mr. ——'s absence this winter; and this shows, among other things, that the assistant-substitute has been well appreciated.

The number of prizes for the scholars, subscribed for by the parishioners, and presented after the examination, shows the interest taken hitherto in the school is not diminished.

———— ————, *Minister of* ————,
and Convener of Presby. Comm.
———— ————, *Minister of* ————.
———— ————, *Minr. of* ————.

APPENDIX IV.

ABSTRACT OF REGULATIONS OF THE DICK BEQUEST, in so far as these relate to the Appointment and Qualifications of PAROCHIAL SCHOOLMASTERS, ASSISTANT-SUBSTITUTES, ASSISTANTS and SUCCESSORS, and ORDINARY and TEMPORARY ASSISTANTS.

I.—PAROCHIAL SCHOOLMASTERS.

1. After a newly-elected schoolmaster has been examined and admitted by the Board of Examiners prescribed by the Statute, he must pass the Examination prescribed by the Trustees before being allowed to participate in the Bequest.

2. A schoolmaster, on going up for examination, must, in the first year, profess at least five branches of study—whereof English, Arithmetic, and Latin must be three.

3. To gain distinction for eminence, a schoolmaster must at first appearance profess all the subjects of trial.

4. Where a schoolmaster's examination extends over more than one year, any modified allowance on partial profession and success is reserved, and not paid till the whole examination is passed.

5. Where the examination of a schoolmaster is not completed in the second year's examination, he must begin his examination *de novo*, excepting only on those subjects on which he shall have received the mark " Good."

6. Where a schoolmaster passes with distinction, an addition is made to his allowance in respect of " Scholarship," which he retains throughout his incumbency, as part of his annual allowance. And the Trustees further, in cases of extraordinary proficiency

displayed at examination, sometimes bestow a single donation in money as a mark of special approbation.

7. When a schoolmaster has not gone up for examination, he can never in any shape participate in the benefits of the Bequest. Thus, in such a case, were he to fall into bad health, the Trustees will not give any aid toward procuring an assistant, nor will they assist him to get rid of the active duties of his office by making him a retiring allowance.

8. Bad health is accepted as a good excuse for not attending the examination; but only if it be pleaded beforehand, and medical certificates produced.

9. The expenses of teachers attending the examinations are paid for two years, but not longer.

10. Where schoolmasters are found to be inefficient, and their schools, consequently, in bad order, the Trustees are in use to restrict their allowances, or to keep them back altogether.

11. Where there appears no hope of amendment, the Trustees are in the practice of endeavouring to persuade the inefficient schoolmasters to retire from the active management of their schools.

The terms on which this is arranged are shown under the head " Assistant-Substitutes," and the Trustees sometimes induce incumbents to retire by making money payments to them, which, however, in no case exceed the aggregate amount of the incumbent's allowances, which had been reserved during the years previous to his retirement.

12. No parochial schoolmaster can participate in the benefits of the Bequest until he is twenty-one years of age.

For regulations as to schoolmasters absent from duty, see page 384 *hereof,* at §§ 1, 2, 3, 4.

II.—ASSISTANT-SUBSTITUTES.

1. In every case where an arrangement is made for the retirement of a schoolmaster and the appointment of an assistant, it is a *sine qua non* that the entire responsibility, and consequently the entire authority, shall rest with the assistant, and, as he thus comes in place of the schoolmaster, he is called the " Assistant-Substitute."

2. The Trustees deem it unnecessary to interfere with the mode of appointing assistant-substitutes, but in every case where they

have had to suggest the mode of appointment, they have recommended that the election should, as in the case of schoolmasters, rest with the minister and heritors.

3. The usual terms of the arrangement with schoolmasters retiring in favour of assistant-substitutes are always embodied in a regular stamped deed of obligation by the incumbent of the Trustees, and are as follows, viz. :—

(1.) The retiring schoolmaster receives the allowances to be provided to him by the heritors, under the Act 24 & 25 Vict. cap. 107, and a retiring allowance from the Trustees of £12 per annum.

(2.) The assistant-substitute receives from the heritors a yearly salary, not under the rate of £35, when there is only one school in the parish, and £25 when there are two or more, along with possession of the dwelling-house and garden. He also receives the school fees and the ordinary allowance from the Bequest.

4. The assistant-substitute is required to produce a certificate of his having been examined and found duly qualified by the Presbytery of the bounds.

5. It is a rule of the Trustees that no private agreement different in its terms from that which they have sanctioned shall be entered into between a schoolmaster and his substitute, and when any such is discovered the allowances of both are retained till it is cancelled.

6. Contrary to the rule in the case of schoolmasters, assistant-substitutes are capable of participating in the Bequest before they are twenty-one years of age.

7. Assistant-substitutes must, on their appointment, submit to examination like regular schoolmasters, but in their case participation is not suspended till the examination is passed in full, and the ordinary allowances are paid under an obligation in writing by the assistant that he will attend the examination till he passes.

8. Where, on examination, assistant-substitutes are found deficient in scholarship, the Trustees do not generally restrict their allowances; but if their deficiencies are such as show it to be hopeless that they will ever pass the examination, due notice is given to enable them to look out for other employment; after which the allowance is wholly withdrawn, so as to compel them to resign. In

some cases allowances past due have been paid only on condition of immediate resignation.

For regulations as to assistant-substitutes absent from duty, see page 384 *hereof,* §§ 1, 2, 3, 4.

III.—Assistants and Successors.

1. Parties elected assistants and successors must undergo examination, and are in other respects treated on the same footing as schoolmasters.

IV.—Ordinary Assistants.

1. The Trustees do not interfere with parties employed by schoolmasters to aid them in the management of their schools in the character of ordinary assistants.

2. In some cases, however, where schools were found to be inefficiently taught, the Trustees have insisted on a schoolmaster obtaining the services of an able assistant, under pain of forfeiture of allowance in case of refusal.

3. The Trustees do not generally give any pecuniary aid towards the assistants' salaries in such cases, the only occasions on which they have given such aid having been where an assistant has been required in consequence of the incumbent being in bad health, or too old for the full discharge of his duties.

V.—Temporary Assistants.

The following regulations were adopted by the Trustees in regard to temporary assistants appointed to take charge of schools during the absence of the schoolmaster or assistant-substitute at college :—

1. By the general rule any schoolmaster who shall absent himself from duty to attend College, or for any other cause, not involving physical disability, suffers abatement proportionate to the duration of his absence. And that regulation was, by the Trustees' Minutes of 30th December 1851, extended (after the end of the session of College in spring 1852) to assistant-substitute teachers, who are to suffer abatement on the ground of absence, in the same way as if they were schoolmasters fully inducted.

2. If any schoolmaster or assistant-substitute shall be absent at College during two or more winters in succession, he shall, for every

winter in succession after the first, forfeit his allowance for the whole year.

3. Every schoolmaster and assistant-substitute proposing to attend College, shall give notice of his intention to the Trustees' clerk at least a month before the commencement of the session, and if such notice is not given in any case the party shall be held to have forfeited his allowance for the whole year.

4. In the case of any teacher forfeiting his allowance for the period of absence only, and not for the whole year, the Trustees will be ready to consider any application to have the forfeited portion of the allowance, or a part of it, made available to the temporary assistant officiating in the absence of the schoolmaster or assistant-substitute, provided the following regulations shall be observed, viz. :—

(1.) Any schoolmaster, or assistant-substitute, intending to go to College, shall, along with the notice of his intention, transmit a copy of the testimonials of the person who is to teach during his absence, and state the amount of the allowance (the same not being less than at the rate of £1 per week) which he proposes to give to such temporary assistant.

(2.) The qualifications of the temporary assistant, and his discharge of the duties, shall be satisfactory to the minister of the parish and the Presbytery of the bounds, of which evidence shall be produced: in order to qualify a temporary assistant to receive any allowance from the Trustees, the report of the Presbytery shall be so specific and minute as to enable the Trustees to judge of the actual condition of the school, and, in particular, to judge of the degree of its efficiency as compared with its condition under the immediate charge of the absent teacher.

(3.) If the Trustees shall be satisfied with the whole arrangement, and that the temporary assistant has been diligent and successful, they will, in their discretion, award to him (to be paid upon a discharge by the schoolmaster) that part of the annual allowance which the incumbent or assistant-substitute would himself have received if not absent, or such part thereof as the Trustees may think fit.

(4.) It has been the practice of the Trustees, so invariable as to amount to a regulation, not to allow a temporary assistant to receive the forfeited allowances unless evidence be produced of his having had a University education, or of his having obtained a Government Certificate of Merit of the first class, second year.

APPENDIX V.

"THE REVISED CODE."

STATEMENT for THE TRUSTEES of the DICK BEQUEST in reference to the probable effects of the CLAUSE regarding ANNUAL ENDOWMENTS in the "REVISED CODE," if applied to the working of the Bequest under their Management.

The funds under the management of the Trustees, which consist of the residuary estate of the late James Dick, Esquire, sometime of Finsbury Square in the city of London, were, by his Last Will and Testament, specially directed to be applied " to the maintenance and assistance of the Country Parochial Schoolmasters as by law established in the three counties of Aberdeen, Banff, and Moray, excluding the royal burghs."

Mr. Dick, in dedicating the bulk of his fortune, which amounts at the present time to £118,787, 11s., exclusive of forfeited and reserved allowances, to this benevolent purpose, laid down the following, *inter alia*, as the principles to be observed by his Trustees in administering the funds, viz. :—

First, " That the Income of the Fund be applied in such manner as not in any manner *to relieve the Heritors or other persons* from their legal obligations to support Parochial Schoolmasters, *or to diminish the extent of such support*, and so as not to interfere with the rights or powers of Heritors and Presbyteries over Schoolmasters, or the schools intrusted to their care, as the same rights or powers are by law insured to them."

Second, " That the Trustees for the time being shall have full power to pay and distribute the Income of the said Fund, from time to time, to or among all or such one or more of the Parochial Schoolmasters aforesaid in such proportions, and generally to dispose of the said Income among them in such manner as to such Trustees shall seem most likely to encourage active Schoolmasters, and gradually to elevate the literary character of the Parochial Schoolmasters and Schools aforesaid ; and for these purposes *to increase, diminish, or altogether to discontinue the salary or allowance to be from time to time made to all or any of such Schoolmasters, without being accountable for so doing."*

The Trustees, with a view to carrying out the intentions of Mr. Dick as thus indicated, have endeavoured to apportion the allowances from the fund under their care in such a way that they shall correspond in each case to the merits of the recipient as a teacher. These accordingly form a direct encouragement to active teachers, and become a means of elevating at once the literary character and material comforts of the schoolmasters within the three counties.

Before a teacher can become a participant in the Dick Bequest, it is imperative that he should pass a stringent examination before examiners appointed by the Trustees on all the branches of a thorough classical and literary education, including English Literature, History, Geography, Arithmetic, Latin and Greek, the higher branches of Mathematics, and Physics.

The funds are divided annually among those teachers who are eligible according to a regular scheme of division, in which effect is given, in accordance with certain fixed rules, to the state of each separate school in respect of (1.) the numbers in attendance, (2.) the branches of education taught, (3.) *the number of scholars taught gratuitously*, (4.) the personal scholarship of the teacher as ascertained by his preliminary examination, and (5.) the general merit and efficiency of the teacher, as appearing from the yearly reports of a visitor of schools employed by the Trustees for the purpose of inspection.

Further, in order to prevent the Bequest from being made a means of " relieving the heritors or other persons from their legal obligation to support the Parochial Schoolmasters," or of " diminishing the extent of such support," the Trustees have made the amount of school salary an element in their scheme of division, increasing or diminishing each teacher's allowance in proportion to the amount of his salary, thus awarding the larger allowance to the teacher who obtains the larger salary, and so creating an inducement to heritors to grant the *maximum* salary to efficient teachers, that they may thereby become entitled to the full enjoyment of the benefits of the Bequest.

The Visitor of schools fixes the number of marks to be allowed in the scheme of division to each teacher in respect of *merit in teaching*, as ascertained by the condition of his school, and this he does, not in relation to any fixed standard of merit, but on a comparison of the state of the particular school with that of the others connected with the Bequest. Thus, a schoolmaster who receives 300 merit marks one year, may in the next receive only 200, not in consequence of any falling off in the actual condition of his school, but from its having failed to advance along with other schools with which it is thus placed in competition.

A teacher's allowance thus fluctuates from year to year, and so strongly does the element of *merit* enter into calculation, that, though the number of scholars, the branches taught, and the various other items above referred to, have an important bearing on fixing the amount of a teacher's allowance, all is of no avail unless his school, by its state of general efficiency, bears a satisfactory testimony to his merits and activity in the discharge of duty. Accordingly, whatever be the number in attendance on a school, if the Trustees have reason to think, that through want of proper care and attention on the teacher's part, its condition is falling off, they are in the constant practice of restricting his allowance to the extent of one-third or one-half, and sometimes, in aggravated cases of neglect, of withdrawing it altogether.

Under such a system, consistently and rigorously carried out, no schoolmaster, merely because he has once participated in the Bequest, can calculate with certainty on doing so in any future year. Allowances are not the right of a teacher in respect of his tenure of office, but are emphatically the reward of merit.

The Dick Bequest has now been in operation for nearly thirty years, and has been instrumental in carrying out in a remarkable degree the views of its founder. Indeed it may be asserted, without fear of contradiction, that this fund, as administered by the Trustees, has raised the literary character of the parochial schoolmasters and schools within the three favoured counties to a position of marked pre-eminence over those of any other part of Scotland.

The Trustees have reason to fear, however, that the usefulness of the Bequest is likely to be very seriously impaired, under the operation of the " Revised Code," recently laid on the table of the House of Commons by the Committee of the Privy Council on Education.

By Article 52 D. of the Code, the value of all " Annual Endowments" is to be deducted in calculating the amount of the Government grant to which any teacher shall be entitled, and the Trustees understand that allowances from the Dick Bequest are to be held by the Committee of Council as endowments falling under the operation of this Clause.

In order fully to appreciate the injury which such a provision is likely to inflict on the Bequest, it is necessary to contrast the regulations in regard to participation by the Trustees on the one hand, and by the Committee of Council on Education on the other.

1. As already seen, the Trustees require as a preliminary to participation that teachers should pass a stringent examination on all the subjects of a high class literary and classical education, and in particular in Latin, Greek, the higher branches of Mathematics, and Physics; while, under the examination for a Government certificate, Latin, Greek, and Physics are not required at all, and the knowledge of Mathematics necessary is of the most elementary character.

2. A teacher's allowance is liable to be restricted or wholly cut off at the discretion of the Trustees, in case, through inattention on his part or otherwise, his school shall fall off to any serious extent in respect of efficiency; while in the case of the Government grant total deprivation is a thing almost unheard of, and the power of restriction given to the Inspectors is limited to one-half, but in practice is never exercised, excepting to the extent of one-tenth only.

It will thus be seen that, unless the allowances from the Dick Bequest far exceeded in amount those awarded out of the Government grant, it would not be worth any man's while to offer himself for the Trustees' examination, or to incur the risks of deprivation or of restriction of allowance, to which necessarily every one is liable who receives the benefits of the Bequest, when he can secure his share of the Privy Council grant free from the risk of any serious fluctuation, and without the trouble of preparing for what is truly a very severe examination.

So far, however, is it from being the case that the allowances from the Bequest are likely to exceed those from the Government grant, that, on the contrary, it appears they will be much smaller in the case of large schools, and about equal in the case of smaller schools in rural and remote parishes. Thus, in the case of the school of ——, where the enrolled scholars amount to 272, it is calculated that the amount of the grant from Government would exceed £90 yearly, while the allowance from the Bequest is no more than £40; and in the case of ——, which is a remote school consisting of only 65 enrolled scholars, the Government grant would be probably about £30, while the allowance from the Bequest would amount to about the same sum.

If, then, in the case first supposed, the schoolmaster of ———, in claiming his share of the Government grant, is obliged to deduct from it the amount which he receives from the Bequest, it is clear that he has no interest whatever in the question whether that allowance shall be greater or smaller, seeing that, if greater, he has still to deduct it from his Government allowance, and if smaller, as a consequence of the standard of excellence being higher with the Trustees than under the " Revised Code," he may hope to receive from Government full compensation for any amount which may be struck off from his allowance under the Bequest.

In the case second supposed, namely that of ———, it is equally clear that the schoolmaster has little interest in the question whether he shall claim from the Bequest or from Government in the first instance, though he too would, in the event of the Trustees putting him on restricted allowance, probably be compensated for the shortcoming by the Government grant.

Indeed the result seems to be, that for the future, in all cases of large schools in populous districts, where the Government grant, under the system prescribed by the Code, would be at the largest rate, the teachers will never dream of connecting themselves with the Bequest at all, and the literary character of the schoolmasters and schools will suffer in consequence.

The Trustees, however, though they have the power of withholding any share of the fund from those schoolmasters who do not comply with their regulations, are under the necessity of apportioning the whole annual income among those connected with the Bequest, who, by obedience to the rules, and by their efficiency as teachers, have qualified themselves to receive it. It may, therefore, be confidently anticipated that, while the teachers of large schools will, under the operation of the Clause 52 D. of the Code, cease to share in the Bequest, and the free income for division among the remainder be thus largely increased, the teachers of smaller schools will throw off the Government grant altogether, in order that they may continue to draw their allowances from the Bequest, for the obvious reason, that under the supposed alteration of circumstances these allowances would, in all probability, come up to the emoluments derived from the grant by the larger school teachers, and, at all events, would very largely exceed any to which their own small number of scholars could ever entitle them under the Code.

Mr. Dick's view, in dedicating his fortune to educational purposes, was to raise the character of the schoolmasters, and the standard of education generally, throughout the three counties, so as to make them an example to other parts of the country. This purpose will, however, as appears from the foregoing statement, be in a great measure frustrated if the allowances from the Bequest are to be viewed as endowments under the "Revised Code." Moreover, though, if the schoolmasters were to draw both the Government grant and the allowance from the Bequest, they would no doubt be better provided for than others of their class in Scotland, still it must not be forgotten that the fund from which the excess is derived is the result of private benevolence, and the allowances from it wholly within the power of the Trustees, and granted as the direct reward of tried merit. Farther, it will surely be a sad perversion of the funds voted by Parliament for educational purposes if, as will be the case in the three counties, they shall ever become the means of lowering, instead of elevating, the literary character of the teachers, and the standard of education within the schools.

It only remains to be remarked that, apart from all other considerations, the Dick Bequest allowances *are not "Endowments," in the proper sense of that term*. *An endowment is properly a sum mortified to a particular school for the benefit of its teachers, and to the proceeds of which an individual becomes entitled by the mere possession of office.* Such, however, can never be said to be the character of a fund which is not provided for the schoolmasters as individuals, but is given for their behoof as a body, with power to Trustees arbitrarily to divide it among such of them only, and subject to such conditions as they shall from time to time see fit.

The Trustees earnestly hope that, on the above grounds, Parliament, in its wisdom, may see cause so to modify the conditions of the "Revised Code" as to except from its operation the Dick Bequest under their management.

(Signed) JAMES HOPE,
Deputy-Keeper of the Signet,
Chairman of the Trustees.

LONDON, 23d February 1864.

APPENDIX VI.

LIST OF PAROCHIAL SCHOOLS, AND OF THE SCHOOLMASTERS AND ASSISTANT-SUBSTITUTES, IN THE COUNTIES OF ABERDEEN, BANFF, AND MORAY, FROM 1854 TO 1864.

Parochial Schools.	Date of Appointment.	Schoolmasters and Assistant-Substitutes.	Cause of Vacancy.
Aberdour, ..	1837	Charles Forbes, .	Died in 1856.
	1856	James L. Ironside.	
,, Auchmedden,	1862*	Wm. F. S. Gordon.	
Aberlour, ..	1844	Charles Grant.	
Abernethy, ..	1845	James Grant.	
Aboyne, ...	1854	George M'Irvine, .	Appointed minister of St. Andrews Church in Mauritius.
	1856	Andrew Gray.	
,, Glentanner,	1847	Andrew Christie, .	Appointed schoolmaster of Alford.
	1864	James Kerr.	
Alford, ...	1833	Hugh M'Connach, .	School declared vacant under Act 24 & 25 Vict. cap. 107.
	1856	Chas. Dunn, Asst.,	Elected schoolmaster.
	1861	Chas. Dunn,	Appointed minister of Birse.
	1864	Andrew Christie.	
Alvah, ...	1850	James Duncan.	
Alves, ...	1854	A. F. Smart.	
Auchindoir, ..	1849	Wm. Gordon, ..	Appointed minister of Glenbucket.
	1854	Robert Smith,	
,, Lumsden, .	1861*	John Wilson, ..	Appointed schoolmaster of St. Andrews-Lhanbryde.
	1864	J. J. Tindal.	
Auchterless, ..	1845	Thos. M. Pirie, .	Appointed minister of Seafield Church, Cullen.
	1864	Andrew Soutter.	
,, Badenscoth,	1864	Alexr. Macharely.	
Banchory Devenick,	1852	Wm. Skinner, ..	Resigned ; now minister of Coull.
	1855	John Black, ..	Appointed one of H. M. Inspectors of Schools.

* Date of admission of school.

Parochial Schools.	Date of Appointment.	Schoolmasters and Assistant-Substitutes.	Cause of Vacancy.
Banchory-Devenick,	1858	Robt. Ogilvie, . .	Appointed Rector of Milne's Free Institution, Fochabers.
	1860	John Garden, . .	Appointed Rector of Elgin Academy.
	1863	Robert Gray.	
Banff Hilton, .	1839	John Soutter, . .	Resigned in 1863; died same year.
	1863	Thomas Gentles.	
Belhelvie, . .	1846	John Jack.	
Bellie, ...	1833	James Milne, . .	Died in 1856.
	1847	A. Anderson, Asst.,	Elected schoolmaster.
	1856	A. Anderson, . .	Appointed minister of Rhynie.
	1858	Alex. Brownie.	
Birnie, . . .	1852	Wm. Masson, . .	Appointed a missionary in Canada.
	1857	Wm. Gordon.	
Birse, ...	1847	Alexr. Esson.	
Boharm, . . .	1853	Wm. Burgess, . .	Appointed to Church of Ardallie, Old Deer.
	1859	Thomas Fraser.	
,, Maggyknockater,	1857*	Wm. MacLeod, .	Died in 1862.
	1862	Alexr. Ross. . .	
Botriphnie, . .	1853	Alexr. Carmichael,	Died in 1859.
	1860	Donald Stewart.	
Bourtie, . . .	1833	James Mearns.	
Boyndie, . . .	1834	George Hepburn.	
Cabrach, . . .	1833	Wm. Ronald.	
,, Invercharrach,	1864*	James Kissach, .	Appointed schoolmaster of Portsoy.
	1865	Thos. Robertson.	
Cairney, . . .	1852	John Annand, . .	Appointed assistant and successor to minister of Cairney.
	1858	James Wilson.	
Chapel Garioch,	1853	George Selbie.	
Clatt, ...	1834	John Minto.	
Cluny, . . .	1851	Robert Milne, . .	Appointed missionary, East Parish, Aberdeen, now minister of Towie.
	1857	Wm. Middleton, .	Appointed minister of *quoad sacra* church at Rosliu, now minister of Church of Scotland at Kurrachee.
	1860	Wm. Harper.	
Coldstone, . .	1833	Francis Beattie, .	Died in 1855.
	1855	J. G. Michie.	

* Date of admission of school.

APP. VI.] LIST OF SCHOOLS AND SCHOOLMASTERS. 393

Parochial Schools.	Date of Appointment.	Schoolmasters and Assistant-Substitutes.	Cause of Vacancy.
Coull, ...	1847	John Rannie, . .	Appointed missionary in Canada in connexion with Colonial Scheme of Church of Scotland.
	1857	Alexr. T. MacLean.	
	1858	John Robbie.	
Crathie, . . .	1848	Joseph Copland.	
Crimond, . . .	1833	James Wattie, . .	School declared vacant under Act 24 & 25 Vict. cap. 107.
	1856	J. G. Niven, Asst.,	Elected schoolmaster.
	1861	J. G. Niven.	
Cromdale-Advie,	1851	James M'Donald, .	Appointed minister of *quoad sacra* church at Daviot.
	1855	William Gordon, .	Appointed schoolmaster of Birnie.
	1857	James Grant.	
,, Dulnan, . .	1858*	James Menzies.	
Cruden, . . .	1851	Robt. Dawson.	
,, Bogbrae, .	1848	Alexr. Black.	
Cullen, . . .	1834	Robt. Innes, . .	Died in 1857.
	1849	A. C. Webster, Asst.,	*See* Kincardine O'Neil, Torphins.
	1857	C. R. H. D. Gordon.	
Culsalmond, . .	1833	Andrew Allan.	
	1861	A. M'William, Asst.,	Appointed missionary in Nova Scotia, in connexion with Church of Scotland.
	1863	Andrew Soutter, do.,	Appointed schoolmaster of Auchterless.
	1864	James Cameron, do.	
Dallas, . . .	1833	James Young.	
Daviot, . . .	1854	J. C. Grant, . .	Appointed schoolmaster of Old Meldrum.
	1859	James Brebner.	
Deskford, . .	1850	James Allan, . .	Appointed minister of *quoad sacra* church at Grantown.
	1856	Lewis Grant, . .	Appointed minister of Grantown.
	1858	James Brander.	
Drainie, . . .	1846	Alexr. Milne, . .	Appointed minister of Fyvie.
	1856	Robt. M'Kerron.	
Drumblade, . .	1844	John Souter, . .	Appointed minister of Inverkeithny.
	1859	Alexr. Thomson, .	Resigned through ill health (died).
	1861	John Robertson.	
Drumoak, . .	1848	John Davidson.	
Duffus, . . .	1854	James Bain.	

* Date of admission of school.

Parochial Schools.	Date of Appointment.	Schoolmasters and Assistant-Substitutes.	Cause of Vacancy.
Duthil, . . .	1853	John Robertson, .	Resigned.
	1861	Charles M'Gregor.	
Dyce, ...	1850	G. W. Kemp.	
Dyke, ...	1833	Wm. Ogilvie, . .	Died in 1855.
	1855	Alexr. Paxton.	
Echt, ...	1846	Wm. Malcolm.	
Edinkillie, . .	1843	John Forbes, . .	School declared vacant under Act 24 & 25 Vict. cap. 107.
	1857	Robt. Ogilvie, Asst.,	Appointed schoolmaster of Banchory-Devenick.
	1858	John Smith, do., .	Appointed assistant-substitute at Tough.
	1859	Wm. Fraser, do., .	Elected schoolmaster.
	1861	Wm. Fraser.	
Ellon, ...	1844	John Davidson.	
,, Tillydeask,	1841	William Hay.	
Fintray, . . .	1842	David Milne.	
Fordyce, . . .	1845	George Stephen.	
,, Portsoy, . .	1847	W. B. Moyés, . .	Appointed a master of Circus Place School, Edinburgh.
	1854	James Davidson, .	Appointed minister of Ord Chapel, Banff.
	1864	James Kissach.	
Forglen, . . .	1833	John Webster, . .	School declared vacant under Act 24 & 25 Vict. cap. 107.
	1851	John Webster, jun., Asst.	Appointed schoolmaster of Rothiemay.
	1856	Wm. M. Philip, do.,	Resigned.
	1859	Wm. S. Caie, do.,	Elected schoolmaster.
	1861	Wm. S. Caie.	
Forgue, . . .	1833	George Webster,	School declared vacant under Act 24 & 25 Vict. cap. 107.
	1851	Wm. Macleod, Asst.,	Resigned on account of ill health.
	1854	David Innes, do., .	Resigned on account of ill health (died).
	1857	Wm. Robertson, do.,	Appointed assistant-substitute of Old Machar.
	1859	Robt. Lippe, do., .	Elected schoolmaster.
	1861	Robt. Lippe.	
,, Wells of Ythan,	1848	Alexr. M'William,	Appointed assistant-substitute at Culsalmond.
	1861	J. Barclay.	
	1862	George Davidson.	
Foveran, . . .	1849	James Anderson.	

LIST OF SCHOOLS AND SCHOOLMASTERS.

Parochial Schools.	Date of Appointment.	Schoolmasters and Assistant-Substitutes.	Cause of Vacancy.
Fraserburgh,	1833 1862	Wm. Woodman, George Murray.	Died in 1862.
Fyvie,	1833	John Stott,	School declared vacant under Act 24 & 25 Vict. cap. 107.
	1851	J. Davidson, Asst.,	Schoolmaster of Portsoy.
	1854	James Kidd, do.,	Resigned.
	1856	Jas. D. Cheyne, do.,	Died in 1859.
	1859	Alexr. Bremner, do.,	Elected schoolmaster.
	1861	Alexr. Bremner,	
Gamrie,	1848	David Chalmers.	
,, Macduff,	1847	Walter Grigor,	Appointed minister of Macduff.
	1860	Alexr. Mathieson,	Resigned.
	1862	Hugh Mair.	
Gartly,	1846	William Smith.	
Glass,	1837	Arthur Stephen.	
Glenbucket,	1839	William Reid.	
Glenmuick,	1833	James Smith,	School declared vacant under Act 24 & 25 Vict. cap. 107.
	1858	D. M'Farlane, Asst.	
	1860	Wm. Murray, do.,	Elected schoolmaster.
	1861	Wm. Murray,	
Grange,	1841	Arthur Gerrard.	
Huntly,	1849	John Macdonald.	
,, Kinmoir,	1857	—— Fowlie,	Resigned for situation as private tutor.
	1858	James Smart,	Died in 1860.
	1860	Wm. D. Frater,	Appointed assistant-substitute at Premnay.
	1862	Walter Milne.	
Insch,	1833	Charles Norrie.	Resigned.
	1855	James Maclachlan.	
Inveravon,	1833	James Chree,	School declared vacant under Act 24 & 25 Vict. cap. 107.
	1853	J. M'Donald, Asst.,	Resigned for medical profession.
	1857	John Stewart, do.,	Appointed schoolmaster of Grantown.
	1860	And. Meldrum, do.,	Elected schoolmaster.
	1861	Andrew Meldrum.	
Inverkeithny,	1833	Alexr. Morrison,	Died in 1856.
	1855	G. F. J. Philip, Asst.,	Elected schoolmaster.
	1856	G. F. J. Philip.	
Inverury,	1833	Geo. Cruickshank,	Died in 1861.
	1861	Alexr. Fowlie.	

* Date of admission of school.

Parochial Schools.	Date of Appointment.	Schoolmasters and Assistant-Substitutes.	Cause of Vacancy.
Keig, ...	1833	Gordon Raeburn, .	Died in 1861.
	1852	Lewis Beaton, Asst.,	Appointed assistant-substitute at Strichen.
	1854	Walter Milne, do.,	Appointed schoolmaster of Huntly Kinnoir in 1862.
	1861	George Chree.	
Keith, . . .	1833	James Smith.	
Keithhall, . .	1843	David Brown.	
Kemnay, . . .	1833	Andw. Stevenson,	Died in 1857.
	1857	George Proctor.	
Kildrummy, .	1833	Wm. Christie.	
	1859	D. Christie, Asst.	
Kincardine O'Neil,	1840	James Hogg, . .	Died in 1854.
	1854	James Clark.	
,, Torphins, .	1833	Alexr. Ross, . .	Resigned in 1861; died in 1862.
	1850	Ben. Reid, Assist.,	
	1857	A. C. Webster, do.,	Left through ill-health; since dead.
	1858	Alex. Millar, do., .	Elected schoolmaster.
	1861	Alex. Millar.	
,, Tornaveen,	1833	George Reid.	
	1858	Wm. Brand, Asst.,	Appointed assistant to minister of Renfrew.
	1859	Wm. M'Rae, do.,	
	1860	James Webster, do.	Appointed assistant-substitute, afterwards schoolmaster, of Shannas, Old Deer.
	1864	John Smith, do	
Kinellar, . . .	1833	John Barclay, . .	School declared vacant under Act 24 & 25 Vict., cap. 107.
	1850	John Joss, Asst., .	Elected schoolmaster.
	1861	John Joss.	
King-Edward, .	1833	James Steinson, .	Died in 1854.
	1852	John Milne, Asst.,	Elected schoolmaster.
	1854	John Milne.	
Kinloss, . . .	1833	James White, . .	Died in 1855.
	1852	John Knight, Asst.,	Resigned.
	1855	R. R. Rannie, do.,	Elected schoolmaster.
	1855	R. R. Rannie.	
Kinnethmont, .	1833	Alexr. Minty, . .	School declared vacant under Act 24 & 25 Vict. cap. 107.
	1851	F. A. Wilson, Asst.	
	1862	Wm. Gerrard.	
Kintore, . . .	1836	John Brotchie.	
	1857	R. Kennedy, Asst.,	Died in 1861.

Parochial Schools.	Date of Appointment.	Schoolmasters and Assistant-Substitutes.	Cause of Vacancy.
Kintore, . . .	1861	W. M. Brown, Asst.,	Appointed by Church of Scotland Committee for Conversion of Jews to school at Constantinople.
	1864	D. M. Cruickshank, Asst.	
Kirkmichael, .	1845	Alexr. Cameron, .	Appointed minister of Kingussie.
	1856	Robert Cameron, .	Died in 1859.
	1859	Donald Robertson.	
,, Tomintoul,	1853	R. B. Burgess, . .	Appointed teacher of a school in Kent.
	1854	James Maclean, .	Appointed rector of Pulteneytown Academy, Wick.
Knockando, . .	1852	Robert Smith, . .	Appointed minister of Rafford.
	1864	John A. Sutor.	
,, Elchies, . .	1848	Lewis Grant, . .	Appointed schoolmaster of Deskford.
	1856	James Fraser.	
Leochel, . . .	1833	Chas. Humphry, .	Resigned.
	1855	Wm. M'Robert.	
,, Cushnie, .	1833	Andw. Malcolm, .	Died in 1857.
	1857	James Reid.	
Leslie, . . .	1854	Alexr. Machardy, .	Appointed a master in Dollar Academy, now schoolmaster of Badenscoth, Auchterless.
	1861	Wm. Macfarlane.	
Logie Buchan, .	1853	Wm. Jaffrey.	
Longside, . .	1854	Wm. Center, . .	Died in 1863.
	1863	Alexr. Center.	
,, Mintlaw, .	1834	John Farquhar.	
,, Rora, . . .	1843	John Beaton.	
Lonmay, . . .	1845	Geo. Robertson.	
,, Kinnimonth,	1833	Alexr. Stronach.	
,, St. Combs, .	1848	Wm. Shand, . .	Resigned.
	1858	Arthur Rettie, . .	Died in 1858.
	1859	Arthur Allan.	
Lumphanan, .	1833	Alexr. Birnie, . .	Died in 1856.
	1852	John Smith, Asst.,	Elected schoolmaster.
	1856	John Smith.	
Marnoch, . .	1846	William Christie.	
Methlic, . . .	1851	Alexr. Gray, . .	Appointed minister of Holburn Church, Aberdeen.
	1857	Joseph Ogilvie.	

Parochial Schools.	Date of Appointment.	Schoolmasters and Assistant-Substitutes.	Cause of Vacancy.
Methlic, Inverbrie,	1850	Alexr. Fraser.	
Midmar, . . .	1833 1860	George Mortimer. J. W. Leith, Asst.	
Monquhitter, .	1833 1850 1861	Alexr. Cheyne, . J. Cameron, Asst. Donald Duff.	School declared vacant under Act 24 & 25 Vict. cap. 107.
Monymusk, . .	1849 1854	Duncan Anderson, Alexr. Ogilvie.	Emigrated to America.
Mortlach, . .	1837	John Macpherson.	
New Deer, . .	1844	Peter Farquharson.	
,, Savoch,	1833 1851 1855 1855 1861	James Mair. Jas. Mair, jr., Asst., George Law, do. George Chree, do., James Moir, do.	Resigned. Appointed assistant-substitute at Old Machar. Appointed schoolmaster of Keig.
,, Whitehills,	1833	Alexr. Greig.	
Newhills, . .	1844	James Stewart.	
New Machar, .	1835 1846 1856	Colin Falconer, . D. M'Hardy, Asst., Donald M'Hardy.	Died in 1856. Elected schoolmaster.
New Spynie, .	1853 1863	John Skeen, . . William Smith.	Appointed minister of Seafield Church, Cullen ; died in 1863.
Old Deer, . .	1850	Robt. Wilson.	
,, Clochan,	1833 1863	James Anderson, . Alexr. Greig.	Died in 1862.
,, Shannas,	1833 1862 1864 1865	David Wood, . . Jas. Cantlay, Asst., James Webster, do., James Webster.	Died in 1864. Resigned. Elected schoolmaster.
Old Machar, .	1833 1855 1856 1859 ... 1861	John Cowie, . . J. Milligan, Asst., George Law, do., . W. Robertson, do., Wm. Robertson, . John Gregory.	Died in 1859. Died in 1856. Resigned. Elected schoolmaster. Resigned.
Old Meldrum, .	1833 1856 1859	George Cooper, . Wm. M. Keay, . J. C. Grant, . .	Died in 1855. Appointed minister of Woodside, Aberdeen. Appointed minister of East Church, Brechin.

LIST OF SCHOOLS AND SCHOOLMASTERS.

Parochial Schools.	Date of Appointment.	Schoolmaster and Assistant-Substitutes.	Cause of Vacancy.
Old Meldrum, .	1862	James Mackenzie.	
Ordiquhill, . .	1833	Wm. Cruickshank.	
	1853	James Smart, Asst.,	Resigned on account of ill-health.
	1855	John Thomson, do.,	Appointed assistant-substitute at Turriff.
	1857	James Brander, do.,	Appointed schoolmaster of Deskford.
	1858	Joseph Mackay, do.,	Resigned.
	1860	John Shand, do.	
Oyne, ...	1833	John Shand, . .	School declared vacant under Act 24 & 25 Vict. cap. 107.
	1848	J. Ledingham, Asst.,	Appointed minister of Seafield Chapel, Cullen.
	1854	William Watt, do.,	Appointed schoolmaster of Rathen.
	1857	Robt. Lippe, do., .	Appointed assistant-substitute at Forgue.
	1859	James Stuart, do.,	Resigned on account of ill-health (died).
	1860	J. R. Anderson, do.,	Elected schoolmaster.
	1861	J. R. Anderson.	
Peterculter, . .	1846	John Smith.	
Peterhead, . .	1844	James Lyall.	
Pitsligo, . . .	1852	Charles Sleigh, .	Appointed schoolmaster of Tarves.
	1864	John Fowlie.	
Premnay, . .	1833	John Mann, . .	School declared vacant under Act 24 & 25 Vict. cap. 107.
	1855	J. Lumsden, Asst.,	Resigned.
	1857	John Wilson, do.,	Resigned.
	1858	Alex. Frater, do.,	Received an appointment in the War Office.
	1861	Wm. D. Frater, do.,	Elected schoolmaster.
	...	Wm. D. Frater, .	Resigned.
	1864	Jonathan M. Grant.	
Rafford, . . .	1838	James Watson.	
Rathen, . . .	1846	John Watt, . . .	Appointed minister of Towie.
	1856	William Watt.	
,, Inverallochy,	1845	Geo. Mathieson.	
Rathven, . .	1849	John Russell.	
Rayne, . . .	1850	G. W. Cruickshank.	
Rhynie, . . .	1841	Geo. Stuart.	
Rothes, . . .	1843	Archd. D. Wright.	
Rothiemay, . .	1833	Wm. Webster,	Died in 1856.
	1856	John Webster,	Appointed minister at Buckie.
	1862	George J. Sim.	

Parochial Schools.	Date of Appointment.	Schoolmasters and Assistant-Substitutes.	Causes of Vacancy.
Skene, . . .	1844　1861　1862	David Smith, . .　A. Youngson, asst.,　Alex. Youngson.	Resigned in 1862.　Elected schoolmaster.
Slains, . . .	1850	James R. Souter.	
Speymouth, . .	1846	James Dawson.	
St. Andrews-　Lhanbryde, }	1851　1864	Charles Bruce.　John Wilson.	
St. Fergus, . .	1833　1849　1855	John Kennedy, . .　James Taylor, asst.,　James Taylor.	Died in 1855.　Elected schoolmaster.
Strathdon, . .	1836	A. G. Anderson.	
Strichen, . . .	1833　1853　1854　1857	John Gordon, . .　Alexr. Ogilvie, asst.,　Lewis Beaton, do.　Lewis Beaton.	Died in 1857.　Appointed schoolmaster of Monymusk.　Elected schoolmaster.
Tarland, . . .	1847　1857　1860	John Reid, . . .　James Adams, . .　Robert Slessor.	Appointed minister of Savoch.　Died in 1860.
Tarves, . . .	1843　1864	George Melvin, . .　Charles Sleigh.	Died in 1864.
,, Barthol Chapel,	1860*	William Wilson.	
Tough, . . .	1833　1854　1855　1857　…　1858　1860	Alexr. Ingram, . .　J. Maclachlan, asst.,　Robt. Kennedy, do.　James Adams, . .　Alexr. Grant, do.　John C. Smith, do.　John C. Smith.	Died in 1859.　Appointed schoolmaster of Insch.　Appointed assistant-substitute at Kintore.　Appointed schoolmaster of Tarland.　Emigrated to New Zealand.　Elected schoolmaster.
Towie, . . .	1833	John Fyfe.	
Tullynessle, . .	1833　1860　1862	James Smith, . .　Hugh Mair, asst., .　James M'C. Pithie.	Died in 1861.　Schoolmaster of Macduff.
Turriff, . . .	1833　1850　1856　1857　1862	John Clark, . . .　Geo. Ogilvie, asst.　Joseph Ogilvie, do.　John Thomson, do.　John Thomson.	School declared vacant under Act 24 & 25 Vict. cap. 107.　Appointed head-master of Stewart's Hospital, Edinburgh.　Appointed schoolmaster of Methlic.　Elected schoolmaster.
Tyrie, ...	1833	William Fowlie, .	School declared vacant under Act 24 & 25 Vict. cap. 107.

* Date of Admission of school.

Parochial Schools.	Date of Appointment.	Schoolmasters and Assistant-Substitutes.	Causes of Vacancy.
Tyrie, ...	1858	Geo. Sturrock, asst.,	Appointed schoolmaster of Kirkden, Forfar.
	1859	G. Ironside, do.	Elected schoolmaster.
	1861	George Ironside.	
,, New Pitsligo,	1846	J. L. Ironside, . .	Appointed schoolmaster of Aberdour.
	1856	—— Strachan, . .	Resigned in 1861.
	1861	David Sturrock.	
Udny, ...	1833	J. R. U. Bisset.	
	1854	James Smith, asst.	
	1863	Charles Low, do.	
Urquhart, . .	1847	John Russell, . .	Appointed minister of Skene.
	1860	Wm. R. Bruce.	

www.ingramcontent.com/pod-product-compliance
Lightning Source LLC
Chambersburg PA
CBHW050845300426
44111CB00010B/1140